DAILY LIFE OF

THE
VIKINGS

The Greenwood Press "Daily Life Through History" Series

DAILY LIFE OF

THE
VIKINGS

KIRSTEN WOLF

The Greenwood Press "Daily Life Through History" Series

GREENWOOD PRESS
Westport, Connecticut • London

Library of Congress Cataloging-in-Publication Data

Wolf, Kirsten, 1959–
  Daily life of the Vikings / Kirsten Wolf.
      p. cm. — (Greenwood Press "Daily life through history" series, ISSN
1080–4749)
  Includes bibliographical references and index.
  ISBN 0–313–32269–4
  1. Vikings. 2. Civilization, Viking. I. Title. II. Series.
  DL65.73   2004
  948'.022—dc22   2004015184

British Library Cataloguing in Publication Data is available.

Library of Congress Catalog Card Number: 2004015184
ISBN: 0–313–32269–4
ISSN: 1080–4749

First published in 2004

Greenwood Press, 88 Post Road West, Westport, CT 06881
An imprint of Greenwood Publishing Group, Inc.
www.greenwood.com

Printed in the United States of America

The paper used in this book complies with the
Permanent Paper Standard issued by the National
Information Standards Organization (Z39.48–1984).

10 9 8 7 6 5 4 3 2 1

Copyright Acknowledgments

The author and publisher gratefully acknowledge permission for use of the
following material:

Excerpts from R.I. Page, *Chronicles of the Vikings*. Toronto, Canada: University of
Toronto Press, 1995. Reprinted with permission.

Excerpts from Adam of Bremen, *History of the Archbishops of Hamburg-Bremen*,
translated by Francis J. Tschan. New York: Columbia University Press, © 1959.
Reprinted with permission.

Poetic excerpts from "Poetry and its changing importance in medieval Icelandic
culture," published in *Old Icelandic Literature and Society*, edited by Margaret
Clunies Ross. *Cambridge Studies in Medieval Literature*. 42. Cambridge: Cambridge
University Press, 2000. Reprinted with the permission of Cambridge University
Press.

Every reasonable effort has been made to trace the owners of copyright materials
in this book, but in some instances this has proven impossible. The author and
publisher will be glad to receive information leading to more complete acknowledgments in subsequent printings of the book and in the meantime extend their
apologies for any omissions.

for Anne, my daughter

Contents

Preface

In accordance with the volumes in The Greenwood Press "Daily Life Through History" series, this book seeks to convey to a nonspecialist readership the facts and flavor of everyday life in Scandinavia during the Viking age. What kind of houses did the Scandinavians live in? How stable was the family? Were they literate? What did they eat? How did they view death? What were their sources of income? Did they share our ideas about romantic love? How did they treat their slaves? What were the attitudes toward women? How did they relax? What kind of clothes did they wear? How did they view old age? What were their means of transport and transportation? These are but some of the questions that are considered, and while they may seem trivial, if not unimportant, when viewed in isolation, they nonetheless merit attention, for it is the sum of such considerations that enables us to get an impression of the mentality of the Scandinavians in the Viking age.

There are, of course, limitations to a book that aims to describe the daily life of the Viking-age Scandinavians. To begin with, the Viking age spanned three centuries, and during this time Scandinavia underwent major changes: the modern kingdoms of Denmark, Norway, and Sweden took shape, the first towns were established, and the pagan Scandinavian religion was abandoned in favor of Christianity. Moreover, the Viking age witnessed rapid technological developments: bridges and fortresses were built, and great advances were made in shipbuilding and navigation, which enabled the Scandinavians to travel long distances and spread wider in the world than any other European people had done and would do until the voyages and colonizations that followed in the wake of the discoveries of Columbus. In the course of the Viking age, the world of the Scandinavians greatly increased in size, and by necessity the picture that is presented of their everyday life does not include more than a small part of that world, for it must, of course, be recognized that the daily life of a Scandinavian trader in Russia or a Viking marauder in England or on the European continent was quite different from that of a farmer or fisherman living in Scandinavia (although also within Scandinavia there were local variations). It is with the daily lives of the latter—the farmers, hunters, fishermen, trappers, and craftsmen, that is, those who remained at home—that this book is primarily concerned, for they were the ones who built and equipped the ships, accumulated the supplies, and obtained the goods required to fill the cargoes of the merchants. In short, they were the ones who made the voyages—and by extension the Viking age—possible.

Other limitations are caused by the source material, of which an outline will be given in the following paragraphs. Our sources for the Viking age are manifold, and a survey of the era necessitates consideration of a great variety of disciplines, including literature, linguistics, runology, onomastics, history, archaeology, art history, numismatics, geography, geology, zoology, and climatology. Each source poses its own problems, and the different kinds of material must continuously be compared and assessed, and often one type of material is used to interpret another.

Written evidence forms an important source of information about the Scandinavians in the Viking age and the activities of the Vikings. Of the greatest importance are, of course, original inscriptions and documents. The former comprise primarily runic inscriptions, and it is in these that the Scandinavians of the Viking age speak directly to posterity without any intermediaries other than the transliterator, transcriber, and translator. Runic inscriptions are found in all of Scandinavia, but they are not uniformly distributed. Scandinavian runic inscriptions have also been found in many of the Norse colonies or along the Scandinavian trade routes in places as far apart as Greenland and Istanbul. Unfortunately, much of what was once inscribed has perished, and the inscriptions, especially on monuments, are typically short and formal in expression. The other category of native written sources, that is, documentary sources, is more voluminous than the runic inscriptions. They comprise charters, land registers, trade agreements, and the like. The earliest date from the end of the eleventh century, but great numbers are not in existence until the thirteenth century, that is, after the end of the Viking age. Much the same may be said about the laws, which are useful sources of information about local and national administration; several Danish, Norwegian, and Swedish provincial laws are extant, but the majority of them were codified after the Viking age.

In addition, there are literary works—poems—dating from the Viking age. This poetry was composed and transmitted orally, and with the exception of a few short pieces in runic text, it was not recorded until well after the Scandinavians had converted to Christianity. Most of the poetry was recorded in Iceland, and it falls broadly into two classes, eddic and skaldic. The eddic poems are chiefly of two kinds, mythical and heroic. Both eddic categories, but especially the former, provide useful information about pagan Scandinavian religion and the social and ethical attitudes of Scandinavians in the Viking age. Many of these poems are summarized or quoted in the so-called *Prose Edda,* a handbook of mythology for budding poets written in the 1220s by the Icelandic politician, historian, and poet Snorri Sturluson. Skaldic poetry differs from eddic poetry in that it is typically ascribed to named authors and has as its subject recent or contemporary events. The composers of skaldic poetry, the skalds, in many ways functioned as historiographers; in their verses, they typically praise a king or chieftain for his courage or generosity either during his lifetime or in a memorial poem after his death, enumerating his battles and other feats of prowess. Several of the skaldic poems rank high as historical sources about the Viking age.

Prose works also provide information about aspects of Viking-age Scandinavia. Many of the earliest works, such as sermons and saints' lives, are based on foreign sources, but indigenous compositions are found as well, in which Scandinavian authors record in Latin or the vernacular their countries' history or their contemporary world. These writings range from annals and chronicles to historical novels. Denmark has a rich high-medieval historiographical tradition, which reached its climax with the early thirteenth-century *Gesta Danorum* ("Deeds of the Danes") by Saxo Grammaticus. Sweden has no historiography comparable to that of Denmark, and the material is meager. Around 1240, three closely connected Västgöta chronicles came into existence; they go back to about 1000, but only for the period 900–1000 are the short notices sometimes expanded into fuller descriptions. Mention may also be made of the mid-thirteenth century *Guta saga,* which relates the history of Gotland from a mythical origin until the thirteenth century. From Norway, three late twelfth-century to early thirteenth-century histories are extant, one in the vernacular and two in Latin. These are: *Agrip af Noregs konunga sogum* ("Summary of the Sagas of the Kings of Norway"), which, in its complete state, appears to have begun with Halfdan the Black, the father of Harald Fairhair (d. 930–940), the king credited with unifying Norway; *Historia de antiquitate regum norwagiensium* ("History of the Ancient Norwegian Kings"), which is a synoptic history of the kings from the ninth century to the twelfth written by a certain Theodoricus; and *Historia Norwegiae* ("History of Norway"), which consists of a prologue, a geographical description of Norway, the Faroe and Orkney Islands, and Iceland, with an excursus on the customs and habits of the Lapps, and a brief history of Norway. In his *Historia de antiquitate regum norwagiensium,* Theodoricus pays tribute to Icelanders, who had preserved the memory of antiquity in ancient verses, and in his *Gesta Danorum* Saxo praises the Icelanders as a repository of ancient tradition. It is a fact that the medieval Icelanders were extremely interested in the history of the Scandinavian countries. The histories composed in Iceland include biographies of Scandinavian royalty and concern especially the kings of Norway from the ninth to the thirteenth centuries, and also the kings of Denmark from roughly the same period. Provincial or regional histories were recorded as well, dating from the first couple of decades of the thirteenth century. These include accounts of the Norse colonies in the North Atlantic, especially the Orkney and Faroe Islands; stories about the half-legendary Jomsvikings, a Baltic Viking community; and a history of the earls of Lade (near Trondheim) in Norway. But the Icelanders also recorded the history of their own country. The first Icelander to write in the vernacular was Ari Thorgilsson, who in the early decades of the twelfth century composed a short epitome of Icelandic history called *Islendingabok* ("Book of Icelanders"), which gives a sober and reliable account of events from the settlement of Iceland around 870 to the early twelfth century. During Ari's days also began the collection of information recorded in *Landnamabok* ("Book of Settlements"), a remarkable work about the colonizers of Iceland and their families and successors around the country. The best-known medieval Icelandic prose writings are, however, the Sagas of Icelanders; but unfortunately they are also the most difficult to evaluate. The Sagas of Icelanders is a modern term for about 40 narratives concerning Icelandic farmer-chieftains from the settlement of Iceland to the mid-eleventh century. The majority of them date from the thirteenth century. Written in a factual style, they present themselves as history and are often seductively realistic; and from the time they became objects of study until well into the twentieth century, scholars generally regarded them as valuable historical sources. However, some of the sagas have been demonstrated to be little more than fiction, and the trend among historians nowadays is to take precautions when relying on information provided by the sagas and to use them primarily for the details they give about social mechanisms and mental attitudes operative between the time they were recorded and the time in which events are said to have taken place. Despite the modern emphasis on the fictionality of the Sagas of Icelanders, it would, however, seem impossible to write about the Viking age without taking these narratives into account. No other sources are as detailed and colorful as the Sagas of Icelanders, and no other sources have had more of an impact on shaping modern conceptions of the Viking age.

A fair amount of contemporary evidence about Scandinavia and Scandinavians, Vikings, and Viking activities is found in writings composed outside of Denmark, Norway, Sweden, and Iceland. The Vikings are referred to in Old English, Old Irish, Latin, Slavic, Greek, and Arabic works. The Christian sources tend to be annals and histories, while the Muslim sources are geographical works. Like many of the native compositions, these writings must obviously be treated with caution, though for different reasons: it is improbable that Christian and Muslim authors would present a fair assessment of the Scandinavian pagans, whom they knew only as brutal plunderers and invaders. Most of these writings treat the Scandinavians abroad, though some are concerned with Scandinavian conditions. A major source is the German cleric Adam of Bremen's *Gesta Hammaburgensis ecclesiae pontificum* ("Activities of the prelates of the Church of Hamburg") written around 1070. The work consists of four books, and in the fourth, Adam describes the Danes and the Swedes, followed by a section on the Baltic Sea with its islands and shores, and a passage on the Norwegians and the islands of the ocean. Adam gives interesting geographical and ethnographical information about Scandinavia and Scandinavians in the eleventh century, but he never visited Scandinavia himself, and although he cites the Danish King Sven Estridsen as an informant and almost certainly relied on eyewitness accounts, a fair amount of material clearly comes from classical sources and popular misconceptions about the Scandinavians; and, as one would expect, Adam writes from a decidedly Christian standpoint and with the cause of his archbishopric's interest in the conversion of Scandinavia in mind. The example of Adam of Bremen does not, of course, imply that foreign accounts of the Viking age should be discriminated against; rather, they show that an author's intentions and prejudices and the directives of genre must be taken into consideration before his declarations of fact can be accepted. Nor does it imply that all non-Scandinavian sources should be approached with utter skepticism. The Greek work usually known by its Latin name of *De administrando imperio* ("On Administering a Realm") written by the Byzantine Emperor Constantine Porphyrogenitos for his heir Romanus, for example, has generally been considered a reliable and quite authoritative source of information about the dominion of the *Rhos* (presumably Swedes or people of Swedish descent), in western Russia in the tenth century, and the accuracy of its description of a dangerous voyage undertaken by the *Rhos* down the river Dnieper to Constantinople has not been questioned.

Place-names and archaeological finds studied in conjunction with the literature are extraordinarily informative. They often corroborate accounts of the emigration and colonization of Scandinavians abroad and throw light on internal relocation and settlement. Scandinavian place-names are found not only in Denmark, Norway, and Sweden, but also in the colonies established by Norwegians and Danes in the North Atlantic, the British Isles, and Normandy, and by Swedes in the Åland islands and the southern and western parts of Finland. Place-names often reveal which areas were settled by Norwegians and which were settled by Danes, as well as providing evidence of settlement. Archaeological finds more than anything else have contributed to our understanding of the life of the Scandinavians in the Viking age through analyses of skeletal remains, ships, weapons, tools, textiles, pottery, jewelry, etc., and the appeal of archaeological evidence is, of course, that it is concrete and datable, though it too must be interpreted. Thousands of graves have been excavated in Scandinavia and other places, and without these finds our knowledge about the daily life (or death) of Scandinavians in the Viking age would be very limited. The graves provide interesting information about burial practices and religious beliefs, and the grave goods can tell us a great deal about what clothing people wore, what tools they used in their everyday life and, accordingly, what their daily activities were, and sometimes what foods they lived on. Because, however, archaeology is a field that is continuously increasing because of ongoing field research, definitions of Scandinavians and Vikings during the Viking age are under continuous revision.

Yet other limitations to the book are its author's training and background. I am a philologist and a literary historian; not a historian or archaeologist. Accordingly, it may be argued perhaps that the book relies rather heavily on the written sources, and it must be emphasized that it makes no attempt to give a formal history of Scandinavia during the Viking age. For its historical and archaeological details, the book may be said to be descriptive rather than analytical (though hopefully not uncritical), and for these it is much indebted to recent studies by scholars with expertise in these fields of study, notably Peter G. Foote and David M. Wilson's *The Viking Achievement* (1970), James Graham-Campbell's *Viking Artefacts* (1980) and *The Viking World* (1980), Else Roesdahl's *The Vikings* (1987), and Eric Christiansen's *The Norsemen in the Viking Age* (2002). R. I. Page's *Chronicles of the Vikings* (1995) also proved to be a most useful work.

Finally, some comments on the difficulties involved in quoting Scandinavian words and names. Although the languages of Denmark, Norway, Sweden, and the Norse colonies in the North Atlantic were quite similar in the Viking age, there were some differences. An attempt has been made to distinguish between East Norse (Danish and Swedish) and West Norse (Norwegian and Icelandic) instead of consistently using Old Norse forms representing the West Norse tradition. Regarding the Old Norse and also the modern Icelandic words and names, it should be noted that accent marks have been ignored and inflectional endings omitted. The characters þ and ð have been replaced by *th* and *d*, respectively; *æ* has been anglicized to *ae/oe*; and *ö, ø, ǫ* are written *o*. These special characters have only been retained when it is necessary to quote the Norse or Scandinavian words in their exact form. As far as place-names are concerned, the forms given are the ones commonly used today except in cases where an anglicized form exists (e.g., Sweden, Zealand, Scania).

It remains to acknowledge the assistance and support of colleagues and friends. Kevin Ohe, Senior Editor of Greenwood Press, invited me to undertake the work and was most collaborative, as was his successor Michael Hermann. Joyce Salisbury, general editor of Greenwood Press's *Encyclopedia of Daily Life* (2004), kindly made available to me her outline for the medieval volume, which I subsequently adopted as a structural framework for this book. My department, The Department of Scandinavian Studies at the University of Wisconsin–Madison, generously granted me two research assistants during the last stages of work on the book, and to these assistants, Milda Ostrauskaite and, especially, Jay Paul Gates, I wish to express my gratitude for their fine work. Last but not least, I thank Wayne Brabender, who listened with patience and good humor to my gripes about the somewhat more challenging sections of this book and who read the entire manuscript.

Chronology

793	Lindisfarne church and monastery raided by Norwegian Vikings.
794–795	Jarrow, Iona, and Lambay raided by Norwegian Vikings.
808	King Godfred of Denmark destroys the Slav trading station of Reric and establishes its merchants in Hedeby. He orders the construction of a large border rampart (Kovirke) just north of Hedeby.
c. 825	First Scandinavian coins struck, probably in Hedeby.
826	King Harald Klak of Denmark baptized in Mainz.
834	Dorestad attacked by Danish Vikings.
835	Island of Sheppey raided by Danish Vikings; Noirmoutier at the mouth of the Loire pillaged by Danish Vikings.
840–841	Vikings establish fortified bases in Ireland and winter there for the first time.
841	Rouen on the Seine sacked by Vikings.
842	Quentowic near modern Étables sacked by Vikings.
843	First recorded wintering of Viking troops on the Continent (Noirmoutier). Nantes on the Loire sacked by Vikings.
844	First documented raid on Spain; Seville and other places conquered.

845	Hamburg plundered and Paris conquered by Vikings.
c. 850	First church built in Denmark, in Hedeby, at Saint Ansgar's instigation.
850–851	First wintering of Viking troops in England (Thanet in the Thames).
851	Danish Vikings invade Norse Dublin.
852	First church built in Sweden, in Birka, at Saint Ansgar's instigation.
859–862	Expedition of Bjorn Ironside and Hasting to Spain, North Africa, Italy, and France.
861	Pisa and Luna sacked by Vikings.
865	A "great heathen host" arrives in England. First Danegeld paid in England. Death of Saint Ansgar, "the Apostle of the North."
866–873	Vikings attack York, Nottingham, Thetford, Reading, London, Torksey, and Repton.
866	King Alfred the Great makes a treaty with Guthrum, which establishes the border between his kingdom and the Danelaw.
870	Settlement of Iceland begins.
879–892	The "Great Army" harries on the Continent.
885–886	Great siege of Paris by Vikings.
c. 890	Ohthere and Wulfstan tell King Alfred the Great of Wessex about their travels.
899	Death of King Alfred the Great.
902	Scandinavians driven out of Dublin but soon return.
911	Viking colony of Normandy established.
c. 921	The Arab traveler Ibn Fadlan visits the Rus on the Middle Volga.
926	Last recorded payment of Danegeld on the Continent.
930	Establishment of the Althing in Iceland.
c. 935	Death of King Harald Fairhair of Norway.
c. 950	Ibrahim b. Ya'qub al-Turtushi, a merchant from Andalusia, visits Hedeby.
954	Death of Erik Bloodaxe, the last Viking king of York.
c. 958	Death of King Gorm the Old of Denmark.

c. 960	King Harald Bluetooth converts the Danes to Christianity.
968	Viking raid on Santiago de Compostella. Building on Danevirke; the Great Wall probably erected.
980	Dublin loses its political independence at the battle of Tara. The Ravning bridge near Jelling as well as the four circular fortresses (Trelleborg, Aggersborg, Fyrkat, and Nonnebakken) constructed around this time.
980–990	Sporadic Viking raids on England.
985/6	Settlement of Greenland begins.
986	North America discovered by Greenlanders of Scandinavian extraction.
c. 987	Death of King Harald Bluetooth of Denmark.
991	Olaf Tryggvason's expedition to England.
995	Olaf Tryggvason becomes king of Norway and begins Christianizing Norway and the Norse colonies in the North Atlantic.
999/1000	Conversion of Iceland to Christianity. Death of King Olaf Tryggvason of Norway in the battle of Svold.
1013	King Sven Forkbeard of Denmark conquers England.
1014	King Sven Forkbeard dies, and the army sails home again.
1016	Knud the Great conquers England and becomes king of England.
1018	Knud the Great becomes king of Denmark.
1022	Death of King Olof Skotkonung of Sweden.
1030	King Olaf Haraldsson of Norway killed in the battle of Stiklestad in Norway; he was later venerated as a saint.
1035	Death of King Knud the Great.
1042	Danish overlordship of England ends.
1066	King Harald Hardruler of Norway attacks England but is defeated at Stamford Bridge by King Harold Godwinsson, who himself is killed in the battle at Hastings against Duke William the Conqueror of Normandy.
c. 1070	Adam of Bremen writes his *Gesta Hammaburgensis ecclesias pontificum.*
1086	King Knud of Denmark killed in St. Alban's Church in Odense on Funen; he was later venerated as a saint.

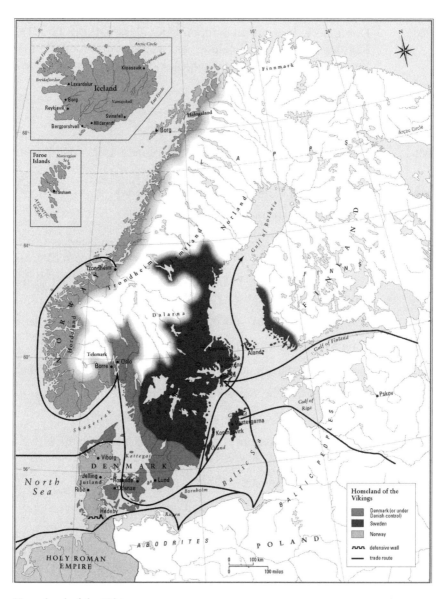

Homeland of the Vikings.

1

Introduction: Time and Space

THE AGE OF THE VIKINGS

"From the fury of the Northmen, O Lord, deliver us." This is alleged to have been the ardent litany chanted in medieval churches and monasteries throughout Europe once the Viking raids had begun. Although the litany is most likely apocryphal—no ninth-century text containing these words has been located—it would seem amply justified, because the fury of the Northmen—Danes, Norwegians, and Swedes—must have been truly terrifying when systematically it was unleashed on Europe. Indeed, writing from Charlemagne's court school in Aachen soon after the unexpected raid in 793 on the church and monastery of Lindisfarne just off the Northumbrian coast, the priest and scholar Alcuin (d. 804) laments in a letter that "never before has such terror appeared in Britain as we have now suffered from a pagan race."[1]

The plundering and destruction of Lindisfarne is cited in most textbooks as the beginning of the Viking age. In the three centuries that followed, the Scandinavians crisscrossed half the world in their longships. As marauders, warriors, traders, and colonists they reached almost every region of the world—known and unknown at that time. In the east, they thrust down the rivers of Russia to the Caspian and Black Sea. In the west, they sailed along the Atlantic coasts, past Arab Spain, through the Straits of Gibraltar, and over the Mediterranean. They reached out across the unknown Atlantic to Iceland, Greenland, and North America. In short, the Scandinavians went almost everywhere there was to go.

As for the end of the Viking age, it has been common to associate that also with a specific historical event: 1066, when the Normans (descendants of the Vikings) crossed the channel to invade England. Since, however, the Scandinavians did not vanish from the British Isles right away, and since the Scandinavian presence continued to be felt in places like Dublin for quite some time, it seems more practical to regard the late eleventh century as marking the end of the Viking age. Broadly speaking, therefore, the Viking age spans the period 800–1100.

"VIKINGS": TOWARD A DEFINITION

The litany and the extract from Alcuin's letter cited above refer to the raiding Scandinavians as Northmen and pagans, respectively. The raiders were called by many names, including also gentiles, foreigners, *Rus,* and Danes. One of the words, "Vikings," has become generally regarded as the appropriate term. Adam of Bremen testifies in his *Gesta Hammaburgensis ecclesiae pontificum* (Activities of the prelates of the Church of Hamburg) that the word was used by the Scandinavians themselves. Adam writes of "the pirates called Vikings by the people of Zealand [the Danes]" but "by our people [the Germans] Ascomanni ['ashmen,' because their ships were made of ash]."[2] Because the word Viking is rarely used in medieval sources outside Scandinavia, it is reasonable to suppose that it is of Norse origin. If this is the case, it may be related to the Old Norse noun *vík,* meaning "bay," "creek," or "inlet." A Viking was therefore someone who kept his ship in a bay either for raiding or trading. In this connection, it might be noted that there is also a place in southern Norway called Vik, which became an early center of Viking raiding fleets. A derivation from the Old Norse verb *víkja* in the sense of "departing," "going away," and "leaving home" has also been suggested, and although this theory may be said not to have won general support, it has the advantage of agreeing with important matters relating to the cause of the Viking voyages. If the word is not of Norse origin, a derivation from the Old English noun *wic* (borrowed from the Latin *vicus*), meaning "camp" or "trading-place," has been proposed. According to this theory, a Viking was, at least to the Anglo-Saxons, a warrior or a trader or both. There is no consensus on the issue, and the matter of the etymology of "Viking" is unresolved.

In addition, "Viking" meant different things to different people of the times. For contemporary Christian communities in Western Europe, the Vikings were barbaric pagans, who suddenly appeared in their ships on foreign shores, where they ruthlessly and brutally maimed and murdered, pillaged and destroyed, raped and enslaved. This image of the Vikings as especially bloodthirsty and cruel is one that can still be found in popular culture, especially the movie industry, which more often than not presents the Vikings as nothing less than terrifying specters. To be sure, the Vikings' ferocity is also emphasized in Norse saga literature and histories written in the Christian era, but to these writers the Vikings symbolized heroism and courage; the Vikings were the epitome of masculine ideals, and a Viking expedition was an opportunity for young men to prove their mettle. To some extent, this attitude still lingers, and Norse saga literature (the Sagas of Icelanders in particular) probably has had more of an impact on shaping conceptions of the Vikings and the Viking age among the Scandinavians themselves than any other sources. From the time the Sagas of Icelanders became objects of study (that is, when the humanism of the Renaissance was taking root in Scandinavia) until well into the twentieth century, scholars generally regarded them as valuable historical sources, and it is almost certainly this past, uncritical use of the sagas that has given rise to the Scandinavians' view of the Vikings as a great civilization and the Viking age as a golden age when Scandinavia exercised a strong power over neighboring countries. The mass media and souvenir industry, which make indiscriminate use of such features as horned helmets, family grave mounds, spectacular drinking horns, harps, and heathen temples, have done much to retain this conception. Indeed, the Vikings have in many ways become a symbol by which Scandinavians identify themselves, and the Vikings have long proved profitable to commercialism.

Regardless of the conflicting attitudes toward the Vikings, there is no doubt that the Vikings were professional pirates and that the name "Vikings" was used as a label for Scandinavian men who banded together to man ships for the purpose of sailing along the coasts to raid ill-defended coastal settlements. But it is doubtful if the term "Viking" should be applied, as has often been done, to the entire population of the Scandinavian countries during the Viking age. Active Vikings at any given time were never more than a tiny fraction of the total population, and the majority of Scandinavians engaged not in raiding abroad but in peaceful activities at home as farmers, fishermen, craftsmen, and the like. Moreover, a man was a Viking only as long as he was on board a Viking ship; when he abandoned that occupation and returned home, he ceased to be a Viking. It seems more practical, therefore, to define "Vikings" somewhat narrowly and limit it to designate those medieval Scandinavians who engaged in banditry, raiding, trading, or military or political action, that is, activities characteristic of the Viking age. It is in this sense the word is employed in this book. For the people of Scandinavia during the Viking age who remained at home, the term "Scandinavians" is used. The term "Norsemen" is used primarily about the pioneering people of Scandinavian descent who discovered and settled new territories.

THE HOMELAND

The word "Scandinavia," the homeland of the Vikings, first occurs in the *Historia naturalis* (Natural history) by the Roman geographer Pliny (d. A.D. 79) as a name for Scania (the southernmost tip of Sweden), which he believed was an island in the Baltic. "Scandinavia" seems not to have been used during the Viking age, and it was not until the eighteenth century that it came to be applied to the area surrounding Scania. In its narrowest sense, it comprises the Scandinavian Peninsula, that is, Norway and Sweden. While this makes geographical sense, it makes no historical, political, and cultural sense, because for a long time Norway was ruled by Danish kings, and a large portion of what is now Sweden belonged to Denmark. Accordingly, "Scandinavia" is generally used in a broader sense to comprise not only Norway and Sweden but also Denmark. Moreover, because the islands in the west—the Faroe Islands and Iceland—were colonized by Scandinavians and share many common cultural traits with the three Scandinavian countries, they too are sometimes included in definitions of Scandinavia. The Faroe Islands came under Norwegian dominion probably in the eleventh century, and Iceland was annexed to the Norwegian crown in 1262. As part of the Norwegian realm, both devolved to the Danish crown in 1380. The Faroe Islands remain a possession of Denmark but have been a self-governing community since 1948. Iceland became an independent republic in 1944.

Scandinavia—in the somewhat broader meaning of the word—is a vast area. It runs from 55° north into the Arctic Ocean, a distance of more than 2,000 km (1,200 miles) and from the western tip of Iceland at 24° west of Greenwich to the eastern border of Norway and Finland at 31° east. Most of this enormous expanse consists of the waters of the North Atlantic and the Baltic, and this has played a vital part in shaping the fates of the Scandinavians and the Scandinavian countries. The sea routes facilitated communication, but at the same time the distances by sea coupled with the often-rugged landmasses have constituted barriers that made it impractical, if not impossible, for Scandinavians to unite under a single government.

Denmark   Scandinavia's southernmost country, Denmark, is the smallest, measuring 43,070 square km (16,629 square miles). The name is derived from its people, the Danes, and it now comprises the peninsula of Jutland (which accounts for almost 70 percent of the land in Denmark) and the islands of Funen and Zealand, which are the largest, together with more than 400 smaller islands, including the island of Bornholm off the southern tip of Sweden. In the Viking age, Danish territory was larger, however, for during that time the three southern Swedish provinces of Scania, Halland, and Blekinge belonged to Denmark, and at the base of Jutland the German border lay at the river Eider, which is further south than the current border. The distance from Skagen, the northernmost tip of Jutland, to the Eider is about 375 km (233 miles).

Denmark is flat; the highest point, the hill of Yding Skovhøj in Jutland, rises only 171 m (561 ft.) above sea level. Much of the country is a patchwork of white coastal beaches, blue lakes, and green fields. During the

Viking age, forests of oak and elm trees covered the land, but most of the original forests have now been felled.

The country's climate was and is generally temperate and moist. In winter, seas are not as cold as land, and in summer they are not as warm. Consequently, west winds from the seas warm Denmark in winter and cool it in summer. Also in winter, west winds bring some warmth from the North Atlantic Current of the Gulf Stream. Because Denmark is a small country, the climate does not differ much from area to area.

Norway, meaning "the way of the north," occupies the western half of the Scandinavian Peninsula. It is a long, nar-row country, measuring 323,900 square km (125,000 square miles). The northern third of the country lies above the Arctic Circle, and the distance from north to south is about 1,800 km (1,118.52 miles), excluding the distant Arctic islands of Svalbard and Jan Mayen, which are Norwegian possessions. The country has a coastline of approximately 2,650 km (1,647 miles); however, if all the fjords and peninsulas are included, the full length of the coast is about 21,351 km (13,267 miles). About 150,000 islands lie off the Norwegian coast, though some of these are only rocky reefs (skerries). The largest island groups are the Lofoten and Vesterålen islands.   **Norway**

About two-thirds of Norway consists of high mountains. The country's average height is more than 457 m (1,500 ft.) above sea level. The highest point is Galdhøpiggen at 2,469 m (8,100 ft.). Large areas of the rugged mountains are bare rock, and forests and woods now cover only about 27 percent of Norway. Farmland is found in the southeastern and Trondheim lowlands, but today agricultural land covers only about 5 percent of the country.

Western Norway has a marine climate with relatively cool summers and mild winters. The warm North Atlantic Current of the Gulf Stream keeps most of the fjords ice free, even in the Arctic region. Eastern Norway, which is sheltered by the mountains, has an inland climate with warm summers and cool winters. The far north (known as the "Land of the Midnight Sun") has continuous daylight from the middle of May through July; in winter the region has a corresponding period of continuous darkness.

Reindeer and other Arctic animals are found throughout Norway. Elk are common in the large forests and red deer on the west coast. In the Viking age, large animals of prey thrived in Norway, but now the wolf and bear are found only in a few regions, primarily in the north. Foxes, otters, and martens are still common, and badgers and beavers live in many areas.

Sweden derives its name from one of the two main prehistoric tribes, the Svear, who are mentioned as early as A.D. 98. Sweden occupies the eastern half of the Scandinavian Peninsula, and it is the largest of the Scandinavian countries. Modern Sweden   **Sweden** measures 449,960 square km (173,730 square miles), and the distance from north to south is about 1,600 km (995.24 miles). Finland lies to the northeast, and a long coastline with sandy beaches in the south and rocky cliffs in the north extends along the Gulf of Bothnia and the Baltic Sea on the east. Several groups of small islands lie off the coasts. The largest islands are Gotland and Öland, both located in the Baltic Sea.

About a twelfth of Sweden consists of lakes. The largest lake is Lake Vänern, which covers 5,584 square km (2,156 square miles). Woodland and forests of fir, pine, and birch cover about 68 percent of modern Sweden. Arable land makes up only 7 percent. While moose, roe deer, foxes, and hares are found throughout Sweden, wolves and bears now only inhabit the northern forests, where large herds of reindeer are also found.

In terms of physical geography, Sweden may be divided into three regions. The northern part is mountainous. The highest point is Kebnekaise, located north of the Arctic Circle, which rises 2,111 m (6,926 ft.) above sea level. The central part consists in the east of lowlands and in the west of highlands. The southern part includes the highlands of Småland and the plains of Scania.

The climate of Sweden varies considerably between the northern and southern parts of the country. From the southwest, winds from the Atlantic Ocean make the weather mild, but changeable. Another influence comes from continental high pressures to the east, which create sunny weather, hot in summer and cold in winter.

NOTES

1. Alcuin is quoted from Dorothy Whitelock, ed., *English Historical Documents, c. 500–1042.* Rev. ed. English Historical Documents, vol. 1 (London: Eyre & Spottiswoode, 1979), p. 776.

2. Adam of Bremen is quoted from Adam of Bremen, *History of the Archbishops of Hamburg-Bremen,* trans. Francis J. Tschan, Records of Civilization: Sources and Studies, vol. 53 (New York: Columbia University Press, 1959), p. 190.

2

Domestic Life

KINSHIP SYSTEM

The rune stones in Viking-age Scandinavia show that the kinship system was a bilateral one. Men erected memorials to their relatives by marriage, and many of the inscriptions include the name of the wife or mother of a dead man, and in some, a husband, when commemorating his wife, names her father and occasionally her grandfather. Medieval Scandinavian laws confirm this type of kinship system. Their rules of inheritance show that kinship was traced through both sexes and acknowledge that women have a right to inherit. Admittedly, sons are given a stronger claim than their sisters, but daughters have priority over their uncles and grandfather. And what is more, women could inherit land from children who died without descendants. It has been suggested that the absence of husbands on military raids or their deaths abroad leaving underage heirs may at least in part have contributed to this, because the needs to secure family property were better served by partnerships between sexes than by patriarchy.

FAMILY STRUCTURE

The nuclear family (a social unit comprising husband, wife, and their children) was the predominant domestic group in Viking-age Scandinavia. This is evident from rune stones, most of which were raised in memory of people by their closest relatives—by spouses for each other, by children for their parents, or by siblings for each other. The two tenth-century Jelling stones in Jutland, for example, were raised by King Gorm the Old (d. 958) in memory of his queen and by their son Harald Bluetooth (d. c. 987) in memory of his parents.

Extended families (the addition of one or more relatives other than children) and especially multigenerational families were less common. The reason for the latter is obvious: the average life expectancy was somewhere between 30 and 40 years at most, and only a small percentage of people lived long enough to enter the role of grandparent. One may assume, however, that there was considerable local variation. In sparsely populated areas, and especially in areas with intensive animal husbandry, grand families (two or more nuclear families living together in the same dwelling) were probably not uncommon and would seem to have been financially advantageous. By practicing joint ownership of a farm, families could avoid splitting up the means of production and could pool family labor. The Sagas of Icelanders and Icelandic laws report several instances of such complex families.

Persons living alone and all persons living in the same dwelling, biologically related or not, constitute a household. Nuclear family and household were often identical units, especially among the lower classes of farmers. Because, however, servants, lodgers, and relatives quite often lived with nuclear families, households tended to be larger social units than the nuclear families. It is difficult to give estimates for the mean household size in the Viking age, but several researchers have suggested 10 to 13 persons. As for the size of nuclear families, five or six persons is probably a fair average, but because there was a high rate of infant mortality, many more children must have been born.

Despite the predominance of the nuclear family structure, family ties extended well beyond the immediate family to include almost the entire clan on both the paternal and maternal sides. The family was a powerful unit of protection. It was from the family that a person would receive assistance or support if he or she got into trouble, and it was to the family that a person owed his or her obligations. This is clear from the laws concerning *wergild* (compensation made to the injured party for the killing of a man). Both the payment and receipt of *wergild* were divided among the families of the perpetrator and the victim in amounts that grew smaller as the degree of kinship became more distant. In Scandinavia this extended far into the branches of the family and in Iceland as far as to fourth cousins, that is, to people sharing a great-great-great-grandfather.

MARRIAGE

In pre-Christian times, marriage was essentially a commercial contract between two families. The prospective bride and groom were expected to be of similar status in birth and means, although the Sagas of Icelanders suggest that wealth could compensate for social prestige, and in such cases the woman usually married down. Emotional attachment or love, as we would call it today, appears not to have played any particular role in a man's choice of a woman.

The arrangement consisted of two steps: the betrothal and the wedding. The initiative was taken by the man or by his father; the woman's father could do nothing to initiate the marriage of his daughter but had to wait for a suitor to appear. If the suitor seemed acceptable, negotiations took place, in which the prospective groom or his spokesman promised to pay a sum known as the bride price and the woman's father or guardian agreed to hand over at the wedding a dowry, the sum of the woman's inheritance. When the agreement had been reached, the conditions were repeated in front of witnesses, and the date of marriage was fixed. The woman was absent from all negotiations; female consent to marriage was not required until Christian times, when a woman could choose to take the veil.

The wedding took the form of a feast at either the bride's or the groom's house, which often lasted several days. The climax, but not necessarily the end, of the feast was the bedding of the bride and groom. The Old Norse term for the marriage ceremony is *brud(h)laup*, a compound word, of which the first element means "bride" and the second "leap" or "run." The origin of the word has been debated. It may refer to the journey of the bride to her new home, but it invariably calls to mind an image of a woman trying to flee or run away from her prospective husband, and it is known that during their expeditions abroad, Viking men obtained women through force, some of whom they brought home as wives.

There is little in the way of documentary evidence regarding age at marriage during the Viking age, but the fact that the Sagas of Icelanders contain a considerable number of cases where girls married at the age of 12 or in their early teens is indicative and makes it clear that there was no normative resistance to such a practice.

Marriage precluded other sexual outlets for women. A wife's adultery was a serious crime, and, according to some **Adultery** of the Danish and Swedish provincial laws, it gave a husband the right to kill both her and her lover if they were caught in the act. Although Norwegian and Icelandic laws also treat unfaithfulness of husbands as a crime, men generally seem to have been free to have extramarital relationships. In his *Gesta Hammaburgensis ecclesiae pontificum* (Activities of the prelates of the Church of Hamburg), the eleventh-century cleric Adam of Bremen says about the Swedes that "in their sexual relations with women...they know no bounds; a man according to his means has two or three or more wives at one time, rich men and princes an unlimited number."[1] Indeed, polygamy was practiced by many of the Scandinavian kings and earls. About the Norwegian King Harald Fairhair (d. 930–940) it is told that he dismissed nine mistresses before marrying the Danish princess Ragnhild. And the Norwegian Earl Hakon of Lade (d.

c. 995) is reported to have had the daughters of his subjects brought home to him, where he lay with them a week or two and then sent them back to their parents. There is nothing to indicate that concubinage or extramarital affairs in general were regarded as improper at any social level before the Church condemned them as sinful; and if a man publicly acknowledged a child born to him out of wedlock, he could give it gifts, which essentially meant that the child became entitled to a share in the inheritance, though with some restrictions.

Sexuality
Heterosexuality was the norm in Viking-age Scandinavia, but that homosexual relations between men were recognized as social phenomena is clear from Old Norse-Icelandic literature, especially the Sagas of Icelanders, in which they are regarded as signs of unmanliness and immorality. As in many societies with a distinct masculine disposition, and particularly where this disposition is combined with the requirements of warfare, homosexuality was equated with effeminacy and cowardice, and it was epitomized by the man who passively tolerated sodomy. Although the later secular laws do not mention homosexuality per se, they do mention verbal accusations of (passive) homosexuality, which were considered a serious crime and punishable by law.

Divorce
The sources suggest that divorces were relatively common and that it was easy for both men and women to obtain a divorce. In the pre-Christian period a formal declaration before witnesses was probably sufficient. In Christian times, divorce was granted only at the bishop's discretion, for, according to the Christian Church, marriage was not a financial agreement between two parties but a sacrament and a monogamous union that could not be dissolved because the couple had promised faithfulness to one another for life. After a divorce, the woman would typically return to her family with her personal belongings, her dowry, and, if her husband was the cause of the divorce, the bride price. The purpose of the return of the dowry, the function of which was to provide maintenance for the wife, was clearly to ensure that a divorcee did not become financially destitute.

WOMEN'S ROLES

In marriage, men and women had well-defined, distinct roles. Basically women managed those of the couple's affairs that pertained within the house, while men were in charge of everything outside and represented the family in society at large. Only men enjoyed legal or judicial responsibilities, and only men could witness and prosecute in law. Only men fought, and only men could speak at the assemblies.

The primary duty of a wife was to provide her husband with offspring, preferably male offspring. In the absence of any reliable method of birth control, there would be little opportunity for respite between pregnancies, and the care of infants and small children must have occupied most of a woman's time. The high mortality of young women in the Viking age has often been attributed to frequent pregnancies and complications associated with childbirth. But this may be an oversimplification, especially in light of the fact that women had as one of their particular tasks the nursing of the elderly and the sick, which obviously meant increased exposure to infectious diseases.

In addition to fulfilling reproductive needs, a woman also fulfilled labor requirements. Upon marriage, a husband would typically turn over the running of the household to his wife. The specific tasks involved in running a household obviously depended upon a couple's social status and whether the couple lived in the countryside or in town. Little is known about women in urban communities, but presumably wives of craftsmen and merchants took some part in their husbands' businesses. We are better informed about women in the countryside, especially those married to landowning men, although also in the farming communities the circumstances of women varied. The smaller the farm, and, consequently, the smaller the size of the household, the greater the amount and variety of work required of husband and wife; and in areas where fishing and handicrafts were subsidiary occupations, women typically did most of the heavy work. On larger farms with a larger household, many jobs, especially the less desirable ones, such as cleaning the pens or milking the cows or sheep, could be delegated to servants or slaves.

Indoor work included the preparation and preservation of food and drink, cleaning and laundering, and the manufacturing of cloth and the production of garments or hangings. The last-mentioned tasks—spinning and weaving—were laborious, and it is likely that men participated in the work. Although linen was produced, wool was by far the commonest woven cloth, and the first step was obviously the shearing or plucking of the sheep or goats followed by the cleaning and grading of the wool. Next, the wool was carded with fingers or a special comb in order to straighten it and separate the fibers. The spinning was done by attaching the carded wool to a distaff. The wool was then teased onto a weighted spindle, and by twisting and turning the spindle as it was thrown to the ground, the yarn was rolled onto the spindle. When sufficient yarn had been spun, it was removed from the spindle and wound into a ball, unless it had to be dyed, in which case it was wound onto a wooden reel to form a skein (although some cloth was presumably dyed after it had been woven). At this point in the process, the weaving could commence. The most common loom was the so-called warp-weighted loom, which is known throughout the world. Admittedly, the loom found in the mid-ninth-century Oseberg ship-burial in Norway—the only loom to survive from the Viking age—is a two-beam vertical loom, but most likely it is atypical; indeed, loomweights, required to place tension on the warps on an upright loom, are common finds. During weaving, the weft was straightened by the use of a weaving-batten. Detailed patterns were made with the help of small combs, thread-pickers, and pin-beaters. After the cloth was cut from the loom, it was sometimes fulled (soaked and pressed in a mixture of fermented urine and hot water). This process caused the cloth to shrink and thicken, and it also reduced the oil content of the wool.

Although women's work pertained within the house, it does not mean that all tasks were performed indoors. Men were generally the ones who tended the animals, but women were in charge of dairy operations. Men were also the ones who sowed and fertilized the home fields, but women, especially in poor families, participated in fieldwork during the harvest. The task of collecting berries, mosses, herbs, seaweed, wild fruit, and eggs from birds, whether domestic or wild, also fell to women, as did the washing of clothes, which was typically done in streams, and the fetching of water for drinking, cooking, and bathing.

Widows In this age of high mortality, widowhood was not an uncommon state. Because it was difficult for a single person to work a holding, rapid remarriage was often a practical necessity if the widow was young and had small children to care for.

Older widows, on the other hand, probably enjoyed considerable freedom, at least if they were women of high or moderately high social status. An older widow was no longer under the authority of her father, and her sons were usually grown and gone. Her dowry and the bride price guaranteed her economic security, and she was in charge of her husband's property. The Sagas of Icelanders contain several examples of independent and powerful older widows. The most famous of these is Unn (alternatively called Aud) the Deepminded, wife of a Norse king in Dublin and daughter of a Norwegian chieftain who went to the Hebrides as an agent for the Norwegian King Harald Fairhair. Around 900, Unn's husband was killed in battle in Ireland, and her son was killed fighting in Scotland. Accordingly, Unn was left responsible for a large number of grandchildren. *Laxdœla saga* (Saga of the people of Laxardal) reports that because of the hostilities between the Scots and the Norsemen, Unn felt that her grandchildren's future prospects in the British Isles were rather dim and so resolved to emigrate to Iceland, where two of her brothers were already living.

She had a *knorr* [= ship] built secretly in the forest. When it was finished, she made the ship ready and set out with substantial wealth. She took along all her kinsmen who were still alive, and people say it is hard to find another example of a woman managing to escape from such a hostile situation with as much wealth and as many followers. It shows what an outstanding woman Unn was.[2]

The saga proceeds to relate that Unn cleverly married her granddaughters to sons of prominent men in the Orkney and Faroe Islands, whose authority she managed to escape by continuing to Iceland, where she laid claim to a large area of land, of which she gave portions to family members and followers. She lived until she had arranged for a suitable wife for her favorite grandson, to whom she bequeathed all her property, and died with dignity during the wedding feast. The resourcefulness and independence exhibited by Unn and others may well have been fostered by the many responsibilities with which women were left when their husbands were away on trading voyages and military expeditions.

Obviously not all women married. Unmarried daughters, who were not needed at home, could choose to work on **Unmarried** another farm or in towns. On farms, a woman could hire **Women** herself out for specific tasks for a specific period of time. The income was probably small, among other reasons because there were slave women, who for the most part had to be content with lodging, food, and clothes in return for their labor. Towns offered a wider range of employment. The trades or types of work in which women engaged were typically female ones: washing, cleaning, baking, brewing, and cloth making.

Viking-age graves indicate that women, especially older ones, commanded considerable respect. Many of the richest **Attitudes** burials in Scandinavia are of women, the most famous being **toward** the Oseberg ship-burial on the shores of Oslo fjord in Nor- **Women** way. That they also enjoyed a measure of freedom of action is suggested, among other things, by the fact that several rune stones in Scandinavia were raised at the initiative of women and some moreover by women in memory of women. A famous example is the stone from Dynna just north of Oslo, which was erected by a woman in memory of her daughter. With its incised decoration of the Magi under the Christmas star riding to find the Christ child, it is clearly a work from the early Christian period. Its inscription reads: "Gunnvor, Thrydrik's daughter, made a bridge in memory of her daughter Astrid. She was the most skilful girl in Hadeland."[3] Other stones were raised by men in memory of women. The women named in the inscriptions on these stones are usually wives and mothers, and the men typically pay tribute to the deceased woman's fine housekeeping and other traditionally female skills, as exemplified by the mid-eleventh-century stone from Hassmyra in Västmanland, Sweden, raised by the farmer Holmgaut in memory of his wife Odindis:

> A better housewife
> will never come
> to Hassmyra
> to run the farm.
> Red Balli carved
> these runes.
> She was a good sister
> to Sigmund.[4]

In addition, several women were buried with pairs of scales as symbols of good housekeeping or with keys to the meal or treasure chest as symbols of their authority in the home.

Foreigners were evidently so struck by the independent behavior of Scandinavian women that they considered it worthy of comment. Al-Ghazal, a ninth-century poet and diplomat from Andalusia (Muslim Spain), who was sent on a mission to an unspecified Viking court (possibly the court of the Norwegian King Turgeis in Ireland or the royal seat in Lejre on Zealand in Denmark) emphasizes the frankness and flirtatiousness of high-ranking Norse women and the legal freedom women had to leave an unsatisfactory marriage. His comment on women's right to divorce is echoed by Ibrahim b. Ya'qub al-Turtushi, a tenth-century merchant or diplomat also from Andalusia, who visited what is probably Hedeby on the inner part of the Schlei fjord in South Schleswig (in what is now Germany). Clearly, such conduct and practice were in stark contrast to that to which these men were accustomed.

CHILDREN

Birth The birth of a baby was exclusively a female affair. The helpers were always women, trained or untrained, although on more isolated farms the husband assisted. It typically took place in the bath chamber or other separate place, evidently in order to provide the prospective mother with privacy and to limit the risk of infection. The normal birth position was for the woman to kneel on the floor. As the birth progressed, she would shift to a knee-elbow position, and the child would be received from behind. Birth chairs appear not to have been used in Scandinavia.

Childbirth was a risky matter in the Viking age. Although there are no figures for childbirth deaths in this period, it is certain that they were considerably higher than they are now. One reason is without doubt early marriage, because young and often not-fully-grown females have a particularly marked pregnancy-related supermortality. In the pre-Christian period, runes and charms were offered as remedies for painful labor and difficult births; in Christian times, appeals were made to the Virgin Mary and the saints Margaret and Dorothy.

Infant mortality was also high and must be seen in light of poor hygienic standards, causing frequent acute gastroenteritis and epidemics of dangerous intestinal diarrheal diseases like dysentery and typhoid fever. Epidemics of other children's diseases, such as measles, diphtheria, whooping cough, and scarlet fever, no doubt also took their toll.

Unwanted Babies Despite the desire for offspring, some babies were unwanted. Such babies were exposed to the elements and left to their fate, and the fact that this practice was prohibited in some Scandinavian laws compiled in the twelfth and thirteenth centuries suggests that it continued well after the introduction of Christianity; indeed, some laws permitted exposure when a baby was deformed.

Runic inscriptions naming the children of a couple show that daughters were considerably fewer than sons. Sons were more useful in the home than daughters, who had to be provided with a dowry to attract a suitable husband, and there are reasons to believe that couples deliberately attempted to limit through exposure or neglect the number of girls who were allowed to live.

Shortly after birth, the baby was given its name, and this was the first formal event in a baby's life. The naming of the baby **Infancy** signified its inclusion in society and—in Christian times—the Church. Even in pre-Christian times, the ceremony appears to have involved sprinkling the baby with water and giving it a present (another gift was given when the baby cut its first tooth). The choice of a name was an important matter, because name, personal qualities, and good fortune were all considered to be closely related. Rune stones and Old Norse-Icelandic literature show that parents often reproduced name-elements in different combination with each child, as with the children of the ninth-century Norwegian Vegeir, who were named Vebjorn, Vedis, Vegest, Vemund, Vestein, Vethorm, and Vethorn. Alternatively, parents repeated the name of a recently deceased relative, commonly a paternal grand-parent. It is possible that notions of metempsychosis to some degree reinforced the latter principle; later popular belief suggests an interrelationship between the naming of a child and impressions of the deceased relative's character. After the eighth century, the cult of Thor led to a great increase in the use of the god's name as one of its elements, so that by the end of the Viking age names such as Thorgrim, Thorsten, Thorgaut, Thordis, as well as shortened forms such as Toki and Tobbi were found all over Scandinavia and in the Norse settlements and colonies. A more random naming practice within families is also observable during this time, such as at the Hunnestad monument in Scania in Sweden, where a number of eleventh-century rune stones give the names of the sons of a certain Gunni: Asbjorn, Tumi, Roi, and Leikfrid.

Babies were breast-fed for a long time, and during the first years of their life children were in female care, though obviously under the authority of their fathers. The appearance in children's graves of bronze jingle bells, small ornaments, and infant clothing testify to the tender feelings of parents for their little ones, and, of course, sentimentality and grief at the loss of a young child. There are, however, no rune stones raised in memory of children, and nothing is known of beliefs about children's afterlife.

The life of children was a combination of learning and play. There is archaeological evidence of model weapons, **Childhood** boats, and animals, and these toys allowed children to imi- **and Youth** tate the activities of adults. Ball games and other outdoor activities were no doubt also common. But childhood was brief in the Viking age, and from an early age children were actively guided toward their anticipated places in society. For girls of the privileged classes, this might mean learning the skills required for household management; for the less privileged cooking, laundry, spinning, and other domestic skills. Boys might be given the tasks of herding or caring for domestic animals or, if they were of royal or well-to-do families, taught the art of hunting and riding and the basics of combat and sailing. The mentors were presumably the children's parents, though the practice of fosterage, that is, having one's child—especially son—raised in another family, was common. Often this was a "political" arrangement between the child's father and the foster father, and, like marriage, it was a way of supplementing blood kinship relationships with nonblood kinship bonds in order to develop new alliances or strengthen existing ones.

OLD AGE

Because the average age at death in the Viking age is usually put below 40, few people reached what we would now consider old age. Retirement did not exist as an official institution, but we occasionally hear of the head of the household transferring his or her property to a son or grandson. Such was the arrangement made by the Icelandic poet and farmer Egil Skallagrimsson, who died shortly before 1000. In his biography, *Egils saga* (Egil's saga), it is told that after his wife died, Egil gave up farming and turned over the estate to his son Thorstein, but because he did not care much for him, he went to live with his stepdaughter Thordis and her husband. Egil was a wealthy man, and we have no means of knowing the fate of elderly or infirm servants or slaves; nor do we know how old age was viewed by the elderly or by the younger generation(s). The impression given by *Egils saga* is that certainly for men old age was undesirable.

Egil Skallagrimsson lived a long life, but in his old age he grew very frail and both his hearing and sight failed. He also suffered from very stiff legs...

One day Egil was walking outdoors alongside the wall when he stumbled and fell. Some women saw this, laughed at him and said, "You're completely finished, Egil, now that you fall over of your own accord."...

Egil went completely blind. One winter day when the weather was cold, he went to warm himself by the fire. The cook said it was astonishing for a man who had been as great as Egil to lie around under people's feet and stop them going about their work.

"Don't grudge me that I warm myself through by the fire," said Egil. "We should make room for each other."

"Stand up," she said, "and go off to your bed and leave us to get on with our work."...

Another time Egil went over to the fire to keep warm, and someone asked him if his legs were cold and told him not to stretch them out too close to the fire.

"I shall do that," said Egil, "but I don't find it easy to control my legs now that I cannot see. Being blind is dismal."

Then Egil spoke a verse:

Time seems long in passing
as I lie alone,
a senile old man
on the king's guard [= back? bed? chest?].
My legs are two
frigid widows,
those women
need some flame.[5]

In his poem, Egil may well speak for other Viking-age men who reached old age; indeed, according to pagan Scandinavian religion, it was considered nobler to die by the sword than from sickness and old age. The lack of sympathy for old age infirmity, which is given clear expression in the comments made by the female servants in *Egils saga*, may also have a basis in reality, and there are indications that some old people were as unwanted or superfluous as some infants. Although there is no documentary evidence of the exposure or killing of old people, the tale in *Ynglinga saga* (Saga of the Ynglings), as related by the Icelandic historian and poet Snorri Sturluson (1178/9–1241) in his *Heimskringla* (Disc of the world), about the ancient King Aun of Uppsala, Sweden, hints at such practice. According to Snorri, Aun had struck a bargain with Odin that the god would grant him 10 years of life for every one of his sons that he sacrificed. He had sacrificed nine of them and grown so old and feeble that he was bedridden and drank out of a horn like an infant. But when it came to the tenth son, the king's subjects said no, and Snorri adds that it was later called Aun's disease when a man died of old age without any sickness. It is also known that in Sweden there was a tradition of "family cliffs," from which men and women were pushed or hurled themselves in times of famine, and of "family cudgels," with which the elderly were knocked on their heads.

NOTES

1. Adam of Bremen is quoted from Adam of Bremen, *History of the Archbishops of Hamburg-Bremen*, trans. Francis J. Tschan, Records of Civilization: Sources and Studies, vol. 53 (New York: Columbia University Press, 1959), p. 203.

2. *Laxdoela saga* is quoted from Viðar Hreinsson, ed. *The Complete Sagas of Icelanders Including 49 Tales* (Reykjavík, Iceland: Leifur Eiríksson Publishing, 1997), 5:3.

3. The inscription on the Dynna stone is quoted from R. I. Page, *Runes* (London: British Museum Publications, 1987), p. 52.

4. The inscription on the Hassmyra stone is quoted from Judith Jesch, *Women in the Viking Age* (Woodbridge: Boydell Press, 1991), p. 65.

5. *Egils saga* is quoted from Viðar Hreinsson, ed. *The Complete Sagas of Icelanders*, 1:174–75.

3

Economic Life

SETTLEMENT CONDITIONS

The economy of the Scandinavian countries was dependent on and conditioned by the local ecology. Agriculture was the mainstay of the economy in most areas, though obviously the farming conditions of Denmark differed considerably from those of, for example, northern Norway and Sweden, for Scandinavia is divided into different ecological zones with different resources. The differences are clearly reflected in the settlement patterns of Scandinavia. Denmark and most of the Swedish coastlands were dominated by village settlements, that is, a cluster of three farms or more. These were generally situated on easily cultivated land. In most of Norway, the Swedish interior, and also the Norse colonies in the North Atlantic, the normal pattern of settlement took the form of separate or individual farms.

The most detailed, contemporary source of information about the settlement conditions in the Scandinavian countries is Adam of Bremen, who in his *Gesta Hammaburgensis ecclesiae pontificum* (Activities of the prelates of the Church of Hamburg), written in the 1070s, includes interesting geographical and ethnographical descriptions of the northern countries. About Denmark he reports as follows:

The principal part of Denmark, called Jutland, extends lengthwise from the Eider River towards the north; it is a journey of three days if you turn aside in the direction of the island of Funen. But if you measure the distance direct from Schleswig to Ålborg, it is a matter of five to seven days' travel... At the Eider Jutland is fairly wide, but thereafter it narrows little by little like a tongue to the point called Wendila [Vendsyssel], where Jutland comes to an end. Thence it is a very short passage to Norway. The soil in Jutland is sterile; except for places close to a river, nearly everything looks like a desert. It is a salt land and a vast wilderness. Furthermore, if Germany as a whole is frightful for its densely wooded highlands, Jutland itself is more frightful in other respects. The land is avoided because of the scarcity of crops, and the sea because it is infested by pirates. Hardly a cultivated spot is to be found anywhere, scarcely a place fit for human habitation. But wherever there is an arm of the sea it has very large cities.

Funen is a fairly important island, lying back of that called Wendila in the entrance of the Barbarian Gulf. It is close to the region named Jutland, from every part of which the passage to Funen is very short. There is the great city of Odense. Small islands encircle it, all abounding in crops. And it is to be observed that if you pass through Jutland into Funen, your route is a straight way to the north. But your course faces east in going through Funen into Zealand. There are two passages to Zealand, one from Funen, the other from Århus; each place is an equal distance from Zealand. The sea is naturally tempestuous and full of two kinds of danger so that, even if you have a fair wind, you can hardly escape the hands of pirates.

Zealand is an island, very large in extent, situated in an inner bight of the Baltic Sea. It is very celebrated as much for the bravery of its men as for the abundance of its crops. It is two days' journey in length and almost the same in breadth. Its largest city is Roskilde, the seat of Danish royalty. This island, equally distant from Funen and from Scania, may be crossed in a night. To the west of it lies Jutland, with the cities of Århus and Ålborg, and Wendila; to the north, where it also is a desert, is the Norwegian strait; to the south, the aforementioned Funen and the Slavic Gulf. On the east it faces the headlands of Scania, where is situated the city of Lund...

From Zealand to Scania there are many routes; the shortest is that to Hälsingborg, which is even within the range of vision. Scania is the province of Denmark fairest to look upon—whence also its name—well provided with men, opulent of crops, rich in merchandise, and now full of churches. Scania is twice as large as Zealand, that is it has three hundred churches, whereas Zealand is said to have half that number, and Funen a third. Scania is the most remote part of Denmark, almost an island, for it is surrounded on all sides by sea except for one reach of land which, becoming mainland on the east, separates Sweden from Denmark. The densely wooded highlands and very rugged mountains, over which the road from Scania into Götaland necessarily runs, make one doubt whether perils by land are more easily avoided than perils by sea, and whether to prefer the former to the latter.[1]

Following his description of Denmark, Adam of Bremen gives an account of Sweden and Norway:

The Swedish country is extremely fertile; the land is rich in fruits and honey besides excelling all others in cattle raising, exceedingly happy in streams and woods, the whole region everywhere full of merchandise from foreign parts. Thus you may say that the Swedes are lacking in none of the riches, except the pride that we love or rather adore. For they regard as nothing every means of vainglory; that is, gold, silver, stately chargers, beaver and marten pelts, which make us lose our minds admiring them...

As Nortmannia is the farthest country of the world, so we properly place consideration of it in the last part of the book. By moderns it is called Norway...In its length that land extends into the farthest northern zone, whence also it takes its name. It begins with towering crags at the sea commonly called the Baltic; then with its main ridge bent toward the north, after following the course of the shore line of a raging ocean, it finally has its bounds in the Riphean Mountains, where the tired world also comes to an end. On account of the roughness of its mountains and the immoderate cold, Norway is the most unproductive of all countries, suited only for herds. They browse their cattle, like the Arabs, far off in the solitudes. In this way do the people make a living from their livestock by using the milk of the flocks or herds for food and the wool for clothing. Consequently, there are produced very valiant fighters who, not softened by any overindulgence in fruits, more often attack others than others trouble them. Even though they are sometimes assailed—not with impunity—by the Danes, who are just as poor, the Norwegians live in terms of amity with their neighbors, the Swedes. Poverty has forced them thus to go all over the world and from piratical raids they bring home in great abundance the riches of the lands. In this way they bear up under the unfruitfulness of their own country. Since accepting Christianity, however, imbued with better teachings, they have already learned to love the truth and peace and to be content with their poverty—indeed to disperse what they had gathered, not as before to gather what had been dispersed...

In many places in Norway and Sweden cattle herdsmen are even men of the highest station, living in the manner of patriarchs and by the work of their own hands. All, indeed, who live in Norway are thoroughly Christian, except those who are removed beyond the arctic tract along the ocean. These people, it is said, are to this day so superior in the magic arts or incantations that they profess to know what every one is doing the world over. Then they also draw great sea monsters to shore with a powerful mumbling of words and do much else of which one reads in the Scriptures about magicians...They use the pelts of wild beasts for clothing and in speaking to one another are said to gnash their teeth rather than to utter words, so that they can hardly be understood by the peoples nearest to them. That mountain region is named by Roman writers the Riphean range, terrible for its perpetual snows. Without these frosty snows the Skritefingi [Sami] cannot live, and in their course over the deepest drifts they fly even faster than the wild beasts. In those same mountains there are such large numbers of big game that the greatest part of the country subsists only on the beasts of the forest. Aurochs, buffaloes, and elk are taken there as in Sweden. Bison, furthermore, are caught in Slavia and Russia. Only in Norway, however, are there black fox and hares, white martens and bears of the same color who live under water like aurochs...

The metropolitan city of the Norwegians is Trondheim, which, now graced with churches, is frequented by a great multitude of peoples. In that city reposes the body of the most blessed Olaf, king and martyr. At this tomb the Lord to this very day works such very great miraculous cures that those who do not despair of being able to get help through the merits of the saint flock together there from far-off lands. But the route is of a kind that, boarding a ship, they may, in a day's journey, cross the sea from Ålborg or Wendila of the Danes to Viken, a city of the Norwegians. Sailing thence toward the left along the coast of Norway, the city called Trondheim is reached on the fifth day. But it is possible also to go another way that leads over a land road from Scania of the Danes to Trondheim. This route, however, is slower in the mountainous country, and travelers avoid it because it is dangerous.[2]

RURAL LIFE

Agriculture
Adam of Bremen's account is not accurate in all its details. The geographical relationship of the Danish islands is not precise, and place-name research shows that there were many villages in Jutland during the Viking age. The best-known and the most thoroughly excavated and examined Danish village is Vorbasse in central Jutland. Its history spans from 100 B.C. to the end of the Viking age, during which it shifted several times within a small area. In the first half of the eighth century, the village of Vorbasse had seven farms on fenced-in square plots each with a wide gateway to a communal street. Six of the farms were of approximately the same size, but the seventh was larger. In layout, however, they were all similar. Each farm had a main building situated in the middle of the yard containing both dwelling and byres. The main building was surrounded by smaller buildings, some situated along the fence. These buildings were probably storage places for food and winter fodder, workshops, and dwellings for servants and slaves. In addition, there was a hayloft and some sunken buildings, and some of the farms also had a smithy and a well.

In the byres of the Vorbasse village, traces of stall partitions show that there had been room for 20 to 30 animals in each farm, which suggests that the economy was based on animal husbandry. Indeed, livestock breeding appears to have occupied a strong position not only in Denmark, but also in Sweden and Norway. For dairy farming, cows were the most important animals, though goats were also used as milk-producing animals. Pigs were raised for their meat, especially in the southern part of Scandinavia, and sheep were bred in some areas for wool and meat. In addition, hens, ducks, and geese were kept; they provided eggs and meat, and their feathers were used for pillows and eiderdowns. Horses were used primarily for transportation and as draft animals, though in pagan times horse meat was eaten. In the mountainous areas of Norway in particular, the practice developed during the Viking age of transferring cattle, sheep, and goats to the mountain pastures (shielings) during the summer months, where the animals could graze on uncultivated land not immediately accessible from the farm. In the fall, the animals were then sorted and driven home, where some would be slaughtered and others kept for the winter.

Around the Vorbasse village cultivated fields were found, and grain appears to have been grown throughout Scandinavia in the Viking age, though especially in Denmark. Barley was the most important crop, but rye and oats were popular too. In addition, peas, beans, cabbage, hops, hemp, and flax were cultivated; the last-mentioned was used for linen making. The smaller fields were cultivated by picks and hoes with iron blades on wooden shafts. On larger fields an ard (a plough without mold-board) was used, which scratched the surface of the soil with a downward-directed point pulled by one or more oxen or horses. It is not known when the proper plough was introduced, but it must have been known in Denmark in the second half of the tenth century, and during the next two centuries it spread to western Sweden and southern Norway. Corn harvesting was done with sickles and haying with scythes consisting of iron blades fitted with wooden handles. Rakes, pitchforks, and other tools needed for hay making, have not survived, so most likely they were made of wood. Other agricultural tools included broad-bladed knives to cut foliage, axes, whetstones, and, of course, objects associated with animal husbandry, such as sheep shears.

The various tools and implements were fabricated locally. Many farms had their own smithies for working iron smelted from bog ore. Norway and Sweden had great resources of bog-iron, which became the basis for a considerable iron trade in the Viking age and of great economic importance. It is known that smiths enjoyed much prestige in Viking-age Scandinavia, and some of the wealthiest graves in Scandinavia are those of iron workers. Such craftsmen had, of course, their own tools necessary for the trade, including bellows, furnace stones (to protect the nozzle of the bellows used to raise the heat of their furnaces), tongs, hammers, metal shears, files, and an anvil.

Hunting as well as sea- and freshwater-fishing were important in all parts of Scandinavia, but especially in areas where people lived in marginal farming territories. The fish resources along the North Atlantic shores of Scandinavia were and are quite unique, not only because they are very rich, but also because they are relatively close to land. Accordingly, fish could be caught with simple fishing equipment (spear, net, and line) and in small boats. In the coastal areas of Norway and in northern Sweden, where grain cultivation and cattle and sheep breeding were minimal due to the climatic conditions, fishing was a staple of the economy. Indeed, traces of fishing stations consisting of small huts or buildings have been found along the coast lines. The finds in these huts include fishing hooks, line sinkers, potsherds, knives, and bones of various fish. Lakes and rivers in Scandinavia also contained a variety of fish, of which salmon was the most important.

Hunting and Fishing

In Denmark, hunting was not a significant source of food or income, but in large areas of Norway and Sweden it gave farmers an extra and often necessary supply of cash and meat. On land, squirrel, ermine, marten, fox, and, in Norway and Sweden, bear were mostly hunted for fur and hides, while deer, elk, reindeer, and hare were also hunted for meat. From the elk and reindeer people took antler, which was used to fabricate combs,

spindle-whorls, spoons, arrowheads, and other small objects. The northernmost part of Scandinavia was, as Adam of Bremen notes, inhabited by
tribes of people often called Lapps, but who call themselves Sami, and
they lived almost exclusively by fishing and hunting, especially reindeer,
which provided them with meat, skins for clothing, boats, and tents, and
antler for implements and ornaments. Bow and spear were the weapons
used to hunt animals. Reindeer, elk, and deer were typically chased over
cliffs or into trenches dug in rows across the tracks of the animals. In addition, snares and a variety of traps were used.

The sea animals that were hunted included whales, seals, and walruses.
Whales were hunted in most of Scandinavia, though especially in Norway.
Several forms of whaling were practiced, the most primitive being to cut
the blubber off beached whales. Other forms of whaling involved har-
pooning the whales on the open sea or scaring them to shore, where they
would be killed with spears and knives. Seals were hunted all over Scandinavia and were typically clubbed or harpooned. Both whale and seal meat
was eaten, but the most important product derived from these sea animals
was their blubber, which was eaten as an alternative to butter. Moreover,
seal oil was used in oil lamps and instead of tar to smear boats. Seal skins
were used for gloves, shoes, bags, and the like. Walrus was hunted especially northeast of Norway, around Murmansk, and later in Greenland for
its valuable ivory, which was used as a substitute for elephant ivory in decorative art, and for its hides, from which strong ropes could be made.

In addition, wild birds were lured and netted or shot with bows and
arrows, and their eggs were collected with a variety of methods. It is also
known that peregrine falcons were tamed and trained to hunt ducks and
seabirds. These birds provided not only meat, but also feathers and down
used for insulation purposes.

TRADE

Some of the agricultural products or products derived from hunting
served as trade goods. Little, if anything, is known of local trade, but most
likely it was fairly extensive and comprised not only perishable commodities, but also minerals, from which tools, jewelry, and other items
could be fashioned, as well as rocks used to make whetstones and grind-
stones. Iron and soapstone in particular seem to have been in demand on
the home market.

Luxury goods—especially fur—were traded over long distances, and
about this kind of international trade we are better informed. Fur was
probably the main export in the Viking age, and fur trade is referred to in
the ninth-century record of Ohthere (an anglicized form of the Norse
name Ottar), a chieftain from Halogaland in northern Norway, who in the
reign of King Alfred the Great (871–899) visited the court in Wessex,
England, and gave accounts of his voyages in Scandinavia and of his way

of living in Norway. His account of life in Norway and his travels is preserved rather by chance. As part of King Alfred's educational program, a group of scholars put together a number of translations of useful books into Old English. One of these books was a translation of Paulus Orosius's world history, the *Historiae adversum paganos* (Histories against the pagans), and into this Old English work Ohthere's account was inserted. Ohthere says that he was a farmer, but because the land was poor he tells that he supplemented his income from reindeer hunting, walrus hunting, whaling, and the tribute enforced from the neighboring Lapps or Sami (a distinct people inhabiting the northernmost part of Scandinavia, who lived by fishing and hunting):

Their wealth comes mostly from the tax the Lapps pay them. This tax consists in the pelts of wild beasts, in birds' down and whale-bone and in ships' cables that are made of the skins of whale and seal. Each pays according to his rank. The highest has to pay the skins of fifteen martens, five reindeer and one bear, and ten bushels of down and a short coat of bear- or otter-skin and two cables—each must be sixty ells long, one of whale-hide and one of seal.[3]

To sell these goods Ohthere sailed to main market places further south, Skiringssal (that is, Kaupang) in Vestfold in southeast Norway, and Hedeby:

Ohthere called the district he lived in Halogaland. He said that nobody lived north of him. But there was a certain market-town in the south of the land called Skiringssal [Kaupang]. He said it took at least a month to get there under sail if you laid up at night and had a favorable wind every day. All the time you must sail along the coast. To starboard there is, first, Ireland; and then the islands that lie between Ireland and England; and then this country until you get to Skiringssal. And to port Norway all the time.

South of this place Skiringssal a great sea opens out into the land, broader than anyone could see across. Opposite on the other side is Jutland and then Zealand. This sea reaches many miles into the land. From Skiringssal he said he sailed in five days to the trading town called Hedeby. This is set between the lands of the Wends, the Saxons, and the Angles, and it owes allegiance centrally to the Danes. When he sailed there from Skiringssal he had Denmark to port and open sea to starboard for three days; then, two days before arriving at Hedeby, he had to starboard Jutland and Zealand and a lot of islands—these are the lands the Angles lived in before they came to England—and for two days there were to port the islands that are part of Denmark.[4]

Ohthere is the only Viking-age merchant whose social status is known from contemporary sources. He was clearly not a professional merchant, and his income came primarily from farming and taxation. Most likely, the majority of Scandinavian merchants in the Viking age were farmer-merchants.

Another important commodity was slaves. Slave trade is mentioned in several literary works. Adam of Bremen makes frequent reference to slave trade in his *Gesta Hammaburgensis ecclesiae ponitificum,* and Arab accounts of the Scandinavian traders living on the Volga make it clear that slaves were among the most important trading goods. Scandinavians bought or captured slaves in Russia and sold them in western Europe or in the east, and it is also known that Viking raiders took prisoners in western Europe and sold them in Scandinavia. In his biography of Saint Ansgar (d. 865), archbishop of Hamburg-Bremen, who is commonly called the "Apostle of the North" and credited with bringing Christianity to Scandinavia, the German writer Rimbert (d. 888) tells, among other things, that Saint Ansgar gave away his horse and its gear to ransom a nun who had been taken captive and enslaved by Vikings.

In addition, the Scandinavians traded walrus ivory, fish, honey, timber, amber, and, as Ohthere points out, down, whale bone, hide ropes, as well as a variety of foreign artifacts acquired either as loot or through gift exchange. The main imports were salt, spices, wine, cloth of wool, silk, pottery, glass, semiprecious stones, weapons, and silver in the form of coins. Pottery, glass, and woolen cloth were bought in western Europe. Cloth of silk was imported from Byzantium. Silver was obtained from the Arabs and was one of the primary imports, especially in the form of *dirhems* (also called Kufic coins because of the inscriptions after the town Kufah southwest of Baghdad in modern-day Iraq). Indeed, more than 85,000 Arab coins dating from the ninth and tenth centuries have been found in Scandinavia. Many of the coins were melted down and transformed into jewelry, but the presence of broken or cut silver (hack-silver) in many hoards (cash reserves of precious metal concealed in the ground) shows that silver in any form was used as a medium of exchange and—at least within Scandinavia—treated as bullion (rather than currency) which was weighed on scales. These scales, which sometimes were also buried, are small folding balances fitted with pans, and the weights are typically kept in small boxes. Silver probably became increasingly common as a means of payment during the Viking age, although it is reasonable to assume that a fair part of Viking-age trade was conducted by barter.

Coins and Coinage
The main period of import of Kufic coins was about 870–960. After the end of the tenth century they were not imported, probably due to a "silver crisis" in the east, as a result of which fewer coins were issued, and often of debased metal. Although these coins played a significant role as means of payment in Scandinavia, they were far from the only coins used. French *deniers*, Anglo-Frisian *sceattas*, and Anglo-Saxon pennies have also been found in Scandinavia. The last-mentioned became especially common at the end of the tenth century and during the first half of the eleventh century for obvious reasons: around this time Viking armies attacked England and forced King Aethelred the Unready (r. 978–1016) to pay tribute (Danegeld) to the invaders. More than 40,000 Anglo-Saxon coins from

the latter half of the tenth and the eleventh centuries have been found in Scandinavia, which is more than what has been found in England.

Moreover, coins were struck within Scandinavia from around 825. These were anonymous imitations of French *deniers* minted in the Frisian town of Dorestad and made, no doubt, in Hedeby. An abbreviated form of Carolus (= Charlemagne) and Dorestad is found on several of these Danish coins. Other coins are stamped with animals, ships, and the like. It was not until around 1000, however, that pennies were issued in the names of Scandinavian kings: Sven Forkbeard (d. 1014) of Denmark, Olaf Tryggvason (d. 999/1000) of Norway, and Olof Skotkonung (d. 1022) of Sweden. These pennies—the only unit of weight to be coined in the Viking age— were based both in weight and design on those of King Aethelred the Unready. For most of the Viking age, the system of weights was based on 1 *mork* = 8 *aurar* = 24 *ortogar* = 240 pennies.

Gradually, the Scandinavians became accustomed to using coins. Jewelry, hack-silver, and ingots or rods cease to appear in the hoards. Toward the end of the Viking age foreign coins disappeared and came to be replaced by native coins, which became the only legal tender.

Not very much is known about the actual trade routes during the Viking age. Descriptions of some can be found in the literary sources. Two accounts from around 890 detail voyages to or from Hedeby, the great mart in South Schleswig. The "eastern route" is described by a certain Wulfstan, apparently an Englishman, in the Old English translation of Paulus Orosius's *Historiae adversum paganos.* Wulfstan's seven-day journey begins at Hedeby and ends across the Baltic in Truso in the Gulf of Danzig (probably Elbing) in what is now Poland, and he tells that he traveled with Wendland to starboard and the Danish islands Langeland, Lolland, Falster, and also Scania to port—then Bornholm, and then Blekinge, Möre, Öland, and Gotland, all Swedish territory. The "western route" is described also in the translation of Orosius, though not by Wulfstan but by the Norwegian Ohthere, who tells of his voyage from his home in northern Norway to Hedeby. He relates that he sailed south along the Norwegian coast to Kaupang in southern Norway. From there he sailed for three days with Denmark to port and open sea to starboard and then for two days with Jutland and the cluster of Danish islands to starboard until he finally reached Hedeby. A third route to Hedeby, the sea route from the trading center Birka on the island of Björkö in Lake Mälaren in Sweden, is amply documented in Rimbert's life of Saint Ansgar. The fact that the ships taking Saint Ansgar to Birka in 829 were attacked by pirates indicates that the route was well established and on a sufficiently grand scale to make piracy worth the time and effort.

To Hedeby goods were brought from the Rhine area, which was an economically advanced part of Europe in the Viking age. Dorestad, which lay at the junction of the river Lek and an arm of the Rhine right in the center of the Netherlands, was the main trading center toward the North Sea, and from here goods were transported by land or sea to southern Scandinavia. The Frisian and German traders probably used land routes, whereas the Scandinavian merchants, who were primarily seafarers, were more likely to sail the goods along the Frisian coast and across Jutland to Hedeby. All traffic from Hedeby northward and eastward almost certainly went by sea and appears to have been controlled exclusively by Scandinavians. Similarly, the trade routes west were sea routes. Danes and Norwegians regularly crossed the North Sea to England from the Limfjord area in Jutland and western Norway, respectively, and it is known that Scandinavians sailed direct from Ireland to Iceland and from Norway to Greenland.

In addition to the account of his voyage to Hedeby, Ohthere also tells of a voyage to the northern tip of Norway (North Cape) and then east along the northern coast until he reached the White Sea:

Once, he said, he determined to explore how much farther north the land stretched or whether anyone lived to the north of the uninhabited land. So he sailed north along the coast. The whole way the waste land was to starboard and the open sea to port; this went on for three days. By then he was as far north as the whale-hunters reach at their farthest. Then he continued north as far as he could sail in the next three days. Then the land curved eastward (or the sea formed an inlet in the land—he didn't know which). All he knew was that he waited there for a west-north-west wind and then sailed east along the coast as far as he could reach in four days. At that point he had to wait for a wind from due north because the land turned south there (or the sea formed an inlet in the land—he didn't know which).

From there he sailed due south along the coast as far as he could reach in five days' sailing. There a great river opened up into the land. So they turned in along it because they did not dare sail beyond the river since they had no secure right of passage there and the land was continuously settled on its far bank. He had not come upon any cultivated land before since he left his own home; but the whole way there was uninhabited territory to starboard—except for nomadic fishermen, fowlers and hunters, and they were all Lapps—and to port was nothing but open sea. The Beormians had made good use of their land, though Ohthere and his crew did not venture ashore there; but the land of the Lapps was quite empty, except where hunters or fishermen or fowlers had their camps...

He made this journey—apart from a desire to explore the country—mostly for the walrus-hunting since they have most excellent ivory in their tusks (some of these tusks he brought to the king), and their skins made excellent ships' cables. This whale (the walrus) is much smaller than other whales—it is not more than seven ells long. But in his own country there is the very best whaling; they are forty-eight ells long and the biggest fifty. He said that he and a group of six others killed sixty of these in two days.[5]

The walrus ivory that Ohthere speaks of and also furs of animals hunted in these northern regions as well as other commodities were shipped by traders either to Hedeby for onward transport to western

Europe or across the Baltic into the Gulf of Finland, which is connected to Lake Ladoga by the river Neva. From here there were two main trade routes eastward.

A northern route reached the upper Volga and Bulgar (near today's Kazan). It was in this region that Scandinavians came into contact with the Arabs, who referred to them as Rus. One of these was Ibn Fadlan, who gave an account of an embassy sent by the caliph in Baghdad to the Bulgars in the early 920s. His account is especially valuable due to its inclusion of an eyewitness description of the Rus merchants—probably Swedes—he encountered on the Volga. A few Scandinavians continued from Bulgar down to the Caspian Sea and even reached Baghdad, where they could touch the long silk route to China and obtain silk, silver, and spices. The Arab author al-Mas'udi (d. 956) tells of an ill-fated Rus expedition to the Caspian in 912, and Rus activity on the Caspian is further mentioned by the historian Ibn Miskawayh (d. 1030). More specifically, he tells that the Rus occupied the town of Bardha'a (Azerbaijan) in 943 but were forced to withdraw due to disease and by the local Muslim ruler. It is believed that it was along this particular route that most of the Arab coins used in Scandinavia had traveled.

A southern route, which is described in the *Russian Primary Chronicle*, went along the river Volkhov to Novgorod and from there to Gnezdovo (the precursor of Smolensk) and along the Dnieper via Kiev to the Black Sea. The goal here was Byzantium (Constantinople), where silk, fruit, wine, jewelry, and other luxury items could be obtained. In a Greek work known by its Latin name of *De administrando imperio* (On administering a realm) written around 944 by the Byzantine Emperor Constantine Porphyrogenitos an account is given of these Scandinavian (Swedish) merchants, here called Rhos, and the route along the Dnieper, which was a most perilous one, is described in detail:

The wooden boats coming down to Constantinople from outer Russia are some from Novgorod (in which Sviatoslav, son of Igor prince of Russia, had his seat), some from the walled town of Smolensk and from Lyubech and Chernigov and from Vyshgorod. All these come along the river Dnieper and converge on the fortress of Kiev (also called Sambatas). The Slavs who are bound to pay the Rhos tribute—those called Krivichians and Lenzanenes and the remaining Slav regions—hew the hulls in their wooded hills during the course of the winter, and when they have them ready, at the season when the frosts dissolve, they bring them to the lakes nearby. Since these discharge into the river Dnieper, these people come into the said river Dnieper, make their way to Kiev, drag their ships along for fitting out and sell them to the Rhos. The Rhos buy the plain hulls, and from their old ships, which they break up, they provide oars, rowlocks and whatever else is needed. So they fit them out. And moving off down the river Dnieper in the month of June they come to Vitichev, a town in alliance with the Rhos, and gather there for two or three days. When all the ships are assembled they set off and make their way down the aforesaid Dnieper. And first they come to the first rapid called Essoupi,

which in Russian and Slavonic means "Don't fall asleep." This barrier is just as narrow as the width of the imperial polo-ground. In the middle of this rapid are rooted
tall rocks, looking like islands. The water comes against them and, flooding up,
dashes down to the depths below with a great and terrifying noise. So the Rhos do
not dare to get through the midst of them but put ashore nearby and set the men on
dry land leaving everything else in the ships. Then they strip off, feeling their way
with their feet to avoid bumping against the rock. This is how they do it; some at the
stem, some amidships, others again at the stern, they push along with poles. And
by this caution they get through this first barrier, round the bend of the river bank.
When they have got past this rapid they take the others from the dry land on board
again and set off, and come down to the second rapid, called in Russian Oulvorsi
and in Slavonic Ostrovouniprach, which means "The islet of the barrier." This one
is like the first, tough and awkward to get through. Again they put the men ashore
and take the ships past just as at the first one. They go through the third rapid in the
same way; this is called Gelandri, which in Slavonic means "Noise of the rapid."
And then the fourth rapid, the huge one, called in Russian Aeifor and in Slavonic
Neasit because pelicans roost among the small rocks of the barrier. At this rapid all
put ashore, stem foremost, and out get all those who are appointed to keep watch.
Ashore they go, and unsleeping they keep sentry-go against the Pechenegs. The
rest of them, picking up the things they have on board the ships, conduct the
wretched slaves in chains six miles by dry land until they are past the barrier. In this
way, some dragging their ships, others carrying them on their shoulders, they get
them through to the far side of the rapid. So, launching the ships back on to the
river and loading their cargo, they get in and again move off. When they come to
the fifth rapid, called in Russian Varouforos and in Slavonic Voulniprach because it
forms a great lake, they edge their ships again round the bank of the river, just as at
the first and second rapids, and so they reach the sixth rapid, called in Russian
Leanti and in Slavonic Veroutzi; that is, "The boiling of the water." This too they
pass in the same way. From there they sail off to the seventh rapid, called in Russian
Stroukoun and in Slavonic Naprezi, which is translated as "Little rapid." This they
pass at the ford named Krarios [later called the ford of Kichkas], where the Cher-
sonites cross from Russia and the Pechenegs to Cherson. The crossing is the width
of the hippodrome, and its height from the bottom up to where the rocks project is
the distance an arrow can be shot from a bow. It is at this point, therefore, that the
Pechenegs come down and attack the Rhos.

    After crossing this place they make the island called St Gregorios; on that island
they conduct their sacrifices...From this island on the Rhos have no fear of the
Pechenegs until they reach the river Selinas [Sulina]. So they set out from there and
travel for four days until they reach the lake forming the mouth of the river, on
which there is the island of St Aitherios [modern Berezan]. Reaching this island
they take a rest there for two or three days. Then they fit out their ships with whatever they need [to make them seaworthy]—sails, masts and steering-oars—which
they have brought on board. Since this lake is the mouth of the river (as has been
said) and since it holds on down to the sea and the island of St Aitherios faces the
sea, they come down from there to the river Dniester; and when they are secure
there they have another rest. And when the weather is suitable they embark again
and come to the river called Aspros, and after a rest there in the same way they
move off again and come to the Selinas, to, as it is said to be, a branch of the river
Danube. Until they are past the river Selinas the Pechenegs run alongside them.

And if as often happens the sea casts one of the ships ashore, the whole lot land to make a common stand against the Pechenegs.

After the Selinas they are afraid of nobody; entering the region of Bulgaria they come to the mouth of the Danube. From the Danube they make for the Konopas and from the Konopas Constanza, from there to the river Varna [Provadiya], and from Varna they come to the river Dichina, all of them in Bulgarian territory. From the Dichina they get to the region of Mesembria, and at last their journey is at an end, full as it was of agony and fear, hardship and danger.[6]

An alternate route to the Black Sea went from the Baltic (Gotland) through the Gulf of Riga. That this route was a well-traveled one is clear from the many hoards of coins found in Latvia and Estonia and the number of Baltic objects found in graves on Gotland. One chronicler called the river Dvina, which runs into the Gulf of Riga, "the route to the Varangians." The Varangians were an elite corps of mercenary Scandinavian soldiers in the service of Byzantine emperors; more specifically, they were members of the famous Varangian Guard, which was established by Basil II around 988 and survived until the fall of Byzantium in 1204. The Guard was composed primarily of Scandinavians, though it included also Franks, Turks, and Englishmen, and on many Swedish rune stones from the ninth century onward, there are references to men who died "eastwards in Greece," that is, in Byzantium or in Russia. At Ed in Uppland, Sweden, a certain Rognvald had a boulder inscribed to his mother's memory. He says little about her and boasts instead of his own accomplishments:

Rognvald had the runes cut in memory of his mother Fastvi, Onam's daughter. She died in Ed. God help her soul. Rognvald had the runes cut. He was in Greece. He was the leader of the host.[7]

The most famous Scandinavian to become a member of the Varangian Guard was the Norwegian King Harald Hardruler (r. 1046–1066), who spent the years 1034–1043 as an officer in the Byzantine army.

A third eastern trade route, the Polish route, passed through either the Oder or the Vistula to link up with the Mainz-Kiev trade route and to the Danube and the markets of central southern Europe and the Mediterranean. As the trade routes through Russia became less important in the late tenth century, these Polish trade routes became increasingly significant, possibly because of the increased importance of the western silver mines.

URBAN LIFE

With the rapid growth in trade during the Viking age, small trading centers came into existence. These trading centers gradually grew into towns, although any real tendencies toward urbanization cannot be detected until the ninth and tenth centuries.

Establishment of Towns

Hedeby
Hedeby (the heath-settlement) was Scandinavia's most southerly mercantile center. It is situated at the inner part of the Schlei fjord south of the town Schleswig (by which it was succeeded in the mid-eleventh century when it was destroyed by fire). It seems to have begun as a small trading center around 800; from the Frankish annals of 804, it is known that the Danish King Godfred destroyed the Slav trading station of Reric (possible Rostock), took the merchants from there away with him, and established them by the site of an early settlement at Hedeby. This was a clever idea, for Hedeby soon prospered, and along with Birka in Sweden it became the most important trading center in Scandinavia in the Viking age and greatly sought after by both the Swedes and the Germans. It is mentioned in several written sources, including Rimbert's life of Saint Ansgar, Adam of Bremen's *Gesta Hammaburgensis ecclesiae pontificum,* and an Arab source. The last-mentioned is the account by Ibrahim b. Ya'qub al-Turtushi, who visited Hedeby around 950 and called it a large town at the very end of the world ocean. These writers all regard Hedeby as an international town, and excavations in the cemeteries do indeed reveal a polyethnic society of Scandinavian, Frisian, Saxon, Frankish, and Slavonic origin.

The reason for Hedeby's success was obviously its geographical location on the neck of the Jutland peninsula near the Schlei fjord, from which rivers flowed into the Eider and the North Sea. Moreover, the Army Road or Ox Route, Jutland's north-south land route, passed through the Danevirke, the system of earthworks that protected the Danish border, near Hedeby. The main settlement itself was enclosed by a semicircular rampart, about 1,300 m (4,265 ft.) long, on three sides—north, west, and south—but to the east it was open to Haddeby Nor, an inlet of the Schlei that provided a sheltered harbor as well as access to the fjord. The rampart was linked to the Danevirke by a connecting wall.

Excavations have been undertaken inside the rampart, in the harbor, and in the cemeteries. A large number of artifacts have been found that testify to multifaceted and extensive trade, especially with Germany and the Baltic, and handicraft production (objects made of iron and other metals, bone and antler, glass, leather, pottery, wood, and textiles). Hedeby very clearly served as a center of both import and export as well as of transit trade, and its population, which has been estimated at around 1,000 during the tenth century, was clearly nonagrarian in production.

Birka
The town of Birka on the small island of Björkö in Lake Mälaren in Sweden was, for about 200 years, the most northerly mercantile center in Scandinavia and the most important harbor of the Baltic, to which it was connected by an extensive system of inland waterways. Like Hedeby, it appears to have been settled around 800, but it was abandoned in the 970s. Some have suggested the rising land level as the cause of Birka's decline, for this would have blocked easy access to the Baltic via the outlet at Södertälje, which required a short overland haul of

the ships. Others have pointed to the fact that the long-range transit trade between the Baltic and the Volga ended around 970, whereby Birka was cut off from its primary source of wealth. In any case, the town of Sigtuna halfway between Birka and Uppsala seems to have succeeded it as an internal market and a manufacturing center; its function as an international trading center was taken over by Gotland. Birka is mentioned in both Rimbert's life of Saint Ansgar and Adam of Bremen's *Gesta Hammaburgensis ecclesiae pontificum*, for just as a church, the first in Denmark, was built at the instigation of Saint Ansgar in Hedeby around 850, so a church, the first in Sweden, was built at the saint's initiative in Birka in 852.

In many ways, Birka resembled Hedeby. It was fortified on the landward side by a semicircular rampart, of which only a portion remains. It encloses an area of about 30 acres, that is, half that of Hedeby, and within this lies the "Black Earth," an occupation deposit; this is the actual site of the town of Birka, which probably averaged 500–700 inhabitants. As at Hedeby, the waterfront was protected by a palisade, and the two natural harbors, Kugghamn (cargo-boat harbor) and Korshamn (cross harbor) provided sheltered accommodation for ships. The construction of an artificial harbor, now known as Salviksgropen, testifies to the high demand for suitable and safe anchoring places. The entire site was dominated by a fortress, Borg, built outside the rampart.

Birka has not been as extensively excavated as Hedeby, but the finds indicate industries that are comparable with those of Hedeby. In addition, many hundreds of bone ice skates have been found in the "Black Earth," which shows that Birka was fed not only by ships and that there was extensive traffic, possibly trade, also during the winter months when the lake was frozen. Excavation of the cemeteries at Birka has revealed a number of inhumation graves containing a variety of luxury goods, such as pottery and glass from the Rhineland; coins from western Europe that had been adapted to serve as ornaments; coins or coin fragments from the East; and traces of silk, of which some appear to have come from China. The finds suggest that Birka's primary contacts were with the Volga rather than the Dnieper.

The third of the early Scandinavian trading centers is Kaupang (marketplace) in southeast Norway, which has been   **Kaupang** dated to the period around 750–920. Although it never became a town and was never as rich as Hedeby and Birka, it was clearly one of the main outlets of trade for Vestfold, and from Ohthere's account it seems reasonable to conclude that northern merchants came to Kaupang with their cargoes of furs, skins, down, walrus ivory, and hide ropes. Kaupang is now situated on a shallow bay sheltered from the open sea by a string of small islands and shoals, some of which were below the surface of the water during the Viking age. (Since the Viking age, the sea level has dropped some 2 m (6.5 ft.), and it is generally believed that this may be the reason why Kaupang was abandoned in the early tenth century.) It is set between rocky hills, which provided a natural defense and therefore made the construction of a fortification unnecessary. Excavations in the "Black Earth" area of Kaupang provide evidence of soapstone and metal (especially iron) processing. The surrounding grave fields revealed artifacts especially from Rhineland and the British Isles, which demonstrates that Kaupang's trade interests were primarily in western Europe.

Other Towns and Trading Centers   Other towns developed at a later date. Aside from Hedeby, Birka, and Kaupang, Ribe and Århus in Denmark are the only Scandinavian towns whose origins can be traced back to well before 1000.

Ribe on the west coast of South Jutland was founded around the mid-eighth century and is considered to be Denmark's oldest town. It is mentioned in Rimbert's life of Saint Ansgar, where it is said that Saint Ansgar received permission from the Danish kings Horik the Older (d. 854) and Horik the Younger (d. 864) to build a church there about 860, and it is known that in 948 Archbishop Adaldag of Hamburg-Bremen consecrated a bishop for the see of Ribe. Recent excavations testify to the existence of several industries in the town: metalworking, shoe making, textile production, bronze casting, comb making, and glass and amber bead production. Most likely, the trading connections of Ribe were with Germany and the Netherlands.

Århus, which is situated on the east coast of the middle of Jutland, was founded around the mid-tenth century. It is first mentioned in 948 when a bishop was consecrated for the see of Århus. The town was protected by a semicircular rampart, and it is possible that originally it was primarily a fort. Excavations have revealed traces of industry, such as wood carving and comb making; pottery, quernstones, soapstone pots, as well as scales and weights indicate trade with the Baltic, Rhineland, and Norway or Sweden.

With the continued development of trade and industries, a number of towns were founded around 1000 or in the course of the eleventh century. These include Viborg, Odense, Roskilde, and Lund in Denmark; Bergen, Oslo, and Trondheim (Nidaros) in Norway; Sigtuna, Lödöse, and Skara in Sweden; and Västergarn on Gotland, which had become exceedingly wealthy in the tenth century because of Baltic trade. Trade was, however, not the sole basis for the existence of these early towns. Royal support probably played a significant role in the establishment of, for example, Hedeby, Birka, and Kaupang, and the early missionary church established itself in Hedeby, Ribe, and Århus. It is impossible to calculate the number of inhabitants in any of these towns, but obviously they were quite small and their populations probably numbered only in the hundreds.

Scandinavian Towns Abroad   The Vikings also founded trading centers and towns in their colonies abroad. Dublin, Ireland, was founded by the Vikings shortly before the middle of the tenth century, and it soon became an exceedingly prosperous and powerful trading center for merchants in the North Atlantic. The

Dublin Vikings appear to have engaged especially in slave trade, and it is believed that Dublin was the prime slave market of western Europe, furnishing customers in the British Isles, Anglo-Saxon as well as Scandinavian, and the Scandinavian countries and Iceland. In addition to slaves, hides and textiles were probably the primary exports. Recent excavations have also revealed the existence of many crafts and industries in Dublin, such as wood carving, shoe making, comb making, shipbuilding, iron forging, bronze casting, and leather work. Imports included walrus ivory, amber, soapstone objects, pottery, glass, jet and other metal ornaments, and silk from Scandinavia, England, the Continent, and the East. Other towns in Ireland—Limerick, Cork, Wexford, and Waterford—also owe their existence to the Vikings, although they never became as important as Dublin.

In England and on the Continent the Vikings settled themselves in already existing towns. The capital of the Vikings in England was York, which was captured by the Vikings in 866. They established a line of kings there, who controlled the city and its kingdom until the mid-tenth century, when the last Viking king was expelled. Scandinavian settlers continued to have a strong impact on York, however, and its development. Excavations show that York had commercial links not only to the Scandinavian countries, but also to western Europe and, via middlemen, to the eastern Mediterranean and the Near and Middle East. Among the commodities brought from these regions were wines from northwestern Europe and silks from Byzantium. They also show that York was an important manufacturing center. Metalwork in particular seems to have been a common industry in York. Other towns in England on which the Vikings exercised strong influence include the Five Boroughs (Lincoln, Nottingham, Derby, Leicester, and Stamford), and Cambridge, Bedford, and Northampton.

In eastern Europe, the Scandinavians (especially Swedes) had established trading centers in the south Baltic before the Viking age. They include Wolin at the mouth of the Oder in the Baltic, which is described by Adam of Bremen as the largest town in Europe (although at that time under Slav rule); Truso on the Vistula in Estonia, which was visited by Wulfstan; and Grobin near modern Liepaja on the Latvian coast, which is mentioned by Rimbert in his life of Saint Ansgar. It is doubtful, however, if the Scandinavians ever formed a sizeable portion of the population of these towns.

There is no real consensus when it comes to assessing the extent of the Scandinavians' involvement in the foundation of trading centers and towns in Russia, but it is generally accepted that for some time they were in control of Staraja Ladoga, Novgorod, Gnezdovo (the precursor of Smolensk), and Kiev, and thereby in control of the route to Byzantium along the Dnieper. According to *Heimskringla* (Disc of the world) by Snorri Sturluson, Staraja Ladoga was taken by the Scandinavians in 997, but archaeological excavations in the town have produced little in terms of Scandinavian material, and it may be that it was merely a stopping-off point, a kind of transit town, on the way to other places, notably Novgorod.

Novgorod is situated on the river Volkhov approximately three miles north of Lake Ilmen and about 185 km (115 miles) south of Staraja Ladoga. Also here, excavations have revealed little to suggest a strong Scandinavian presence, but in its account of the history of the town the Hypatian text of the *Russian Primary Chronicle* is unambiguous about the role played by the Scandinavians in its foundation. It tells that a Rus by the name of Rurik was invited to settle in Novgorod, and the way he and his brothers are described in the company of other Scandinavians suggests that they were Scandinavian or of Scandinavian descent:

[Year] 6367 [i.e., 859]. The Varangians [i.e., Scandinavians] from beyond the sea imposed tribute upon the Chuds, the Slavs, the Merians, the Ves', and the Krivichians.... [Year] 6368–6370 [i.e., 860–862]. The tributaries of the Varangians drove them back beyond the sea and, refusing them further tribute, set out to govern themselves. There was no law among them, but tribe rose against tribe. Discord thus ensued among them, and they began to war one against another. They said to themselves, "Let us seek a prince who may rule over us and judge us according to the Law." They accordingly went overseas to the Varangian Russes: these particular Varangians were known as Russes, just as some are called Swedes, and others Normans, English, and Gotlanders, for they were thus named. The Chuds, the Slavs, the Krivichians, and the Ves' then said to the people of Rus': "Our land is great and rich, but there is no order in it. Come to rule and reign over us." They thus selected three brothers, with their kinsfolk, who took with them all the Russes and migrated. The oldest, Rurik, located himself in Novgorod; the second, Sineus, at Beloozero; and the third, Truvor, in Izborsk. On account of these Varangians, the district of Novgorod became known as the land of Rus'. The present inhabitants of Novgorod are descended from the Varangian race, but aforetime they were Slavs.[8]

Two Swedish runic inscriptions may be mentioned in this connection, because they were erected in memory of Swedish men who died in Novgorod (or Holmgard as it was known to the Scandinavians). One stone, a natural boulder at Esta in Södermanland, has the following inscription:

Ingifast had this stone cut in memory of his father Sigvid.
He fell in Holmgard,
A ship's captain with his crew.[9]

The other, a granite block at Sjusta in Skokloster, Uppland, is even more interesting, for its eleventh-century inscription suggests that the Scandinavians in Novgorod had a church dedicated to the Norwegian King and Saint Olaf Haraldsson, who, incidentally, had been to Novgorod himself. The inscription reads as follows:

Runa had this memorial made after Spiallbudi and Svein and Andvett and Ragnar, her sons by Helgi, and Sigrid after her husband Spiallbudi. He met his death in Holmgard in Olaf's church. Opir cut the runes.[10]

Rurik, who settled in Novgorod, is said to have been the ancestor of the old Russian dynasty, and it is told that after his death his kinsman Oleg seized power in Kiev too. "Oleg," it is related, "set himself up as prince in Kiev and said that it should be the mother of Russian cities." As with Staraja Ladoga and Novgorod there is, however, little archaeological material to substantiate the information given in the *Russian Primary Chronicle* and little to suggest a large Scandinavian population in Kiev, but it may be that the number of Scandinavians who lived permanently in Russia quickly assimilated to the Slavs and to Slav culture. At Gnezdovo, a large cemetery has been examined, and of the burials that have so far been excavated only very few are decidedly Scandinavian. Yet it is known that Gnezdovo was one of the most significant trading stations in Russia.

The inhabitants of towns made their living from a full range of trades and crafts. Most of our information about **Crafts and** crafts and industries comes from archaeological finds, and **Industries** while they give a detailed and broad picture of production and products, they provide little information about the producer, the artisan, and his workshop. Written sources show that there was a clear distinction between the craftsman, who made a living from his products, and the person whose workmanship was aimed at personal or household use. To some extent this distinction was gender-based: the artisan who manufactured goods for sale was male, while the household producer was female. There is, however, no indication that these craftsmen formed a new or separate class of (urban) citizens during the Viking age, because much of the work could be done in rural communities and could be combined with other occupations, and while one may speak of specialization one cannot speak of true industrialization.

The Scandinavian crafts and industries were, of course, largely determined by available resources and demand. Metalworking was clearly an important trade, and the smith was a vital part of every community, for only he had the skills and also the equipment for manufacturing and repairing metal goods. Iron, which could be found in Scandinavia, was the most common metal and was used for tools, weapons, domestic utensils, nails and rivets, and riding equipment. Some of the smiths were evidently also very skilled artists. Some of their products—especially sword-hilts, spurs, and stirrups—are decorated with elaborate patterns and motifs. Encrustation (covering a surface with silver or copper wire pressed and hammered to form a pattern) was clearly quite common.

A variety of metals was used for jewelry and other decorative items, such as buckles, keys, and tableware. Gold and silver were imported, but copper was mined in Sweden. The copper was alloyed with other metals, such as lead and tin, which may have been imported. Bronze was especially common, and bronze-casting was carried out all over Scandinavia. Several clay and iron molds used for casting bronze ornaments have been found. These clay molds obviously had to be broken open to release the casting quite unlike the molds of stone and antler used for casting silver, tin, lead, and pewter, for which lower temperatures are needed. Other tools used by the jeweler included crucibles for smelting, bellows, tongs, molds for ingots, light hammers, dies, metal shears, pinches for filigree work, dies for impressing foils, and engraving and chasing tools.

The quarrying of steatite, a rock also known as soapstone that is quite soft when quarried but which hardens in the air, and the manufacture of soapstone vessels and pots, molds, crucibles, loom-weights, and other artifacts were a major industry in Norway, from where the products were exported. In many parts of Norway and Sweden there were also rocks from which high-quality whetstones could be made. These were necessary for sharpening weapons, knives, and tools and were distributed throughout Scandinavia and even exported.

Pottery seems to have become common only toward the end of the Viking age. Very little is known about the details of this craft, and it appears to have been a rural craft more than an urban industry and situated near clay deposits, such as those on Zealand in Denmark.

The production of bone, horn, and antler objects was yet another important industry and was most likely carried out by professional craftsmen. The antlers of red deer were widely used to make combs. The method used was to cut a pair of long, flat, and relatively thin plates to form the back of the comb, and between these plates a number of smaller plates were fastened, into which the teeth were cut. Antler was also used for many other products, such as arrowheads, handles for knives and tools, gaming pieces, dice, and vices. Animal bone was used for skates, pins, spindle-whorls, handles, bodkins, and the like. Animal horn was used especially for drinking vessels, which might also be decorated with carving. In contrast to wood carving, carving in bone, horn, and tusk was limited to small objects by nature of the size of the material. Nonetheless, the same methods of carving are found in bone, horn, and tusk as in wood carving: incised work, openwork, relief, and sculpture.

Amber and glass were used mostly for ornamental objects. Amber was available in the southern Baltic and along the coast of southwest Jutland. It was used for making small objects, such as pendants, beads, and gaming pieces. Excavations in Ribe revealed no less than 4 pounds (1.8 kg) of rough amber. The raw material for glass was imported from abroad. The preserved glass objects are mostly beads.

Woodworking was probably not a specialized craft per se, although the construction and maintenance of ships and boats as well as the building of large houses and churches would have required substantial training, skill, and experience. Moreover, the very high quality of some of the woodcarvings points to the existence of highly competent craftsmen. The tools of the carpenter are demonstrated by the contents of a wooden chest found at Mästermyr on Gotland. Included are, among other things, a hacksaw, a large saw with a wooden handle, an ax, an adze, spoon bits for an auger, and a wedge. The chest also contained tools for metalworking, and most likely, the owner of the chest was an itinerant craftsman.

Like woodworking, the production of textile, the preparation of leather, and the manufacture of ropes and nets were probably home industries that were carried out in both rural and urban communities, although shoemakers and saddle makers may have been urban professionals or semiprofessionals. Leather off-cuts found in Hedeby and Ribe certainly reveal the existence of shoemakers in these towns. As far as the manufacture of cloth and clothing is concerned, grave finds and literary sources make it clear that it was mainly the domain of women. Wool and linen were the most common materials used, and spinning and weaving must have been part of the daily domestic chores. By the end of the Viking age, homespun (in Norse commonly known as *wadmal* meaning "cloth measure") had become an industry in Iceland and was exported to Norway. Its significance for the Icelandic economy is among other things clear from the fact that the harbor tolls, which the Icelanders were charged in Norway, were payable in cloth, coats, or silver.

MONASTIC LIFE

Following the conversion of the Scandinavian countries to Christianity, monasteries were eventually founded, in which men (and later women) could seclude themselves from the secular world and dedicate themselves to austere lives devoted to prayer and holy contemplation in order to achieve greater personal perfection and sanctification than is normally possible in the world. During the Viking age, this kind of life probably did not appeal to very many people, and we know of only a few monasteries founded before 1100. Around 1095, the Benedictine monastic chapter of Odense on Funen in Denmark was established. It was a daughter house of Evesham Abbey in England and was founded by monks from Evesham at the request of the Danish King Erik Ever-good (r. 1095–1103). The church in Odense was where the Danish King (and later Saint) Knud the Holy (r. 1080–1086) was martyred, and it was dedicated to Saint Alban, the protomartyr of Britain. It is also known that around 1100 the monastic centers of Selja near Bergen and Nidarholm on an island outside of Trondheim in Norway were established. Generally, it is impossible to determine the date of the foundation of the early Scandinavian monasteries. However, the ones near the cathedral towns of Ribe, Schleswig, and Lund may date from shortly before the end of the Viking age.

NOTES

1. Adam of Bremen is quoted from Adam of Bremen, *History of the Archbishops of Hamburg-Bremen,* trans. Francis J. Tschan, Records of Civilization: Sources and Studies, vol. 53 (New York: Columbia University Press, 1959), pp. 186–87.

2. Adam of Bremen, *History of the Archbishops of Hamburg-Bremen*, pp. 189–91, 202–3, 210–14.

3. Ohthere is quoted from R. I. Page, *Chronicles of the Vikings: Records, Memorials, and Myths* (Toronto: University of Toronto Press, 1995), pp. 47–48.

4. Ohthere, quoted from Page, *Chronicles of the Vikings*, pp. 47–48.

5. Ohthere, quoted from Page, *Chronicles of the Vikings*, pp. 46–47.

6. Constantine Porphyrogenitos is quoted from Page, *Chronicles of the Vikings*, pp. 94–96.

7. The inscription on the Ed rune stone is quoted from David M. Wilson, *The Vikings and Their Origins: Scandinavia in the First Millennium* (London: Thames and Hudson, 1970), p. 112.

8. *The Russian Primary Chronicle* is quoted from Samuel Hazzard Cross and Olgerd P. Sherbowitz-Wetzor, eds. and trans., *The Russian Primary Chronicle: Laurentian Text* (Cambridge, MA: Medieval Academy of America, [n.d.]), pp. 59–61.

9. The inscription on the Esta stone is quoted from Page, *Chronicles of the Vikings*, p. 81.

10. The inscription on the Sjusta stone is quoted from Page, *Chronicles of the Vikings*, p. 83.

4

Intellectual Life

LANGUAGE

Linguists usually refer to the language of Scandinavia in the Viking age as North Germanic. The term implies that by the beginning of the Viking age the language showed sufficient individual traits to distinguish itself from the West Germanic dialect that became Low and High German, Frisian, Dutch, and English, as well as the East Germanic dialect that is mainly known to us through the extinct Gothic.

In the Viking age, Scandinavian was spoken over an area that comprises what are now Denmark and southern and central Norway and Sweden (including Gotland and Åland). As the Scandinavians gradually established themselves in Normandy, the British Isles, the islands in the North Atlantic, Greenland, and in the Finnish and Estonian coastal areas, the language also came to be spoken in these regions. Indeed, in the Orkney and Shetland Islands, the Faroe Islands, and Iceland, it became the dominant language, although in the Orkney and Shetland Islands it later yielded to Lowland Scots. In Greenland, Scandinavian died out as a result of the demise of the Norse colony.

It is generally believed that the Scandinavian language was quite uniform throughout the vast area where it was spoken, and the period 700–1050 is therefore often referred to as "Common Scandinavian." However, this impression may be false, due to the paucity of surviving texts. Certainly by the end of the Viking age, a split is observable between the areas that faced the Atlantic and those that looked to the Baltic. Linguists generally speak of two branches: West Scandinavian and East Scandinavian. West Scandinavian (also called Old Norse) comprises Old Norwegian and its daughter languages Icelandic and Faroese as well as the now extinct Orkney and Shetland Norn. East Scandinavian comprises Old Swedish, Old Danish, and Old Gutnish (the language spoken and written on the island of Gotland).

The similarity vis-à-vis dissimilarity between West and East Scandinavian and the relationship of West and East Scandinavian to Germanic may be illustrated by the famous inscription on the fifth-century Gallehus horn found near Tønder in South Jutland, Denmark, in 1734. The horn, which was of gold, was one of a pair, for a similar horn was discovered nearby a century earlier. The treasure was sent to the royal collection, whence it was stolen in 1802 and melted down, but fortunately not before drawings had been made of the horn and of the inscription. The inscription is shown below in transliteration into the Latin alphabet and then in a word-for-word translation into West Scandinavian (Old Norse) and East Scandinavian (Old Swedish). The time between Germanic and Common Scandinavian was a period of great change, and one of the major changes was syncope (the loss of many unstressed syllables), which resulted in a shortening of words. Because West and East Scandinavian are inflected languages, the word order is of less significance than the inflections of the individual words. Each word consists of a stem, which only occasionally changes, and an ending, which usually does. As far as nouns, pronouns, and adjectives are concerned, the endings show the gender, case, and number of the word. Regarding verbs, the endings indicate person, number, tense, and mode.

Germanic	*ek*	*HlewagastiR*	*holtijaR*	*horna*	*tawido*
	I	Hlewagastir	from Holt	(the) horn	made
Old Norse	ek	Hlégestr	Hyltir	horn(it)	táða
Old Swedish	iak	Lægiæster	Hyltir	horn(it)	taþe[1]

ek: The pronoun *ek* ("I") keeps its vowel in West Scandinavian, but in East Scandinavian it is "broken," that is, it is split into a falling diphthong (*ia/ja*) by *a* in the next syllable (the Germanic or Proto-Scandinavian form of *ek* was *eka*). In this quotation *ek* is the subject of the sentence and therefore in the nominative case.

HlewagastiR: The name qualifies *ek* and is in the nominative case. It is a compound of *hlewa* (famous) and *gastiR* (guest). The former is not attested in later developments of the language, and so the word is cited in Old Norse and Old Swedish according to the forms it would have had if it had survived. In Old Swedish, initial *h* was lost before *l* (*Hl-/L-*). The effect of syncope is seen in the disappearance of the consonants -*w*- between the vowels *e* and *a*, taking the following vowel (*a*) with it (*Hlé-/Læ*). Along with syncope went the emergence of new vowels in the stressed syllables, a process known as vowel mutation. If, for example, a stressed nonfront vowel (for instance, *a*, *o*, or *u*) were followed by an unstressed *i* or *j*, it was fronted (to *e/æ*, *ø*, and *y*); accordingly, *gastiR* became *gestr/giæstr*. The latter East Scandinavian form is due to the fact that *g* was fronted before front vowels, which resulted in the spelling *gi*. Moreover, the *–R* that marks the ending of the nominative case developed a new vowel between itself and the preceding consonant; in East Scandinavian the vowel was *e*, while in Old Norse (at a later stage) it was *u*; hence the forms *gestr/giæster*.

holtijaR: This adjective, which qualifies *ek HlewagastiR*, is not attested in later developments of the language, and the Old Norse and Old Swedish forms are reconstructed, taking into account syncope and vowel mutation.

horna: This noun is the object of the sentence and therefore in the accusative case. The effect of syncope is seen in the loss of *–a*. To the noun in Old Norse and Old Swedish the definite article (the) has been added. The definite article developed during the Common Scandinavian period and was suffixed. *Horn* is a neuter noun, and in the neuter accusative singular the definite article had the form *–it*, which was originally a separate word meaning "that."

tawido: The verb must have had the infinitive *tawian* (which we find in Gothic as *taujan*), but in later Scandinavian it does not occur. The Old Norse and Old Swedish forms given are reconstructed forms. Again, we see the disappearance of *-w-* between vowels (*a* and *i*), taking the following vowel (*i*) with it. We also see the fronting of (long) *o* to *a* (which is the ending showing that the verb is in the first person in the preterite tense) and the replacing of *a* by *e* in Old Swedish.

Word order: Finally, it should be noted that the word order of the inscription is atypical for Scandinavian, in which the verb normally stands before the object. The order may be an old Germanic feature, which was abandoned in the later languages.

The speakers of these West and East Scandinavian languages, or, more accurately, groups of dialects, made no particular distinction, however, and used the term "Danish tongue" about all the variations of North Germanic. The term is believed to have originated outside of Scandinavia and then been adopted by the Scandinavians themselves. The choice probably stems from the fact that the Danes lived in closer proximity to other language communities than the other Scandinavian people.

Later in the Middle Ages, the east-west division of the Viking age was supplemented or replaced by a north-south division, which first separated Danish from Norwegian and Swedish and later separated insular Nordic

(Icelandic and Faroese) from what may be called Scandinavian (Danish, Norwegian, and Swedish). The relationship among the languages as it is today may be illustrated in chart form.[2]

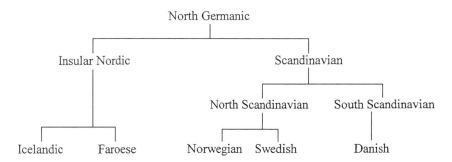

Within Scandinavia, speakers normally expect to be understood when speaking their native language. The insular languages, however, differ sufficiently from the mainland languages to require mutual learning for comprehension, but they are unmistakably Scandinavian, and Icelandic in particular has preserved many features that have been lost in the mainland languages. The similarity between the five modern Scandinavian languages, whose spelling is often etymological and quite deceptive with regard to pronunciation, may be shown by citing again the inscription on the Gallehus horn. Here the usual word for "make" (*gera/gjøre/göra/gøre*) has been substituted, and *Hyltir* has been replaced by the phrase "from Holt."

Icelandic	ég	Hlégestur	frá Holti	horn(ið)	gerði
Faroese	eg	Lægestur	frá Holti	horn(ið)	gjørði
Norwegian	jeg	Legjest	fra Holt	horn(et)	gjorde
Swedish	jag	Lägäst	från Holt	horn(et)	gjorde
Danish	jeg	Lægæst	fra Holt	horn(et)	gjorde[3]

NAMES

Personal names and naming customs in Viking-age Scandinavia differed from those in the rest of Europe. This makes it relatively easy to distinguish Scandinavian place names from other names in the Viking colonies, because one element (usually the first) is frequently a Scandinavian personal name.

Of forenames, there were two types: compound names and simplex names. The former are made up of two words, of which one or both are often drawn from pagan Scandinavian religion (*Thor*stein, *Frey*dis, *As*laug), the animal kingdom (Styr*bjorn* [= bear], Kveld*ulf* [= wolf]), or warfare (*Geir*finn [= spear], Svan*hild* [= battle], Hildi*gunn* [= battle]). The latter consist of only one element. Male names that were common throughout Scandinavia include Ulf, Grim, Karl, Harald, Svein/Sven, Olaf, Knut/Knud, and Hakon; among popular female names can be mentioned Sigrid, Asa, Ingrid, Thora, Tove, and Gunhild. The names Harald, Sven, and Knud were much used in the Danish royal family in the late Viking age, whereas the Norwegian royal family appears to have favored Harald and Olaf. Forenames often alternate between generations within families, because the practice of naming a boy or a girl after his/her grandparents was widespread.

Many people also had by-names, and in contrast to forenames they had a lexical meaning and characterized their bearers. By-names of relationships, especially patronymics, were the most common. They usually comprise the father's forename plus the words for son (*-son/-søn/ -sen*) and daughter (*-dottir/-datter*). If a man by the name of Thorstein had a son called Egil and a daughter called Sigrid, their by-names would therefore be Thorsteinsson and Thorsteinsdottir, respectively. Names expressing relationship to a place, such as Per *Jude* (from Jutland), or occupation, such as Sten *Bonde* (farmer), were also relatively common. Finally, some people had by-names describing their physical or mental characteristics; the better-known examples of this kind are those of some of the Scandinavian kings, including Harald Fairhair, Sven Forkbeard, Harald Bluetooth, and Ivar the Boneless. Most likely, these names were invented by later generations and not used when the dignitaries were alive.

As a result of the Scandinavians' commercial activity in southern and central Europe and the introduction of Christianity, foreign names were introduced, especially biblical names and names of popular saints. By the end of the Viking age, names such as Maria, Birgitta, Katarina, Johannes, Petrus, Benedikt, and Andreas had become the most popular forenames in most of Scandinavia.

WRITING

It is often said that the Viking-age Scandinavians were illiterate until they became Christian and the Church of Rome brought to them the art of reading and writing. This is only partially true, because, like other Germanic-speaking people, the Scandinavians had their own way of writing with an alphabet called runic. The origin of the runes has been hotly debated, but most scholars today agree that runic writing was created by the Germanic people themselves in the second century A.D. under direct or indirect influence of the Greek and/or Roman alphabets.

Earlier studies of the runes tended to emphasize the magical or ritual aspect. According to Old Norse mythology—or, more specifically, the eddic poem *Havamal* (Sayings of the High One)—the runes were divine. Odin (the "High One"), the father of gods and men, had passed the threshold of death when he hung from the tree Yggdrasill for nine nights wounded by a spear. From the world of death he received the runes and the secret wisdom that goes with them and later gave the runes to humans. This approach to the runes is now outdated, and most runologists are of the opinion that the runes were simply a script used for everyday purposes as well as for charms.

The oldest runic alphabet, called the *futhark* (after the phonetic values of its first six letters: *f, u, th, a, r, k*), consists of 24 characters. Each runic character had a name, which normally began with the sound that the rune represented. The letter of the *futhark* with the value *t*, for example, had the name *TiwaR* (Old Norse *Tyr*), god of war; the *f*-rune was called *fehu* (Old Norse *fe*) meaning "cattle" or "money"; the *d*-rune was called *dagaR* (Old Norse *dagr*) meaning "day"; and the *n*-rune had the name *naudiR* (Old Norse *naud*) meaning "need." With much conciseness, each rune could therefore represent not only its sound but also the entity for which it was named.

The *futhark* was once used by all the Germanic people. The characters are made up of vertical and diagonal lines, which make them especially suitable for carving on wood. Curves, which would be difficult to cut in grainy material, are avoided, as are horizontal strokes, which would mingle with the grain. There are, however, many variations in the letter forms of the Germanic runic alphabet, and this makes it virtually impossible to give a standard pattern for the alphabet, which underwent significant changes. In the areas settled by the Anglo-Saxons and Frisians, for example, new runic letters were created to fill new linguistic needs, whereas in Scandinavia a number of runic letters were discarded. Indeed, by the ninth century, the runic characters had been reduced from 24 to 16, and many of the forms had been simplified so that they would be quicker and easier to carve. Of this new alphabet, called the younger *futhark*, there were two main variants: the Danish (or common) runes and the Swedo-Norwegian (or short-twig) runes. The geographical names of the two variant *futharks* are somewhat misleading, because they were not restricted to specific regions, and both types were used over large areas. Generally, it seems that the Danish runes were used for inscriptions on monuments while the Swedo-Norwegian runes were used for everyday communication, though some inscriptions are mixed, using some forms from one *futhark* and some from the other. The two alphabets are shown below (though some runes have variant forms that are not given here). Above are the Danish runes, and below are the Swedo-Norwegian runes. In between, the corresponding Roman letters are given, though it must be stressed that the correspondences are only approximate.

It is not known why the new runic alphabet of only 16 characters developed. It certainly raised problems of representing sounds. There is, for example, no *e, o, d, g,* or *p*, and clearly a single rune had to denote several sounds. On the other hand, there are two types of *r*-rune (*r* and *R*) and two runes for similar pronunciations of *a* (*a* and *ą*). As a result, many runic inscriptions are difficult to understand.

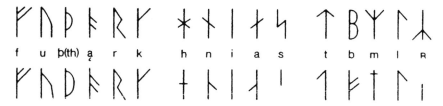

Runes.

We do not know if the ability to use and interpret the runes was a privilege of the select few or if there was a general acquaintance with runes among common people. The fact that rune stones were as a rule erected in public places, beside roads and bridges, or at parish or farm boundaries, suggests that they were intended to be seen or read, and, by extension, that a good number, if not the majority, of Viking-age Scandinavians were able to interpret runes. Two famous examples are the tenth-century Jelling stones in Jutland, which form part of a group of monuments in which two kings, Gorm the Old and his son Harald Bluetooth, display their magnificence. The smaller rune stone, which is not ornamented, is the earlier and has the following inscription:

> King Gorm
> made this monument
> in memory of his wife Thorvi,
> Denmark's adornment.[4]

The larger rune stone is a large boulder with three sides, two of which have relief carving, of a crucified Christ and a lion entwined with a snake. Most of the inscription is on the third side, but there is a further line along the bottom of each of the carved sides. It reads:

> King Harald ordered this monument
> to be made in memory of his father Gorm
> and his mother Thorvi.
> This was the Harald who won all Denmark for himself
> and Norway,
> and made the Danes Christian.[5]

Rune stones are a hallmark of the Viking age. There are about 180 Viking-age and early medieval rune stones in what is now Denmark. In Norway, about 45 such monuments are extant. In Sweden, no fewer than approximately 2,500 rune stones have been preserved from this time period. The eleventh century is a particularly rich period for Swedish runes, and in the province of Uppland alone some 1,300 monuments have been recorded. Nearly 30 stones are found in the Lake Mälaren area raised in memory of men who accompanied Yngvar the Far-traveler on an ill-fated expedition to the East. The noblest of these stones is at Gripsholm in Södermanland. It reads: "Tola had this stone set up in memory of her son Harald, Ingvar's brother." And then comes in verse:

> Like men they went far to seek gold,
> and in the east they fed the eagle,
> died in the south in Serkland [the Arab caliphates].[6]

Moreover, a number of Scandinavian runic inscriptions have been found in the Viking colonies; the tiny Isle of Man, in particular, has a remarkably large collection of rune stones.

Runic inscriptions are by no means limited to epigraphic texts on stone monuments. They occur on a variety of objects, such as jewelry, weapons, tools, and utensils, made of wood, bone, antler, or metal. There is even an inscription dating from around 800 on a human skull. Most of these inscriptions have been found in towns and trading posts, including Ribe and Schleswig in Denmark; Trondheim and Bergen in Norway; and Lund, Old Lödöse, Skara, Nyköping, Söderköping, and Uppsala in Sweden. Excavations in Bryggen, Bergen, in the decades after the mid-twentieth

The larger Jelling rune stone. Face A has most of the inscription. Photo courtesy of the National Museum of Denmark.

century brought to light an exceptionally large number of rune-inscribed objects, although they date mostly from 1150–1350. The majority are wooden sticks, of which many are ownership tags or deal in other ways with mercantile transactions. These finds show that runes were an important tool for communication, especially after the Viking age had come to an end, and that certainly at that time the ability to read and write runes must have been widespread.

The Roman alphabet accompanied the conversion to Christianity, but for some time this alphabet, which was mastered primarily by clerics and the nobility, was used only for writing in Latin. Christians did not disapprove of the runes despite their pagan origin, and Christians themselves used runes on baptismal fonts and memorial stones. It appears that for quite some time the two alphabets complemented each other and served different functions: texts of a permanent character, such as royal edicts and legal texts, were written in Roman letters on parchment, whereas notes of importance for only a limited time were inscribed with runes on bones or twigs.

LITERATURE

Although literacy is not exactly a feature commonly associated with Viking-age Scandinavians, it is a fact that they had a literature. Verse appears to have been the preferred means of literary expression. It was composed and transmitted orally, and with the exception of a few short pieces in runic text, it was not recorded until after the Scandinavians had converted to Christianity. Most of the poetry was recorded in Iceland, and it falls broadly into two classes, called eddic and skaldic. Although these terms are somewhat misleading—some skaldic poems have characteristics appropriate to eddic—the distinction is a convenient one.

Eddic poetry derives its name from the word *Edda,* which among other things, means "poetics," and which is the title of a **Eddic** textbook on the traditional poetry of the Icelanders written in **Poetry** the 1220s by the Icelandic politician, historian, and poet Snorri Sturluson. In the seventeenth century, however, the title *Edda* was also applied to an Icelandic manuscript, the Codex Regius, in which most of the early poems are preserved and which, erroneously, was believed to be Snorri Sturluson's source. Nonetheless, the name *Edda* has stuck to the poems gathered in the Codex Regius, though most people now refer to the volume as the *Poetic Edda* or speak of the eddic poems.

The Codex Regius or *Poetic Edda* may be characterized as an anthology of 29 loosely related poems. Eleven of them are on mythological topics and 16 (plus 2 fragments) are on legendary heroes of Germanic folklore. Additional eddic poems and fragments are contained in manuscripts of Snorri Sturluson's *Edda;* in *Flateyjarbok* (Book of Flatey), an Icelandic manuscript from the late fourteenth century; and in a number of late-medieval

Icelandic texts known as mythical-heroic sagas. Most likely, the body of eddic poetry was once quite large.

The place and date of the composition of the individual eddic poems have been sources of debate. The poems are all anonymous, and it is hard, if not impossible, to localize their composition. Some of them are most likely from the Viking age, whereas others may date from as late as the twelfth century. The Codex Regius itself has been dated to about 1270–1280, that is, almost three centuries after Iceland officially became Christian, but the manuscript was evidently copied from an exemplar (or exemplars) at least some decades older.

The heroic poems of the *Poetic Edda* have counterparts in other Germanic literatures and treat heroes who lived in central Europe in the so-called Migration Age. Admittedly, some of the heroes are unknown to history, but others are famous men mentioned in reliable chronicles: Ermanaric, king of the Ostrogoths; Gundaharius, king of the Burgundians; and Attila, king of the Huns. The heroic poems may be divided into three cycles. The first concerns two exclusively Norse heroes, Helgi Hjorvardsson and Helgi Hundingsbani (killer of Hunding). The second deals with Sigurd the Dragon-slayer of the Volsung clan, the most glorious of Germanic heroes. The poems concerning Sigurd are more numerous than those on the two Helgis, but in the Codex Regius the two cycles are linked by making Helgi Hundingsbani Sigurd's older half-brother (both are said to be sons of a certain King Sigmund). The poems detail Sigurd's life and death, focusing on his acquisition of the gold treasure, his marriage to Gudrun, daughter of the Burgundian King Gjuki, and his fall at the hands of his brothers-in-law. The third cycle of poems treats Attila (in Old Norse Atli) the Hun and Ermanaric (in Old Norse Jormunrek) the Goth, and the link between the cycles is Gudrun, Sigurd's wife, who reluctantly marries Atli. More specifically, it gives an account of the events leading up to and detailing the fall of the Burgundians (also called Niflungs) and the deaths of Hamdir and Sorli, Gudrun's sons by a certain King Jonak.

Unlike the heroic poems, the poems about the pagan gods are specifically Nordic. They are not devotional poems comparable to Christian hymns; rather, they are narrative works, in which the gods' fates and adventures are recounted, or didactic works, in which the mysteries of the universe and of gods and humans are disclosed. *Voluspa* (Prophecy of the seeress), which is placed at the beginning of the Codex Regius, is a didactic poem and probably the most renowned of the divine poems. It surpasses all other poems in prophetic power and force, and there is no poem in early Germanic literature of such scope. It relates that Odin, chief of the gods, fears the impending Ragnarok, the end of the world and the old gods' regime. Accordingly, he goes to an ancient seeress, who can foretell the future, in order to gain wisdom and prepare himself for what is in store. She begins by calling for silence, for her audience consists of both gods and humans, and then addresses Odin specifically:

> Attention I ask from all the sacred people [= gods],
> greater and lesser, the offspring of Heimdall [= humans];
> Father of the Slain [= Odin], you wished that I should declare
> the ancient histories of men and gods, those which I
> remember from the first.[7]

She demonstrates her age and remembrance by telling of the creation of earth by the sons of Bur—Odin and his two brothers—who lifted the world from the sea and fashioned Midgard (the middle yard), where they established their own home. She goes on to describe how the gods, enjoying a golden age, were content at work and play and created the first human beings, Ask and Embla, from two tree trunks, which they endowed with breath, wit, hearing, vision, and other qualities of life. But gradually their world darkened, because a mysterious female, Gullveig (intoxication of gold), who appears to symbolize avarice, manifested herself among the gods, and the gods eventually found themselves at war with her tribe, the Vanir. The war ended with the fall of the gods' fortress wall, and they were forced to hire a giant builder, whom they subsequently killed because they could not afford his wages (the sun, the moon, and the goddess Freyja). Here the seeress pauses to pass moral judgments on the gods' oathbreaking and then mocks Odin with the refrain "do you understand yet, or what more?"[8] It is at this point that the poem really begins, for the seeress, who claims to know everything, now speaks of the future. She tells of the death of Odin's son Baldr, the corruption among the gods, the breaking free of monsters, the collapse of moral order, and universal fear among gods and humans:

> Brother will fight brother and be his slayer,
> brother and sister will violate the bond of kinship;
> hard it is in the world, there is much adultery;
> axe-age, sword-age, shields are cleft asunder,
> wind-age, wolf-age, before the world plunges headlong;
> no man will spare another.[9]

The world tree Yggdrasill will tremble and the giants converge from three directions. The battle will begin, and Odin and Thor will be killed by their enemies. The earth will sink into the sea and the heavens be consumed by fire. But the earth will rise anew to be ruled by the innocent gods Baldr and Hod and inhabited by trustworthy men; and a single mighty ruler will come from above to the judgment-place of the gods. However, as the seeress sinks out of her trance, she reintroduces in the final verse the sinister dragon Nidhogg, flying up from black mountains with corpses in its plumage, suggesting, perhaps, that evil, too, will be reborn.

Another much celebrated poem is *Havamal* (Sayings of the High One). It is by far the longest poem in the Codex Regius, although it is incorrect to refer to it as a single poem, for it seems to have been compiled from various poems or fragments of poems that can no longer be distinguished with certainty. The man responsible for bringing them together clearly considered them all uttered by Odin—hence the title "Sayings of the High One [= Odin]"—and some of the more mythical or ritual verses do indeed have Odin as their narrative voice. These include his account of how he hung for nine nights from a rootless tree, wounded by a spear, and how he seduced and later abandoned a woman, Gunnlod, to steal the poetic mead from the giants (see chapter 8). But most of the poem consists of gnomic verse and counsels on the more common situations of life. Some of these are of an almost proverbial character. They may strike the modern reader as mundane, but they provide a rare glimpse of the everyday life and conduct of the Viking-age Scandinavians—not Viking life itself, but life in Scandinavia, more specifically Norway, in a period of social and political upheaval caused by the Viking expansion. A fair number of verses concern social behavior: a man should be washed and fed before he enters the company of others; a man should not visit his friends when he is half starved, gaping at every morsel; no one must try the hospitality of his friends too hard, but instead move on, for by the third day the loved guest is loathed, and when he comes another day, they may tell him that the ale is all drunk or not yet brewed. The need for moderation in eating, drinking, and even wisdom, and the value of circumspection in one's dealings with others are emphasized: if a man trusts his friends, he should be loyal to them, but if he does not trust them, he should pretend that he does, laugh with them just the same, but not let them know what he thinks. Despite the tone of cynicism and misanthropy in many of the verses, much stress is laid on companionship and friendship:

> I was young once, I travelled alone,
> then I found myself going astray;
> rich I thought myself when I met someone else,
> for man is the joy of man.[10]

The poem has very little to say about the heroic. Fighting and warfare are barely mentioned, and feuds and the duty of vengeance for kinsmen not at all. There is no hint of cult, superstition, and an afterlife, and the gods play no part in people's lives: a man must not attempt to keep out of battle nor go in fear of his life, for death, whether by the spear or old age, is its inevitable conclusion; a man has nothing to hope for except that his son will raise a cairn in his memory. And yet, out of this negative background comes the noblest of northern thoughts of death succinctly expressed in what are probably the most magnificent verses in the entire *Poetic Edda*:

> Cattle die, kinsmen die,
> the self must also die;
> but glory never dies,
> for the man who is able to achieve it.

> Cattle die, kinsmen die,
> the self must also die;
> I know one thing which never dies:
> the reputation of each dead man.[11]

Lighthearted and amusing, *Thrymskvida* (Thrym's poem) is an altogether different kind of literary composition. It tells that Thor wakes up to find his hammer, Mjollnir, missing. Without the hammer the gods are helpless against the giants. Accordingly, Thor and Loki go to the home of the goddess Freyja and ask to borrow her feather cloak, so that one of them can fly over the earth in search of the hammer. Freyja happily lends it, and Loki flies to the land of the giants. He happens to meet the giant Thrym, who boasts that he has hidden it and refuses to return the hammer unless he is given Freyja as his bride. Loki and Thor pass on the news to Freyja, who is outraged at the suggestion that she might marry a giant (although her reputation for promiscuity is such that sexual love with a giant would not seem out of the question). In their distress, the gods convene, and Heimdall has a bright idea: Thor must dress up in women's clothes and go to the land of giants, pretending to be Freyja. Thor, the most masculine of gods, is greatly displeased, but eventually he gives in. Decked out as a bride and with Loki disguised as his handmaid, he travels to the land of the giants. Thrym prepares a feast for his wife-to-be, during which the not very intelligent Thor almost gives the game away by drinking three casks of mead and eating one whole ox, eight salmon, and all the dainties reserved for the women. Thrym expresses great surprise at his bride's enormous appetite, but Loki's quick wit saves Thor: "Freyja" has longed so much for the land of the giants that she has not eaten for eight days. Thrym then bends under the veil wanting to kiss his bride, but he is terrified of her burning eyes. Again Loki comes to the rescue: "Freyja" has longed so much for the land of the giants that she has not slept for eight days. Finally, Thrym orders the hammer to be brought in so that he may sanctify the bride, but at this point Thor no longer conceals his identity:

> Thor's heart laughed in his breast,
> when he, stern in courage, recognized the hammer;
> first he struck Thrym, lord of ogres,
> and battered all the race of giants.[12]

The poems of the *Poetic Edda* are stanzaic, and their meters, which are derived from common Germanic meter, are quite simple. The following four lines from *Voluspa* illustrate the features of this metrical tradition:

> Leika **M**íms synir   enn **m**jǫtuðr kyndisk
> at enu **g**amla   **G**jallarhorni;
> **h**átt blæss **H**eimdallr,   **h**orn er á lopti,
> **m**ælir Oðinn   við **M**íms hǫfuð.

> [The sons of Mim are at play and fate catches fire
> at the ancient Gjallar-horn;
> Heimdal blows loudly, his horn is in the air,
> Odin speaks with Mim's head.][13]

Each line consists of two half-lines divided by a metrical caesura (the gap in the middle shows the boundary between the half-lines). The first half-line is called the "a-line" and the second half-line the "b-line." An a-line can have one or two alliterating syllables (the practice of having syllables begin with the same sound); a b-line has only one alliterating syllable. In the example from *Voluspa,* the alliterating stressed syllables are in bold type. This verse is in a meter called *fornyrdislag* (old-story-measure), and it is composed both with and without a fixed number of syllables to the line. It is the most common narrative meter, particularly in heroic poetry. It is also the meter generally used in the rune poems. Some skaldic poems use *fornyrdislag,* but generally it was not favored by that genre. *Ljodahatt* (song-meter) is much used in mythological poetry and especially in that of the didactic kind. It differs from *fornyrdislag* by having a three-part rather than a two-part structure: two alliterating half-lines (which resemble those of *fornyrdislag*) are followed by a "full verse" with no boundaries. All lines show variety in number of syllables. The following four lines from *Hava-mal* serve as an example of *ljodahatt:*

> **H**jarðir þat vitu   nær **þ**ær **h**eim skulu
> ok **g**anga þá af **g**rasi;
> en **ó**sviðr maðr   kann **æ**vagi
> síns um **m**ál **m**aga.

> [Cattle know when they ought to go home,
> and then they leave the pasture;
> but the foolish man never knows
> the measure of his own stomach.][14]

Malahatt (speech-meter) and *galdralag* (spell-measure) are different again but less commonly used. The former is found in the heroic poem *Atlamal* (Atli's poem). The latter occurs in *Havamal,* and it is also found in the runic inscription on the Eggjum stone from Sogn, Norway, which has been dated to around 700.

In terms of language, the eddic poems are relatively easy to read, for the poets availed themselves of a traditional poetic **Skaldic** vocabulary. Not so the skaldic poems, which often present diffi- **Poetry** culties for the modern reader due to their highly specialized diction.

The word "skaldic" derives from the Old Norse *skald* meaning "poet." As it is used today, the term skaldic poetry defines all the early Old Norse-Icelandic alliterative poetry that is not eddic. The earliest skaldic poems have been dated to the ninth century, but, like eddic poetry, the extant verses are transmitted in manuscripts dating from the thirteenth century and later, and most of them are preserved as quotations in prose works. A single complete skaldic stanza survives in written form from the Viking age. It is found on the Karlevi stone on the Swedish island of Öland in the Baltic. The stone was raised around 1000 in the memory of a certain Sibbi, son of Fuldar. Unlike eddic poetry, the majority of skaldic poems are attributed to named poets; and whereas eddic poetry takes its themes from a heroic and mythological past, skaldic poetry makes recent or contemporary events, such as a glorious victory or heroic defeat, its primary subject matter. The bulk of the skaldic poems are in praise of living or recently dead dignitaries, but in a not insignificant number of verses the skalds speak of themselves, boasting of successes or lamenting losses, and express their emotions.

One of the characteristics of skaldic poetry is the use of circumlocutions. Such expressions are not used much in eddic poetry, and the ones that occur are fairly simple. The circumlocutions are usually divided into two categories: *heiti* and kennings. The former, *heiti*, may be translated as "appellations" and covers nouns used in poetry but not in everyday speech or in written prose. The term kenning derives from the Old Norse verb *kenna* (to know, recognize), which in the phrase *kenna X vid Y* means "to call X by Y's name." A kenning consists of basically two elements, both of which are nouns, as in, for example, "surf horse." One of the nouns (here "horse") is the baseword and the other (here "surf") the determinant. In the baseword the object is named, and in the determinant it is qualified. At first sight, the two nouns often appear incongruous, but their meaning can be perceived from their relationship to one another. A third object (here "ship," for a ship is what one rides over the surf) is thereby suggested, and this is the meaning of the kenning.

"Surf horse" is a simple kenning, because some kennings consist of more than two elements. Such kennings are called *tvikennt* (double) or *rekit* (extended) kennings. In a double kenning, the determinant is itself a kenning, as in "stave of the icicle of battle," where "icicle of battle" is a kenning for "sword" and "stave of the sword" is a kenning for "warrior."

In an extended kenning, a kenning forms the determinant to a further kenning, which is determinant to yet another kenning, as in "stave of the icicle of the tumult of axes," where "tumult of axes" is a kenning for "battle," "icicle of the tumult of axes" a kenning for "sword," and "stave of the sword," as noted above, a kenning for "warrior." Although Snorri Sturluson and other critics argued that the kennings within a kenning should not exceed five in number, six-unit kennings do occur. The longest kenning on record is a kenning for "man" devised by the eleventh-century poet Thord Saereksson: "the sword-swinger in driven snow [= battle], with the troll [= ax] of the shield, like a protective moon on the side of the steed of the boathouse [= ship]."

More often than not, the kennings were drawn from mythology, that is, the myths that were often the topic of eddic poetry were used to provide a framework for the skaldic kennings. Such kennings require intimate knowledge of religious belief or legend. "Frodi's corn" is quite easy, but only if the listener or reader knows that Frodi, a legendary king of Denmark, was the owner of a mill named Grotti, which would grind out whatever he asked of it, and gold was the first thing he requested; hence the expression is a kenning for gold. "Kvasir's blood" does not present problems either, provided the listener or reader knows that Kvasir was a wise creature whose blood the dwarfs made into a special kind of mead that gives poetic inspiration (see chapter 8); hence the expression is a kenning for poem.

Not only does skaldic poetry have a complex diction, but it also has a very elaborate combination of verse forms, rhymes, and alliteration, which make it difficult for modern readers to understand. The earliest and most commonly used meter is *drottkvaett* (court meter), which serves as the basis of most other skaldic meters. Below is shown a typical *drottkvaett* stanza taken from the early eleventh-century poem *Austrfararvisur* (Verses on a journey to the east) by the famous skald Sighvat Thordarson:

> Jór rennr aptanskæru
> allsvangr gǫtur langar,
> vǫll kná hófr til hallar
> hǫfum lítinn dag slíta;
> nú's, þat's blakkr of bekki
> berr mik Dǫnum ferri;
> fákr laust drengs í díki
> dœgr mœtask nú fæti.[15]

Each stanza has eight lines and falls into two halves. Each half is complete in metrical form and usually in syntax. The basic unit is therefore the half-stanza of four lines. Each of these lines has six syllables, three stressed and three unstressed, and every line ends in a trochee, consisting of a long stressed syllable followed by a short unstressed syllable. There are two alliterative syllables in the a-line and one in the b-line; the latter must fall on the first syllable of the b-line. In the example above, alliteration is in bold type. Unlike the eddic poets, the skalds used rhyme and half-rhyme (consonance). In full rhyme both the vowel and the following consonant must be identical; in half-rhyme the post-vocalic consonants agree, but the vowels that precede them do not. In the example above, the full and half-rhymes are italicized. The earliest skalds tended to distribute full rhymes and half-rhymes rather freely, but gradually it became the practice to use half-rhyme in the a-line and full rhyme in the b-line. The rhyme or half-rhyme regularly falls on the last stressed, penultimate syllable of the line, and on one stressed (or half-stressed) syllable preceding it.

The sentence structure of skaldic poetry is often complex, because it indulges in extreme liberty of word position within a sentence, and it is often difficult to know which words go with which. Because Old Norse is a heavily inflected language, greater freedom is allowed than in, for example, English, where the sense often depends on the word order. Below, a *drottkvaett* stanza is cited, followed by a reconstructed prose form and a translation into English. The stanza is taken from the beginning of the fragmentary *Ragnarsdrapa* (Ragnar's poem) by Bragi Boddason the Old, a Norwegian poet probably of the second half of the ninth century, who is considered to be the oldest named skald whose poetry has survived. His *Ragnarsdrapa* is a so-called shield-poem, giving verbal expression to pictures and mythological subjects painted on a shield that was given to him by his patron, a certain Ragnar.

> Vilið, Hrafnketill, heyra
> hvé hreingróit steini
> þrúðar skalk ok þengil
> þjólfs ilja blað leyfa?

> Vilið heyra, Hrafnketill, hvé skalk leyfa ilja blað þjófs þrúðar, hreingróit steini, ok þengil?

> [Do you want to hear, Hrafnketill, how I'll praise the footsole leaf of the thief of Thrud (the daughter of Thor > the giant Hrungnir > the shield), brightly planted with color, and the ruler?][16]

From this, it is evident that the skaldic verse-forms are the product of a highly developed artistic movement, which has no counterpart in other Germanic literatures. As the British scholar Gabriel Turville-Petre puts it, it was sufficient to be born a poet to compose eddic poetry.[17] But to compose skaldic poetry, a long training and a thorough education in poetic diction, metrics, and mythology were necessary. Skaldic poetry is the poetry of the professional and not of the amateur.

Most likely, many, if not most, Scandinavians had problems understanding this highly complicated and artificial form of verse. And it was for this reason that the poet and historian Snorri Sturluson composed his

Edda, because he feared that the art of skaldic poetry would die out and wanted contemporary thirteenth-century poets to understand and be able to compose similar poetry. His *Edda,* which is a unique and original work, is comprised of four parts: a prologue, *Gylfaginning* (The deluding of Gylfi), *Skaldskaparmal* (Language of poetry), and *Hattatal* (List of verse forms). The prologue gives an account of the origin of pagan religions and an explanation of the Norse gods as kings descended from King Priam of Troy in Turkey, who migrated to Scandinavia and came to be worshiped as gods by ignorant people. From these incomers from Asia—who were therefore called "Aesir" (sing. "As"), which is the usual Old Norse word for "gods"—the great kings of Scandinavia were descended. The second part, *Gylfaginning,* comprises a systematic account of Norse mythology from the creation of the world to its end, and its purpose was clearly to give an account of the mythology that underlies many of the kennings found in skaldic poetry. The story is presented in the form of a dialogue, which involves three kings, who answer questions put to them by a certain King Gylfi of Sweden, who wished to find out about the Aesir. Accordingly, he set off disguised as a tramp by the name of Gangleri. However, the Aesir saw him approaching and devised an illusion for him (hence the title "The deluding of Gylfi"). When he arrived in the Aesir's land, he saw an enormous hall, at one end of which there were three thrones occupied by three kings, High, Just-as-High, and Third. The three are prepared to answer Gylfi's questions about the gods and the universe, and the dialogue takes the form of a wisdom contest, but Gylfi is cheated of his victory in the contest when he suddenly discovers that the hall in which the dialogue took place has vanished. The third part, *Skaldskaparmal,* is also in the form of a dialogue, although this time it is between Aegir, god of the sea, and Bragi, god of poetry. Bragi first relates some myths, but this then leads to the myth of the origin of poetical inspiration. Then the origin of some kennings is given, and Bragi begins a systematic overview of kennings for various beings and things interspersed with tales giving the alleged sources of some of them. The final part, *Hattatal,* consists of a poem in 102 stanzas that demonstrates a variety of verse forms composed by Snorri himself along with a prose commentary that explains the meters and devices used, such as rhyme and alliteration.

EDUCATION

Snorri's textbook dates from the thirteenth century, that is, well after the introduction of Christianity and the Latin alphabet and after the Viking age had come to an end. About training and education in the Viking age we know next to nothing. Presumably home schooling or training in various disciplines was the general practice, but on this matter, as on so many others, the Viking-age Scandinavians have left no traces.

Formal, scholarly education was a late phenomenon that followed in the wake of the introduction of Christianity. The Christian Church was without question the most significant educational institution during the Middle Ages, and it was also the primary employer of educated personnel. Generally, three types of schools may be distinguished: cathedral schools, monastic schools, and town schools. However, it is known that in eleventh-century Iceland a kind of formal homeschooling took place; the sources report that learned priests, such as Teit Isleifsson in Haukadal (d. 1110) and Saemund Sigfusson in Oddi (d. 1133), educated young men for the priesthood. Monastic and town schools date from after the end of the Viking age, and so do most of the cathedral schools, although the year of the establishment of the various cathedral schools is known in only a few cases. One of the cathedral schools in Denmark, that of Lund, in what is now southern Sweden, may date from before the end of the Viking age; it is first mentioned in 1085 and with certainty in 1123. The two cathedral schools in Iceland appear to have come into existence shortly after the establishment of the bishop's seats at Skalholt in the mid-eleventh century and Holar in 1106. About Iceland's first bishop, Isleif Gissurarson of Skalholt (1006–1080; consecrated 1056), it is known that he studied for the priesthood at Herford in Westphalia, Germany, as did his eldest son, Gissur Isleifsson (1042–1118), who succeeded him as bishop in 1082. About the first bishop of Holar, Jon Ogmundarson (1052–1121; consecrated 1106), it is known that he had studied under the bishop of Skalholt, and that at Holar he appointed foreign teachers to instruct in reading, writing, Latin, singing, and versification.

The disciplines of the cathedral schools were the liberal arts and, more specifically, the *trivium* (grammar, rhetoric, and dialectics). To this, courses in Christianity and logic were added. The subjects of the *quadrivium* (arithmetic, geometry, astronomy, and music) appear to have had low priority, although it is reasonable to assume that in the curriculum there had much variation, both over time and regionally. Although little is known about pedagogical methods and aims, the education no doubt consisted mainly of rote learning and recitation. By modern North American standards it was rather brutal; corporal punishment, such as birching, whipping, and caning, was considered acceptable and appears to have been common when the pupils broke rules or behaved dishonorably. The education was a two- to three-year program followed by an additional two-year course under the school's supervision for prospective priests. Although the purpose of cathedral schools was first and foremost to educate priests, the schools also trained pupils for political or civil service positions.

We do not know even approximately how many pupils graduated from a specific cathedral school in a given year. Probably only the more prosperous families, who did not need their children's contribution to the family income, could afford to send their children to secondary school. It is also reasonable to assume that girls were excluded from receiving an education. Girls did not need preparation for public life, for a girl who would grow up to be a married woman like her mother could obtain her training at home, although it has generally been acknowledged—usually with reference to a charming vignette in the Icelandic monk Gunnlaug Leifsson's (d. 1218/19) biography of Bishop Jon Ogmundarson (*Jons saga helga*) about a certain Ingunn, who studied at the cathedral school at Holar, where Latin books were read to her while she sewed or played games—that a few women were given the opportunity to study.

SCIENCE

There is ample evidence that the Viking-age Scandinavians possessed considerable knowledge about the natural world. Old Norse-Icelandic literature testifies to an early interest in geography, zoology, astronomy, medicine, computistics, and other subjects that are now labeled as scientific, but there is little to suggest deliberate research by the Scandinavians in the Viking age. Accordingly, the discussion here is limited to the fields of geography and astronomy, in which the Scandinavians may be said to have made independent inquiry.

Geography The Viking-age Scandinavians made no maps and did not leave any artifacts that could be described as maps, but as far as we can tell, their picture of the earth was that of a round one. It was either flat or slightly saucer shaped. Central to it was an inner sea, the Atlantic Ocean and its contiguous waters, and it was surrounded by a land ring. The Norsemen were quite convinced of this, and in many ways it must have been a comforting thought to them that wherever they sailed they were always enclosed by land. From experience, the Viking-age Scandinavians knew that this land ring started somewhere east of northern Norway and went over the White Sea right around the top of the frozen world, came to Greenland, and then proceeded to come down on the other side. When later Latin Christian learning reached Scandinavia, this notion of the earth was somewhat revised, and by the end of the Viking age three separate continents, all thought to lie in the northern hemisphere, are distinguished: Asia, Africa, and Europe. The southern hemisphere was usually considered to be one big unspecified but inhabited area. Europe, separated from Africa by the Mediterranean Sea and from Asia by the River Don, included the islands in the Atlantic as well as Greenland, which was joined to Russia by a strip of land, making the Atlantic Ocean a kind of Scandinavian inland sea. The three North American regions named by the Icelandic explorer Leif the Lucky—Helluland, Markland, and Vinland—were considered to be located south of Greenland and to stretch out from Africa.

The Viking-age Scandinavians' interest in and knowledge of geography can be gleaned from travel writings. One of the oldest examples is the ninth-century record of Ohthere, a chieftain from Halogaland in northern

Norway, who visited King Alfred the Great's court in Wessex, England, and told of his voyages in Scandinavia and his way of living in Norway. Here is an extract from Ohthere's description of Norway.

Ohthere told his lord, King Alfred, that the farm he lived on lay further north than that of any other Norwegian. He said he lived in the north of the country on the Atlantic coast. Yet, he said, the country stretched a very long way farther north but it is all uninhabited, save that here and there Lapps had their encampments, hunting in winter and in summer fishing along the sea-coast...

He said that Norway was very long and narrow. All the land fit for grazing or arable lies along the sea-coast and that is very rocky in places. To the east and higher up, wild fells lie alongside the worked land. In these fells live the Lapps. The worked land is broadest in the south, and the further north you get the narrower it becomes. In the south it may be sixty miles across or more; in the middle thirty or more; and in the north, he said, where it is narrowest, it may be three miles to the fell. And then the fell is in some parts as broad as can be crossed in two weeks, and in other parts as broad as can be crossed in six days. Alongside the southern part of this land, beyond the fells, is Sweden, extending up to the north of the land.[18]

Although most of the indigenous geographical works date from after the Viking age, they obviously draw on information acquired much earlier. Most famous among them are, of course, the two so-called Vinland sagas, *Groenlendinga saga* (Saga of the Greenlanders) and *Eiriks saga rauda* (Saga of Erik the Red), which record the voyages of discovery to North America in the late tenth century. There are also accounts of crusades to the Holy Land.

Astronomy Astronomy seems not to have been a matter of particular interest until the twelfth century, when in the north of Iceland a man by the name of Star-Oddi Helgason took lunar and solar observations, recording azimuth tables. Around the same time, another Icelander, Abbot Niculas Bergsson (d. 1159/1160), reports in his *Leidarvisir* (Guide), which is an account of his itinerary to the Holy Land, how, by the banks of the Jordan, he lay on his back and used his knee, fist, and thumb to measure the angle of elevation of the Polaris.

Considering the fact that the Viking-age Scandinavians were skilled sailors, it is, however, reasonable to assume use of basic celestial observation—in clear skies, that is—when voyaging out of sight of land. On the whole, though, very little is known about the navigational methods used; but it is likely that, for example, courses were steered relative to the Polaris on a clear night, and that estimates for directions of north and south were checked at noon with the sun at its highest or in northern latitudes at midnight with the sun at its lowest.

Calendar and Time-Reckoning Basic lunar and solar observations obviously determined the Viking-age Scandinavians' conceptions of time. To them, a year consisted of a time of light (summer) and a time of darkness (winter). "Summer" lasted from around mid-April to mid-October, and "winter" from around mid-October to mid-April. A new year was considered to begin at the start of the winter semester, and for this reason people's ages were given in terms of number of winters.

The summer semester was production time and the winter semester consumption time. This is clearly reflected in the Old Norse names of the months, although months were not months in our sense of the word but rather indicators of seasonal activities. For example, the first month of winter, *gormanud* (gore month), derives its name from the slaughtering of beasts for winter store, and the third month of winter, *morsug* (marrow-sucker) clearly implies that around this time people typically ran low on food supplies. The name of the first month of summer, *varonn* (spring work), shows that activities connected with production began, though during the summer season a division into weeks appears to have been the norm.

The day, too, was divided into a time of light and a time of darkness. The day was defined by the movements of the sun, and this is given clear expression in the Old Norse term for the 24 hours that comprise a day and a night: *solarhring* (sun-ring). In addition to the day and night division, the *solarhring* was further divided into *eykt*, that is, intervals of approximately three hours from 6 A.M. to midnight. Each *eykt* had a name, which either referred to a physical fact, such as *hadegi* (midday), or, more commonly, a meal, that is, *dagmal* (day-meal) at 9 A.M. or *nattmal* (night-meal) at 9 P.M. In Old Norse, *mal* meant also "measure," which shows that meals were considered means of measuring the time of day.

Only for Iceland do we have a detailed written account of the old calendar before the introduction of Christianity and of the efforts made to adjust the calendar to the solar year and later to the Julian calendar. When in 930 the Icelandic Commonwealth was established through the creation of the Althing (the Icelandic parliament), fixed times for annual assembly meetings had to be determined. The very size of Iceland made it difficult to send out special announcements about the forthcoming session of the Althing each year, so this had to be determined at least one year in advance. Because the Icelanders' time reckoning was not exact, this turned out to be a problem. The Icelanders divided the year into 52 weeks, which makes 364 days. Accordingly, the year was one or two days shorter than the solar year. This distortion was eventually observed. The early twelfth-century historian Ari Thorgilsson says in his *Islendingabok* (Book of Icelanders) that "men noticed by the course of the sun that summer was moving backwards into spring."[19] For that reason, a serious study of chronology was undertaken and, according to Ari Thorgilsson, it was made law that an extra or intercalary week, called summer supplement, should be added to the summer semester every seventh year in order to guarantee that the seasons corresponded with the calendar. Winter was given 25 weeks and 5 days and summer 26 weeks and 2 days, plus the intercalary week if it was the year for it. The supplement was added to all years ending on a Monday, as well as those ending on a Sunday, if they were followed by a leap year.

HEALTH AND MEDICINE

It is difficult to make an assessment of the health conditions among the Viking-age Scandinavians, and the sources are too few to give us any concrete idea how they perceived health and sickness, except that there were no clear boundaries between the domains of medicine and religion. Not only did health mean freedom from disease; it also entailed the presence of good fortune. This good fortune could, however, be taken away by sorcery or the ill will of supernatural beings, in which case the restoration of health sometimes involved the aid of a healer, who could identify the sickness and cure it.

Little is known about the types of illnesses that were prevalent among the Viking-age Scandinavians, but poor **Sickness** sanitation and malnutrition were probably the causes of many ailments. Deficiency diseases, such as scurvy, must have been widespread, especially in the winter when food was often scarce. From skeletal evidence it is also clear that osteoarthritis was common among adults. People frequently lacked one or more teeth, but dental cavities are rarely found (clearly because of the absence of white sugar in the diet). As for epidemics, tuberculosis, typhus, relapsing fever, leprosy, and dysentery would seem probable candidates. Indeed, it is known that an epidemic of leprosy and bloody discharge occurred among the Vikings in Dublin, Ireland, in 949, and the historian William of Malmesbury (d. c. 1143) tells of an outbreak of what was probably dysentery among the Danes in Kent, England. However, there is nothing to suggest the occurrence of plague epidemics in the Viking age that caused severe population reduction in any given area. Within Scandinavia and in the Norse colonies in the North Atlantic, people lived on farms scattered over a vast area or in small settlements, and the cities were few and far between and relatively small. This type of isolation probably offered some protection against contagious diseases, but it also left the local community unprotected when a new disease was carried in from another community. Once a person had contracted an infectious illness, it was likely to spread rapidly, for the sanitary conditions were deplorable, and certainly in the countryside, it was the custom that the whole household slept together in the same room. It is also known that some people had farm animals in the houses where they lived, which would tend to increase the number of rats and fleas—both disseminators of disease—living in the immediate proximity of the household. Two of the Sagas of Icelanders, *Eiriks saga rauda* and *Eyrbyggja saga* (Saga of the people of Eyri), contain accounts of farmsteads hit by epidemics. In *Eiriks saga rauda*, it is told that the people at Thorstein and

Sigrid's farm in Lysufjord in Greenland are stricken with a disease. The first to die is the foreman, and soon other inhabitants contract the illness one after the other. The epidemic eventually leads to the extinction of almost the entire household. In *Eyrbyggja saga*, it is related that the Froda farm in Iceland battles an epidemic, which claims the lives of no fewer than 18 servants. The disease is said to have been brought to the farm by Thorgunna, a visitor from the Hebrides, who is the first on the farm to die, and its spread is attributed to the fact that the mistress of the farm neglects to burn Thorgunna's bedclothes. The burning of the deceased person's bedclothes and bedstraws appears to have been the custom in Scandinavia, evidently in an attempt to prevent contagious diseases from spreading.

Health Care and Medicine While epidemic disease appears to have been met with passive submission, there is evidence that efforts were made to treat other ailments either through herbal remedies, or through diets, steam baths, purges, bloodletting (phlebotomy), or, in the case of acute illnesses, through surgical intervention. Not to be overlooked in terms of treatment and care is also faith healing. In pagan times, such healing efforts involved the recitation of charms, consultation with a religious specialist, or the following of prescribed ritual procedures. In Christian times, they consisted of the invocation of God, Christ, the Virgin Mary, or various saints, especially the Fourteen Holy Helpers (a group of saints known for the efficacy of their intercession against various diseases and especially at the hour of death).

The use of herbal medicine was clearly common. Several herbs from classical Greek or Roman medicine were known and used in Scandinavia in the Viking age, and to this knowledge were added local tradition and the use of local herbs. In his biography of the Norwegian King Olaf Haraldsson (*Olafs saga helga*) in *Heimskringla* (Disc of the world), Snorri Sturluson includes an account of a healer's attempt to treat Thormod, the king's poet, by using herbal remedies. It is related that in the battle of Stiklestad, Norway, in 1030, Thormod was struck right in the heart by an iron-tipped arrow, and that a healer, who ministered to the wounded fighters, offered to treat his wounds.

And when she inspected his wounds she looked closely at the wound he had in his side. She noticed that there was an iron in it, but did not know which path it had taken. She had made a concoction in a stone kettle in which she had mashed leeks and other herbs and boiled them together, and that she gave the wounded men to eat. In that manner she tried to find out if they had wounds in vital parts, because she could smell the leek through a wound which went into the body cavity. She brought some of it to Thormod and told him to eat it.[20]

What the healer clearly attempted to do was make a diagnosis on the basis of a test meal. A smell of leeks and herbs from a wound in Thormod's stomach would prove that his intestines had been pierced. But Thormod was well aware of the fact that the wound was in his heart and not in his stomach, hence his refusal to eat the mixture with the comment that he did not suffer from "porridge illness." Accordingly, he requested a surgical approach, that is, instructed the healer to cut away the flesh around the piece of iron, and subsequently grasped some tongs and wrenched out the arrowhead himself. Shortly after, however, he died—either from the severity of the wound or because of infections resulting from the surgery.

The healer in this story is a female, and in pagan times medical treatment appears to have been the province of women, who relied on their own observations, experiences, and, not least, health advice passed along by word of mouth from previous generations. Indeed, a stanza in the eddic poem *Havamal* includes recommendations for the use of a variety of substances in order to maintain general health and serves as an example of the kind of lore that must have been widespread among the Scandinavians in the Viking age:

> I advise you, Loddfafnir, to take this advice,
> it will be useful if you learn it,
> do you good, if you have it:
> where you drink ale, choose the power of earth!
> For earth is good against drunkenness, and fire against sickness,
> oak against constipation, an ear of corn against witchcraft,
> the hall against household strife, for hatred the moon
> should be invoked—
> earthworms for a bite or sting, and runes against evil;
> soil you should use against flood.[21]

Women may also have been the primary practitioners of magical medicine, in which charms play a central role. A number of eddic poems mention the use of incantations, and these are typically chanted by females. The eddic poem *Oddrunargrat* (Oddrun's lament), for example, tells of a midwife, the noblewoman Oddrun, who recites charms in an attempt to ease the painful labor of Borgny: "strongly Oddrun sang, powerfully Oddrun sang, / bitter spells for Borgny."[22] The charm itself is not included in the poem, and it is difficult to know if charms were intended to cure particular ailments or were more general attempts to retain or restore good fortune.

Runes were also considered to possess healing powers, as exemplified by the following stanzas from the eddic poem *Sigrdrifumal* (Lay of Sigrdrifa), in which the valkyrie Sigrdrifa provides Sigurd the Dragon-slayer with runic wisdom:

> Helping-runes you must know if you want to assist
> and release children from women;

they shall be cut on the palms and clasped on the joints,
and then the *disir* asked for help.

Limb-runes you must know if you want to be a healer
and know how to see to wounds;
on bark they must be cut and of the tree of the wood,
on those whose branches bend east.[23]

A practical example of the use of runes to cure "a wasting sickness" is
found in *Egils saga* (Egil's saga). It is told that Egil orders the patient, who
is a young woman, to be lifted out of her bed and placed on clean sheets.
He then examines the bed and finds a whalebone with runes carved on it
by a local farmer's son, who had previously attempted to cure her. Egil
inspects the runes and realizes that they are incorrectly executed. Accordingly, he shaves the runes off into the fire (presumably to render them
powerless) and has the patient's bedclothes aired. He then reinscribes
some runes and places the new inscription under the pillow of the bed
where she is lying. Soon her recovery begins.

**Physicians and
Hospitals**
It is not until the end of the Viking age that educated
medical practitioners can be identified. The earliest
mention of physicians is found in Snorri Sturluson's
biography of Magnus Olafsson the Good (*Magnuss saga
goda*), who was king of Norway (1035–1047) and Denmark (1042–1047), in
Heimskringla. It is told that when King Magnus won his victory over the
Wends at Lyrskov Moor in Jutland in 1043, many of his men were
wounded. Because there was a lack of healers, the king selected twelve
men with especially soft hands to bandage the wounds of their fellow soldiers. All of these men subsequently became excellent physicians. Among
them was an Icelander, Atli, whose great-grandson, Hrafn Sveinbjarnar-
son (d. 1213), traveled to the Continent to obtain medical training and
became Iceland's most famous physician of early times.

Otherwise, Scandinavia appears to have had little in the way of physicians. After the introduction of Christianity, most medical service was provided by men of the Church, because many of them had some medical
knowledge and were able to practice according to the principles of
monastery medicine from central and southern Europe. Indeed, the first
hospitals were established in connection with monasteries or churches,
but almost all of these date from after the Viking age.

NOTES

1. The inscription on the Gallehus horn along with the translation into East and
West Scandinavian and the modern Scandinavian languages is quoted (with some
modifications) from Einar Haugen, *The Scandinavian Languages*, Wisconsin Intro-
ductions to Scandinavia, no. 1–2 (Madison: Department of Scandinavian Studies,
[n.d.]), p. 13.

2. The diagram is from Lars S. Vikør, *The Nordic Languages: Their Status and Interrelations,* Nordic Language Secretariat Publication, no. 4 (Oslo: Novus Press, 1995), p. 43.

3. Quoted from Haugen, *The Scandinavian Languages,* p. 13.

4. The inscriptions on the Jelling stones are quoted from R.I. Page, *Runes* (London: British Museum Publications, 1987), pp. 45–46.

5. Quoted from Page, *Runes,* pp. 45–46.

6. The inscription on the Gripsholm stone is quoted from Page, *Runes,* p. 49.

7. The stanzas from *Voluspa* are quoted from Carolyne Larrington, trans., *The Poetic Edda* (Oxford: Oxford University Press, 1996), p. 4.

8. Quoted from Larrington, trans., *The Poetic Edda,* p. 7.

9. Quoted from Larrington, trans., *The Poetic Edda,* p. 10.

10. The stanzas from *Havamal* are quoted from Larrington, trans., *The Poetic Edda,* p. 20.

11. Quoted from Larrington, trans., *The Poetic Edda,* p. 24.

12. The stanza from *Thrymskvida* is quoted from Larrington, trans., *The Poetic Edda,* p. 101.

13. The stanza from *Voluspa* is quoted from Kari Ellen Gade, "Poetry and Its Changing Importance in Medieval Icelandic Culture," in *Old Icelandic Literature and Society,* ed. Margaret Clunies Ross, Cambridge Studies in Medieval Literature, vol. 42 (Cambridge: Cambridge University Press, 2000), pp. 61–95, at p. 62.

14. The stanza from *Havamal* is quoted from Carolyne Larrington, trans., *The Poetic Edda,* p. xxvii.

15. The stanza by Sighvat Thordarson is cited from Lee M. Hollander, *The Skalds: A Selection of Their Poems* (Ann Arbor: University of Michigan Press, 1968), p. 10.

16. The stanza by Bragi Boddason (along with the prose order and the English translation) is cited from "Norse-Icelandic Skaldic Poetry of the Scandinavian Middle Ages: Editors' Manual," compiled by Margaret Clunies Ross, Kari Ellen Gade, Edith Marold, Guðrún Nordal, and Diana Whaley (2000).

17. Here reference is made to Gabriel Turville-Petre, *Origins of Icelandic Literature* (Oxford: Clarendon Press, 1953), p. 26.

18. Ohthere's description is quoted from R.I. Page, *Chronicles of the Vikings: Records, Memorials, and Myths* (Toronto: University of Toronto Press, 1995), pp. 46–48.

19. The *Book of Icelanders* is quoted from Ari Thorgilsson, *The Book of the Icelanders (Íslendingabók),* ed. and trans. Halldor Hermannsson, Islandica, vol. 20 (Ithaca: Cornell University Library, 1930), p. 62.

20. *Olafs saga helga* is quoted from Snorri Sturluson, *Heimskringla: History of the Kings of Norway,* trans. Lee M. Hollander (Austin: University of Texas Press, 1964), p. 520.

21. The stanza from *Havamal* is quoted from Larrington, trans., *The Poetic Edda,* p. 34.

22. The stanza from *Oddrunargrat* is quoted from Larrington, trans., *The Poetic Edda,* p. 206.

23. The stanza from *Sigrdrifumal* is quoted from Larrington, trans., *The Poetic Edda,* pp. 167–68.

5

Material Life

HOUSES

Climatic conditions differ within Scandinavian and the Norse settlements in the North Atlantic. Accordingly, there was no single pattern of house in the Viking age. The mode of constructing houses was determined largely by the surroundings. Treeless regions necessitated use of stone, turf (peat cuttings), clay, straw, and hay, while wooded areas prompted the building of timber houses. In addition, the cold climate of northern Scandinavia, Iceland, and, not least, Greenland required considerably more insulation of house walls than did the somewhat milder climate of Denmark and southern Norway and Sweden.

Farmhouses are relatively well known to us from archaeological excavations. Typically, a farm had one main rectangular longhouse. While a width of 4–7 m (13.1–22.9 ft.) appears to have been standard, the length varied from 15 m (49.2 ft.) to 75 m (246 ft.) and obviously reflected the farmer's social and economic position. And while some houses consisted of only one room, other houses were divided by partition walls into several rooms, which could be closed off. One end of the house was reserved for domestic animals (the presence of animals helped keep the cold away). The living room and sometimes a room for cooking and storage were at the other end. In Iceland, the plan of the longhouse was extended by adding rooms to it, such as a lobby, a kitchen, a pantry, a lavatory, and in this way a new pattern was created: a longhouse with annexes. Some farms also had smaller outbuildings with particular functions, such as byres for wintering the ani-

Rural Housing

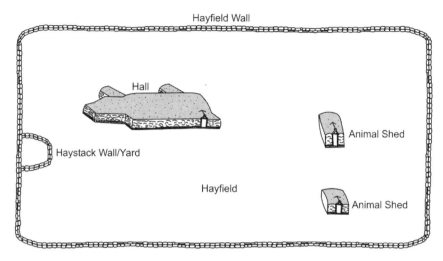

Typical farm layout.

mals, barns for their fodder, stables, storehouses, bathhouses, and smithies, which were grouped around the main longhouse.

The houses always had an inner frame consisting of two rows of interior wooden posts situated in pairs and placed in holes dug into the ground. As construction techniques became more sophisticated, the posts were placed on stones to prevent them from rotting. These posts were connected by beams that ran both transversely and longitudinally to a stable frame. Such a construction was sturdy enough to support the roof, which could be made solely of wood or thatched (covered with sod or birch bark). The walls were built in various ways and of various materials. Some were made of logs with wattle-and-daub in-filling. Others were formed of staves or planks standing side by side in wall ditches. Yet others were made only of stone or turf, and in cold regions, these materials— stone and turf—were typically piled up as an outer embankment for insulation purposes. The walls could be either straight or bowed outward. The latter, which were constructed of halved tree trunks set together in upright rows and with the curved face placed externally, is known from the Danish royal fortresses Trelleborg on Zealand and Fyrkat in north Jutland as well as from ordinary farms in Norway, Sweden, Denmark, and the Norse settlements in the North Atlantic. Such houses also had a curved roof ridge and sometimes rounded corners, which made them look like ships turned upside down. The doors were typically in the long sides at either end. They might be decorated with carvings or iron fittings and could typically be locked with wooden or iron locks. Windows were nonexistent in the longhouses with their thick walls of stone and turf and most likely began in the wooden houses as narrow peepholes protected by inside shutters or glazed with a translucent membrane. It is not until the end of the Viking age that properly glazed windows are recorded. The floors, which were sometimes sunken, were of stamped earth and often strewn with straw or hay.

Especially well preserved remains of a longhouse are found in Thjorsardal in southern Iceland. This farmstead, Stöng, is an example of the home of a wealthy farmer with a household of approximately 20 people. It was abandoned about 1104, when an eruption of the nearby volcano Hekla laid waste to as many as 20 farms and caused the valley to be covered with ash from the eruption. The excavation of Stöng, which began in 1939, revealed two large longhouses (main hall and living room), which were connected end to end. The length of the two longhouses was about 30 m (98.4 ft.). The main hall, which was just over 12 m (39.36 ft.) long, opens off a lobby or entrance hall through the house's one exterior door. In one corner of this lobby was a small rectangular structure, which may have served as a storage room. Against the back wall of the main hall was a bed closet for the head of the household and his wife. The living room, which was about 8 m (26.2 ft.) long, led directly off the hall, and at the back of the house were two rooms, which had been added later. One room, which was entered from the end of the main hall, was evidently a dairy, for there are impressions in the ground for three vats. The other room, which had its entrance from the lobby, was most likely a latrine, for it has trenches on either side. To the east of the house was the byre, and nearby was the barn.

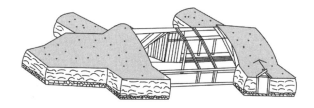

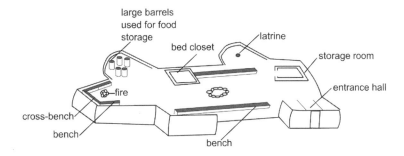

The farm at Stöng.

Standing apart from this complex is what was probably a smithy, because it contained, among other things, an anvil, a basin to quench the hot iron, and a small quern that may have been used for making red dye from volcanic ash.

Urban Housing
Houses in urban communities differed in size and construction. Like farm complexes, they were normally situated on a fenced-in plot, usually rectangular in shape, sometimes with one or more additional outbuildings for cooking, commercial purposes, crafts, and the like. Unlike farm complexes, urban houses were packed close together. They could belong to a single owner or be divided into subordinate divisions as tenements or holdings.

Excavations in Hedeby in South Schleswig in the 1930s and again in the 1960s revealed a number of houses from the ninth and tenth centuries. In size, the houses varied from 7 by 17.5 m (22.96 by 57.41 ft.) to 3 by 2.9 m (9.8 by 9.5 ft.). Most likely, however, the latter did not serve as living quarters for people. The smallest house believed to have been a home measures 7 by

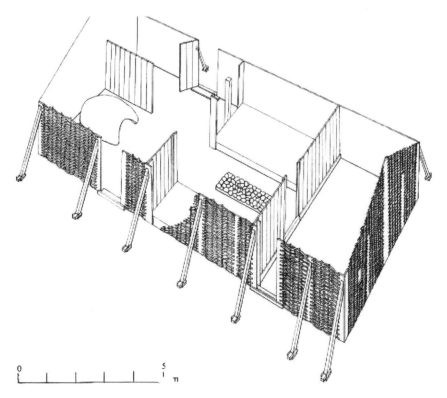

Reconstruction of a ninth-century house based on excavations at Hedeby. From James Graham-Campbell and Dafydd Kidd, *The Vikings* (London: British Museum Publications, 1980). Photograph courtesy of The British Museum Press, a division of The British Museum Company Ltd.

3.5 m (22.96 by 11.48 ft.), that is, an area of approximately 25 square meters! Some of the houses were constructed of horizontal planking; others were stave built with vertical planking normally consisting of wedge-shaped portions of tree trunks; yet others were timber framed with wattle-and-daub in-filling. The roofs appear to have been thatched with straw or reeds with a hole either above the hearth in the middle of the house or at the top of the gable end to allow smoke to escape, for, like farmhouses, they had no chimneys. Some of the houses had partition walls. A rather well preserved house had three rooms: a living room in the middle and two smaller rooms (one containing a bread oven) at either end.

Ibrahim b. Ya'qub al-Turtushi, the tenth-century merchant or diplomat from Andalusia, who visited Hedeby, reports that in the town there were freshwater wells. Excavations not only confirm his statement, but also reveal that most houses had their own wells. Of these wells, which were typically situated behind the houses, there were at least three types: one was box-shaped, built of boards around four cornerposts; another was circular, built of barrel staves; and a third type consisted of a hollowed-out tree trunk. These wells were often at least 2 m (6.56 ft.) deep.

The streets in Hedeby were narrow. In terms of construction, they were simple. They consisted of two parallel rods with a distance of about 1 m (3.3 ft.) between them. Across these were placed boards fastened with wooden rivets on either side. The boards jutted out over the beams, making the roads just over 1 m (3.3 ft.) wide. No streets were therefore wide enough for vehicular traffic; the broadest street was only about 1.5 m (4.9 ft.) wide. One of the streets crossed a brook via a 6 m (19.68 ft.) long bridge, charred wood remains of which were found in the bed of the brook itself. In several places steps led down to the stream, and because a number of hairpins were found in these areas, it is believed that women did their washing there. The remains of a washtub on top of one of these stairs

Reconstruction of a street at Hedeby. From Henning S. Eriksson, *Hedeby* (Copenhagen: Gjellerup, 1967). Image courtesy of Gjellerup.

confirms this supposition. In addition to these through streets, most houses had "private roads." The houses were typically built a little back from, but facing, the streets. A catwalk from the entrance in the gable end of the house across the courtyard to the street was therefore necessary; sometimes the wood-block paving of these walks was replaced by stones.

DOMESTIC INTERIORS

Daily life centered around the fire in the middle of the floor of the living quarters, which gave light and warmth. The fire was on a slightly raised, stone-lined hearth. Because of its rectangular shape, it was called a long hearth or fire. The fire was fed with peat or wood kept outside the house. At night, it had to be banked, so that it could be easily relit in the morning. If it went out, it had to be rekindled with flint and steel in tinder. Some houses had a small oven or roasting pit against the wall instead of, or in addition to, an open hearth. The ovens were made on a framework of wattle and shaped like a dome.

When the light from the fire did not provide sufficient illumination, lamps of soapstone, iron, or clay filled with oil were used. These lamps were simple, open bowls, which stood on a flat surface or were suspended with loops or were mounted on an iron spike stuck in the ground. Wax candles appear to have been a rare and expensive commodity and are known only from wealthy graves, such as at Jelling and Mammen in Jutland, Denmark.

Raised platforms along the long walls of the house served as seats and beds close to the fire, though for sleeping accommodation some houses had built-in bed closets, which provided at least some privacy. Presumably, these platforms were covered with furs, skins, or woolen blankets. The central section of one platform (usually at the inner end) was the so-called high seat of the head of the household. Although it is referred to in English as the high seat, it was not necessarily higher in elevation, only in honor. The guest of honor was seated opposite the head of the household. The high seat was flanked by pillars, which were often adorned, and from Old Norse-Icelandic literature it is known that the high-seat pillars had religious significance. There are several reports of how men emigrating from Norway to Iceland took their high-seat pillars with them. Once they sighted land, they threw the pillars overboard in the belief that the gods would guide them to the place where they were destined to settle.

The walls appear to have been wainscoted, and in some houses the panels were adorned with incised carving or woven hangings or tapestries (narrow strips of cloth with embroidered or woven decoration). The latter, which were a privilege of the wealthier members of society, served the dual purpose of decoration and insulation.

FURNISHINGS

The average house had little furniture. Sleeping, sitting, and eating typically took place on the platforms along the walls. Stools and chairs seem to have been uncommon, though they certainly existed. A rectangular wooden board with corner perforations for four legs was found in Hedeby, and three-legged stools are known from Lund, Sweden, and Dublin, Ireland. Of chairs, there were basically two types. One, a bench-type chair with a square back, was found in the Oseberg ship-burial in Norway. The other type, round with a swung back made from a thick tree trunk, is known from Sweden. Common to both stools and chairs is that they are quite low. As for tables, it is known from literary sources that they were used at least on special occasions. Only one table has been discovered, however, in a woman's grave under Hørning church in northern Jutland, Denmark. It is a small table made of oak for a washbasin. It consists of a heavy frame of logs, which are slotted into each other and held together with wooden dowels, and the top of the table sits in the bottom frame. Moveable beds are also known from archaeological finds, but it is unlikely that they were commonly used and it may be that they were intended for traveling; well-to-do people would have had bed closets partitioned off from the house. The Oseberg ship-burial contained remains of at least five beds, of which the largest measures 2.2 by 1.9 m (7.2 by 6.2 ft.) at the bottom. It is a substantial and beautifully crafted bed: the bedposts at the head of the bed are high and end in carved, bowed animal heads. Horizontal boards inside the bed suggest that it must have had a mattress, and, indeed, mattresses have been found at Tune, Norway. The bedding, or what remains of it, was filled with down, and that such luxury was also enjoyed elsewhere in Scandinavia is confirmed by a down-filled pillow found in a grave at Mammen in Denmark.

Cupboards were unknown. Many objects, such as household utensils and weapons, were stored on shelves or hung on the walls. Wooden pails, soapstone bowls, and clay pots were used to store dry foods and liquids. The only kind of furniture for storage was the chest, in which people would keep personal belongings, such as clothing or tools and utensils of various kinds, both while at home and when traveling; it has been suggested that on board a ship such chests may sometimes have served as rowing benches. Several chests have been preserved, including a very fine specimen found in the Oseberg ship-burial. Smaller caskets and boxes were used for valuables, such as jewelry, and they typically belonged to women. Some of them had built-in locks, though barrel-shaped padlocks have also been found.

PERSONAL APPEARANCE

In appearance, Viking-age Scandinavians were not much different from Scandinavians today except that they were slightly smaller in stature. The

Arab traveler Ibn Fadlan, who in the early 920s set out as secretary of an embassy from the Calif of Baghdad to the king of the Bulgars of the Middle Volga and who there came into contact with the Rus (Swedish Vikings), claims that they are "perfect physical specimens, tall as date palms, blond and ruddy."[1] Contemporary figurative art suggests that men had moustaches and beards and well-groomed hair, which might be held in place by a band across the head. Young girls and unmarried women wore their hair loose, but married women typically had their long hair gathered into a knot at the back of the head.

Archaeological discoveries of toilet implements, such as ear-spoons (for cleaning the ears), tweezers (for removing unwanted hair, though they may also have been used for embroidery with metal threads), toothpicks, combs of antler and bone, and washing bowls, suggest that men and women paid close attention to their general appearance. Indeed, Ibrahim b. Ya'qub al-Turtushi reports that the inhabitants of Hedeby fabricated artificial eye makeup to enhance their looks.

Nonetheless, the Viking-age Scandinavians' personal hygiene was probably low, at least by our modern Western standards—and also by medieval Muslim ones. Ibn Fadlan comments on the Rus's lack of sanitary efforts and goes so far as to call them the filthiest of Allah's creatures. He substantiates his point by drawing attention to the fact that they do not wash after urinating, defecating, ejaculating, or eating, and when once a day they do wash, they all use the same water, into which they also spit and blow their noses. It is, however, possible that within Scandinavia and in the Norse colonies in the North Atlantic people were a little more concerned about personal cleanliness. Indeed, the eddic poem *Havamal* (Sayings of the High One) tells that a guest should be greeted at the table with water and a towel, and it also specifies that a man should be washed before going to the assembly. Moreover, Old Norse-Icelandic literature regularly makes reference to saunas and hot baths in Norway and Iceland. In *Eyrbyggja saga* (Saga of the people of Eyri), the sauna at Hraun in Iceland is described as being partly dug into the ground and with a hole in the top for pouring water on the stove from the outside.

CLOTHING AND ACCESSORIES

Archaeological evidence for clothing in Viking-age Scandinavia is quite limited, for textiles do not normally survive well in the ground. Two kinds of evidence may be distinguished. One comprises scraps of cloth that have been preserved through contact with brooches, and these fragments provide information about the types of fabric used. Moreover, the placement of the brooches, which were used primarily as dress fasteners, on a fully clothed corpse offer hints about the designs and cuts of the clothes. The other consists of contemporary figurative art, such as the Gotlandic picture stones erected between the fifth and the eleventh century, figure pendants, and the tapestry found in the Oseberg ship-burial, which depicts what is probably a procession in connection with a religious ritual. The scanty knowledge afforded by archaeological finds can, however, be supplemented by descriptions of clothing in the literary sources.

The primary fabric was wool, which is warm, durable, and water-resistant. It also takes dyes well, though local dyes made **Fabrics** from vegetables and minerals were not of a high quality and faded after a short while. Varieties of color could, however, be provided by the wool itself, because some wools are naturally shades of gray, brown, and black. Linen appears to have been somewhat less common, though it is reasonable to assume that it was a preferred fabric for undergarments, because it is more comfortable on the skin than wool. Canvas, a heavy and coarse material made from flax, is not particularly well represented in the archaeological finds, but it may be due to the fact that vegetable fibers decompose faster than animal fibers. Silk was a luxury and reserved for the wealthy, for it was imported and costly.

The weave of the domestic fabrics was of two kinds, tabby and twill. Tabby is a weave in which the filling threads and the warp threads interlace alternately, forming a checkerboard pattern. In twill, the filling threads pass over one warp thread and then under two or more others, producing a fabric with diagonal parallel ribs. Sometimes short lengths of wool were inserted into the warp during weaving to give the fabric a shaggy look and feel. Such weave was used for cloaks and appears to have been especially common in Iceland, which exported such shaggy cloaks.

A variety of furs was used, in particular for cloaks and trimmings. In addition to fur trimmings, clothes might also be decorated with embroidery of various kinds and tablet-woven bands containing gold or silver threads. A number of such bands have been preserved due to their use of metal threads. In tablet weaving, the warp threads are passed through holes at the four corners of rectangular plaques of wood. These plaques are then moved a quarter-turn at a time to change the position of the warp threads.

There was considerably more variety in male clothes than in female clothes, which seem rather undiversified and con-   **Men's** servative. It appears that certainly merchants, who traveled   **Clothing** widely, liked to introduce new and foreign fashions in their clothing, while women, who were evidently less fashion-conscious, typically stuck to traditional Scandinavian designs even after they had moved to the colonies in the east and west.

A typical male outfit probably consisted of an undershirt and underbreeches (long or short) of wool or linen, though concrete evidence for the existence of men's and women's underwear is lacking. On top of the shirt, a knee-length, sleeved tunic or kaftan-like jacket was worn, which, if the man was wealthy, might have decorative silk borders and embroideries with gold and silver thread. A bead was sometimes used as a button to

Male dress. From *Vikingernes Verden* by Else
Roesdahl (Copenhagen: Gyldendal, 1989).
Reprinted by permission of Orla Svendsen.

close the opening at the neck. Such tunics or jackets could be tight fitting
or loose. The small bronze buttons found in graves in Birka on Lake
Mälaren in Sweden presumably belonged to tight-fitting garments. A belt
or sash was worn around the middle, fastened with buckles of bronze or
silver. A knife and a purse were normally attached to the belt, though
sometimes the knife was carried on a cord around the neck.

A coat or cloak of heavier material—fur, hide, or wool—was worn on
top of the tunic, and it was fastened over the right shoulder either by a
large penannular brooch or pin or by ties, so that the sword arm could be
kept free. The cloak might have decorative borders or fur trimmings; the
finds in the rich graves of Birka reveal that furs from beavers and martens
were used for such purposes. The less fortunate, such as slaves, obviously
did not have such fancy outer clothes and were more simply dressed in
undyed, coarse woolen clothes. One imagines a blanketlike cloak with a
hole in the center for the head. Children may have been dressed in a similar way, though very little is known about their clothing.

The fashion in trousers or breeches, which were kept up by a belt, seems to have varied considerably. The Gotlandic picture stones show ankle-length as well as mid-calf-length trousers, and narrow as well as baggy trousers. The shorter type was obviously worn with stockings or leggings known as hose. Long hose were held up by cords or laces attached to the top, with which the hose were secured to the breeches-belt. Short or knee-high hose were held up by laces or bands wound around the legs. The hose were typically made of wool and worn with shoes or ankle boots, though some were made of hide and therefore did not require shoes.

Boots and shoes were made of leather and of simple patterns that were common all over Scandinavia. The soles were always flat, without heels, but both round and pointed toes are in evidence. A simple slip-on shoe with no fastenings found at Ribe in Jutland, Denmark, is considered a typical Viking-age shoe in its method of manufacture. The upper part is made from a single piece of goat hide, side seamed at the instep, which is blind stitched to a single-thickness sole. An ankle boot found in York, England, is quite similar in terms of design and is made from a single piece of cowhide blind stitched to a single-thickness sole. But the heel is finished off by fitting a pointed extension to the sole in a v-shaped cut in the back of the upper. Moreover, the upper has an instep flap that is fastened with the help of a toggle and a loop. Such soles with pointed heels and uppers with instep flaps were common, though other types of fastenings are also in evidence. The ankle boot found in the Oseberg ship-burial has a lace that passes through slits or holes in the opening and is bound around the ankle.

Gloves or mittens and hats or hoods of wool or leather would have completed the outfit of a man in cool weather.

Like men, women wore an outfit consisting of layers. The first layer was a long woolen or linen chemise with or without sleeves. The chemise might be finely pleated and fastened at the neck with a small disc or penannular brooch.

Women's Clothing

Over the chemise a woolen dress or gown, possibly decorated with bands or borders, was worn. It consisted of a rectangular piece of fabric, which was wrapped around the woman's body from armpit to mid-calf or longer. The dress, which was tight fitting, was worn suspended from shoulder straps. These straps were sewn on at the back and joined to paired loops attached to the front by a pair of oval brooches, the pins of which passed through the loops. From one of these brooches, usually the right, textile implements like scissors, tweezers, an awl, or a needle case, might hang on straps, and between the brooches festoons of beads might be suspended sometimes with the addition of amber or silver pendants. Around the waist a belt was worn with knife and purse and, if the woman was a housekeeper, keys to the meal or treasury chest. Married women might also wear a tall headdress or a scarf around their hair.

For outdoors, a woman would wear a shawl or a sleeved cloak, held together either by a brooch, usually equal-armed, trefoil, or disc-shaped, or

Female dress. From *Vikingernes Verden* by Else Roesdahl (Copenhagen: Gyldendal, 1989). Reprinted by
permission of Orla Svendsen.

a pin, and, of course, hose kept up with ties. Footwear as well as gloves or
mittens appear not to have differed much, if at all, from those worn by men.

Jewelry   The Viking-age Scandinavians liked splendor, and a considerable amount of jewelry has survived. Most of it comes from
hoards and graves. A variety of metals was used. Iron, copper,
lead, and tin may have been mined in Scandinavia, but silver, gold, and
also zinc, probably already alloyed to produce brass or bronze, were
imported.

Brooches were what one may call obligatory jewelry in that they had a
function in the costumes as fasteners. Many brooches have been found
ranging from individualized items of precious metals to mass-produced
items of base and inexpensive materials. The latter were sometimes gilded
to give them the appearance of gold and silver. The domed, oval brooches
used by women to fasten their dresses are the most common. Worn in
pairs, they are usually 10–12 cm (3.9–4.7 in.) long with bold relief decoration and sometimes ornamented with filigree. The ornament is typically a

kind of "gripping beast" decoration (see the description in the Visual Art section). Brooches used to fasten a chemise, shawl, or cloak and worn singly are the next most common. There were a variety of shapes, but the more usual ones were trefoil, which is Frankish in origin.

Neck rings, arm rings, finger rings, and even toe rings made of silver, gold, or, occasionally, jet, served the dual function of ornamentation and bullion. Such rings were typically made according to weight and from hammering out ingots of gold and silver. They normally consisted of broad bands stamped with patterns or of two, three, or more rods twisted together. In commercial transactions they could, therefore, easily be cut up.

Necklaces, either complete or strung between oval brooches, were frequently used by women. Glass and amber beads, some of which were domestic products, appear to have been the most common, but beads made from imported semiprecious stones, such as crystal, cornelian, and obsidian, were also used. Gold, silver, and bronze beads were considerably less common. Genuine pearls were extremely rare; those that have been found are of poor quality.

Pendants, too, seem to have been popular and were made from a variety of materials. Some pendants consisted of rings or coins often acquired abroad. Others were key shaped and may have served a functional purpose as well as an ornamental one. Yet others served amuletic purposes and comprise miniature weapons, miniature seats or thrones (generally believed to be associated with the cult of Odin), Thor's hammers, and crucifixes.

FOOD AND DRINK

Viking-age Scandinavians ate two meals a day, one in the morning and one in the evening. The food was served in the main hall, and people ate sitting on the raised platforms along the long walls of the house. Well-to-do people probably had tables and tablecloths.

People normally ate with their fingers off flat wooden trenchers. A short-bladed knife, which they typically carried around with them, was used to chop up the food. Some **Tableware** foods, such as porridge, soups, and stews, were served in wooden bowls and eaten with spoons of wood or antler. Ale and mead were drunk from the horns of cattle, which might be ornamented with metal mounts. One problem involved in drinking from a horn is, of course, that it cannot be put down, so a horn must have had to be drained at once or else circulated. Other beverages were drunk from wooden cups or silver bowls. The latter were probably reserved for wine. Glasses, which had to be imported, were uncommon and used only by wealthy people.

The types of food consumed obviously varied from region to region and depended on available resources, but it is reasonable to **Diet** assume that the diet was based primarily on dairy produce, meat, and fish.

Dairy Produce

Milk from cows, sheep, or goats was drunk or used in the preparation of various dishes or processed. It was often separated into curds and whey or buttermilk and made into butter and cheese. Whey, too, was a popular drink and was, moreover, used for pickling. Milk and whey were kept in large vats, from which they were ladled out into vessels.

Meat

In the areas where agriculture was predominant, meat came primarily from domestic animals: pigs, cows, sheep, lambs, goats, and horses. The slaughtering of the animals typically took place in the fall, so that they would not have to be fed during the winter. Hens and geese offered the possibility of fresh meat throughout the year and, of course, also provided eggs.

Other birds and animals were hunted. These included seabirds of all kinds, hares, rabbits, wild boar, elk, deer, seals, whales, and, in the north, reindeer. Both whale and seal meat were considered delicacies, and the oil was used for lamps and, in the case of seal oil, as an alternative to butter.

The meat was prepared in a variety of ways. It might be boiled in a cauldron of iron or soapstone suspended over the open fire from a tripod or hung on chains from a roof beam. It might also be spit roasted or baked in pits filled with hot stones. For preservation, meat was pickled in whey or brine, smoked, dried, or salted. Salt was obtained from boiling seawater or seaweed after which the crystals were gathered.

Fish

Nets, hooks, line winders, floats, and weights found in many settlements show that fish played an important part in the diet. Cod and coalfish were the most important fish in Norway, western Jutland in Denmark, and in the Norse colonies in the North Atlantic. In the Baltic and in the Danish waters, herring was the most important fish. When not eaten fresh, herring was typically salted, whereas cod was, at least in northern Scandinavia and in the colonies in the North Atlantic, wind dried. The dried cod was called stockfish because it hung over a rod, or stock, while drying, and by the end of the Viking age, stockfish was exported. Freshwater fish, such as salmon, perch, and pike, was also consumed, as was shellfish, such as shrimp, mussels, and oysters.

Cereal

Barley was the main cereal; indeed, in Iceland it was probably the only grain cultivated. It was used for making porridge and for baking bread. Malted barley was used for making ale, to which hops might be added for flavor. Rye, too, was commonly used for baking bread, as was oat, which was also used for porridge. Although wheat was grown in Scandinavia, it appears to have been rare and expensive, and "white bread" was probably a luxury reserved for the wealthy.

Bread has been found in a number of graves. Some breads were unleavened while others were leavened with yeast. Barley is the main ingredient, but some breads are mixed with other grains, linseed, pea flour, or pine bark. The flour was ground in hand querns made of local stone or imported lava querns of higher quality. The dough was kneaded in wooden troughs, placed on long-handled, circular pans of iron, and baked on the hot ashes of an open fire. Bread might also be baked in dome-shaped ovens made on a framework of wattle. The ovens were heated up and the embers raked out, where the bread dough was later put and baked. Such ovens have been excavated in both Hedeby in South Schleswig and Lund in Sweden and may have been urban phenomena.

Vegetables and Fruits

Vegetables, fruits, berries, and nuts provided important nutritional supplements. The most common vegetables were probably cabbages, onions, peas, beans, beets, and endives, which were all locally grown. Wild fruits, such as apples, pears, cherries, plums, blueberries, cloudberries, raspberries, blackberries, and strawberries, were found in large areas of Scandinavia and could be picked wherever they grew. They were eaten raw or dried and may also have been used to make fruit wine (grape wine had to be imported and was expensive). The only wild nut known in Scandinavia in the Viking age was hazelnut. Shells of walnuts have been found in excavations, but these nuts are believed to have been imported.

Seasonings

To season the foods, salt, herbs, and spices were used. Cumin, mustard, and horseradish were found in the Oseberg ship-burial. To these types of seasonings parsley, dill, cress, mint, marjoram, thyme, angelica, and wild garlic may probably have been added. Other more exotic spices would have been imported. Honey was the traditional sweetener and was used as the base for sweet, fermented mead.

TECHNOLOGY

The fortresses, bridges, and ships that have been found testify to the fact that the Viking-age Scandinavians were at a technologically advanced stage of development.

Boat building and maritime skill were the greatest technological achievements of the Scandinavians in the Viking age, and the **Ships** ship was the summit of their material culture. Indeed, the ship has become a symbol of the Viking age, for it was the ship that facilitated the expansion of the Scandinavians from their homelands and gave them the ability to raid, trade, and cross the open seas.

The best-known and also the best-preserved ships are the two burial ships found at Oseberg and Gokstad on the shores of Oslo fjord in Norway dating from the early ninth century and the late ninth or early tenth century, respectively. Together with the five eleventh-century Skuldelev ships excavated from Roskilde fjord in Denmark (the ships had been deliberately sunk to blockade the fjord and thereby protect the town of Roskilde from an enemy fleet), these ships are the primary sources for our knowledge about early Viking-age ships and boatbuilding, although many other ships have been excavated. In addition, contemporary pictorial representations on stone or embroidery and descriptions in Old Norse-Icelandic literature provide useful information.

Common to these ships is that they all have a clinker-built hull of overlapping planks or strakes, which are fastened with iron nails and caulked with tarred animal hair (to keep the hull watertight). The top planks have a distinctive upward curve at the ends, making the ship higher fore and aft than amidships. The bottom planks are attached to the slightly curved keel, which extends into the curved fore stem and after stem at the bow and stern. To stabilize the shape and to add stiffness to the shell, ribs are inserted inside the planking made from naturally curved timbers. The hull is further strengthened with crossbeams placed across the width of the hull, and floor timbers are attached to the planking. The upper crossbeams could be used as rowing benches with the rower's feet resting on the lower crossbeams. Oarholes are cut at either end or in a continuous line along the length of the ship, and on some ships the oarholes can be closed by wooden covers. The mast is slotted into a hole cut in the keelson (a wooden structure resting on the keel), which distributes the weight of the mast, and a "mast partner," which is a heavy block of wood resting on the crossbeam, provides additional support. On some ships, this mast partner has a long opening facing aft, so that the mast can be lowered or raised at will without having to be lifted vertically out of its socket. In later ships this mast partner is omitted, and the mast is instead supported by an upper crossbeam. The sail was square, and literary sources suggest that sails were frequently striped. They were made of wool, and for strength a double thickness was generally used. The methods of rigging and reefing are obscure and remain open to speculation, for all the ships that have been recovered by archaeology have been little more than hulls, and contemporary representations of ships are not sufficiently detailed. A side rudder or steering oar is mounted on the starboard side near the stern. During beaching, the steering oar, which extends below the keel, could be swiveled upward and thereby raised, so that it would not be damaged. Anchors were used, and those that have been found are made of iron and in form, typically T-shaped with curved arms that taper to points.

Boatbuilding   Oak was the preferred timber for boatbuilding. Where oak was not available, as in northern Scandinavia, pine and ash were used, especially, it seems, for the top planks or strakes. As far as possible, timber was matched to the job at hand: the timber whose grain followed the shape of the finished pieces was given preference. Accordingly, stems, keels, and ribs were made from timber with a curve, whereas straight-grained logs were used for planks, keels, keelsons, masts, and crossbeams. The woodworkers did not use saws, and so, using beech or hafted metal wedges, split the log radially first in 2, then 4, then 8, and finally 16 wedge-shaped planks or "cloveboards" of uniform breadth, which were axed and then scraped to the desired shape. For very long and wide planks and stringers, the trunk was split in two, each half then worked down to one tangentially oriented plank. For beams and stringers, the trunk was split in four, and each quarter worked down to one element. Keels, stems, and frames were typically cut directly from the trunk. The planks obviously had to be long, and because it can be hard to split very long timbers, individual planks were scarfed from one or more pieces. The ends of the fitting pieces were worked to a sharp edge and then joined, and in order to minimize leakage, the scarfs always had their opening facing aft. Therefore, a substantial amount of wood was necessary to build a ship, for wood was required also for trenails (or wooden pegs), oars, rudders, bailers, gangplanks, and other equipment. It has been estimated that for an average-size Viking ship, that is, a 20–25 m (65.6–82 ft.) longship, about eleven trees (approximately 1 m [3.3 ft.] in diameter and 5 m [16.4 ft.] in length) and another tall tree (15–18 m [49.2–59 ft.] in length) for the keel were required.

Ships served a variety of purposes, ranging from warfare and trade to the transportation of people and cargo across the **Warships** sea. Warships were built for speed and maneuverability. They were slender, had oarholes in a continuous line along the length of the ship, and a mast that could be lowered. They also distinguished themselves from other types of ships by having a shield-batten on the outer side of the top strake, and some ships were furnished with dragon heads (and sometimes tails), which were attached to the prows (and sterns). Two of the Skuldelev ships (known as Skuldelev 2 and 5) are considered representative of warships. Skuldelev 5, which probably had a length of about 17 m (55.77 ft.) and a beam of about 2.5 m (8.2 ft.), is the smaller ship and believed to have carried between 20 and 30 men. Skuldelev 5, of which only fragments survive, was considerably larger: its length is thought to have been 28–29 m (91.86–95.14 ft.) and its beam about 4 m (3.1 ft.). It probably had a crew of 40 or 50 men and can therefore be classified as a longship (a term used about warships with more than 32 oars). The largest ship recorded in Old Norse-Icelandic literature is the Long Serpent built for the Norwegian King Olaf Tryggvason in 998. It is said to have had 34 pairs of oars and to have carried more than 200 men at the king's final sea battle at Svold (the location is uncertain) in Norway in 999/1000.

Although the Oseberg and Gokstad ships have many of the characteristics of warships, they were most likely used more for **Travel** travel than warfare. The Oseberg ship seems to have been a lux- **Ships** ury yacht designed for sheltered waters, a kind of status symbol of the chieftain who owned it. It is a very light ship, about 22 m (72.17 ft.)

long and 5 m (16.4 ft.) broad. It has 15 oars on either side and was therefore rowed by 30 men, for in the larger ships each man pulled only one oar.
These men probably sat on their sea chests because no traces of rowing
benches remain. This suggests that rowing was not the normal means of
propulsion and that oars were used only when the ship was becalmed or
had to be maneuvered in shallow waters. The most characteristic features
of the Oseberg ship are its elaborately carved prow and stern, which arch
up to 5 m (16.4 ft.) above the waterline.

The Gokstad ship, which is by far the finest and most famous Viking ship,
is sturdier and more seaworthy than the Oseberg ship and was constructed
with much skill. It is 23.3 m (76.44 ft.) long and 5.2 m (17.06 ft.) broad. Its
empty weight is about 8.5 tons, and when fully laden with about 10 tons its
draft is less than 1 m (3.28 ft.). The keel is made from an oak log, and thin oak
planking is built up from the keel to form a clinker-built hull, which is made
up of 16 strakes. The mast is a pine, 30 cm (11.8 in.) in diameter, but the top has
rotted away, so its height remains unknown. Sail and rigging have not survived. There are oarholes for 16 pairs of oars, and each oarhole has a shutter.
The oars are made of pine, which were cut to different lengths, so that they
would all strike the water simultaneously. This suggests a crew of 32 men, but
because the ship was found with 64 shields, it probably carried a double crew,
one resting while the other rowed. Like the Oseberg ship, it has no fixed seats.

The Gokstad ship in the museum at Bygdøy in Norway. © University Museum of
Cultural Heritage, University of Oslo, Norway. Erik Irgens Johnson, photogra-
pher. Used with permission.

Cargo ships are a somewhat later development and reflect an
increasing demand for ships that could carry heavy loads. The **Cargo**
cargo ships differ from warships in that they did not have their **Ships**
speed and maneuverability. They were deeper, wider in the
beam, more capacious, heavier, and more suitable for oceangoing travel.
They typically had an open cargo hold amidships with a permanent
deck and oarholes only fore and aft and either a fixed mast or a
more firmly placed mast designed to be lowered only on rare occasions.
Cargo ships relied almost exclusively on their sails for propulsion, and
the few oars were used only when the ship was becalmed or had to be
maneuvered near landing places. Accordingly, they required only a
small crew: a helmsman, one or two men to bail (the ships did not have
pumps), and a few others to handle the sail. On coastal voyages, a small
boat, which was towed astern, enabled the crew to go ashore to sleep
in tents or cook. On voyages across the open sea to, for example, England, the Faroe Islands, Iceland, or Greenland, this would, of course, not
have been possible, and the crew and passengers (and livestock) would
have had to sleep on the deck and live on the food they brought with
them.

Skuldelev 1 and 3 are considered representative of cargo ships. Skuldelev 3, which is built of oak, is about 13.8 m (42.27 ft.) long and 3.4 m
(11.15 ft.) broad. It was mainly a sailing ship with provisions for a few
oars as auxiliary power. It was light enough for land portage when empty
of its cargo and shallow enough to sail in rivers. Yet, it had enough keel to
sail on the open sea, and it could carry about 4.6 tons of cargo. Skuldelev
1, which is made of pine (though oak is used for the keel, stems, bottom
timbers, and keelson), is 16.5 m (54.13 ft.) long and 4.6 m (15.09 ft.) broad
with a half-deck fore and aft, separated by a hold amidships. It could
carry 24 tons of cargo and drew only about 1.25 m (4.1 ft.) when fully
laden. An even larger ship of the same type, but somewhat longer and
with about double the cargo capacity has been found in the harbor of
Hedeby.

Not all Viking-age vessels looked like the Oseberg, Gokstad, and Skuldelev ships, and some types of water trans- **Ferries and**
port required different kinds of boats. The flat-bottomed **Boats**
boat found at Egernsund on the Flensburg fjord in
Schleswig-Holstein, which has been dated to the end of the eleventh century, was probably a ferry designed for inland waterways. Small boats, of
which several fragments have been found in Sweden and Norway, were
probably used by lake or river dwellers. These include a little one-person
rowboat found at Årby near Uppsala in Sweden, which has been dated to
somewhere between 850 and 950. It is made of a keel plank with two
strakes on each side, and it has three timbers fastened directly to the shell
with trenails. The boat was rowed by a person sitting amidships and was
also equipped with a paddle.

Sailing Techniques and Navigation

Several experiments with replicas of Viking ships show that the ships had virtually no limits as far as seaworthiness is concerned and that they were remarkably fast.

Shortly after the discovery of the Gokstad ship in 1880, the first replica of a Viking ship set sail for North America. The ship, called Viking, left Bergen, Norway, on April 30, 1893, with a crew of 12 and reached Newfoundland 28 days later. It skimmed over the waves at an average of 10 knots and achieved 12 knots in fine weather. The side rudder (which had seemed peculiar to the archaeologists) had proven itself highly efficient as a steering tool even in stormy weather, and the Norwegian captain, Magnus Andersen, also noted the ship's extraordinary flexibility and ability to stay watertight:

The bottom together with the keel gave with every movement of the ship, and in a strong head-sea the keel could move up and down as much as three-quarters of an inch [1.9 cm.]. But strangely enough the ship stayed completely watertight. The ship's remarkable elasticity was also apparent in other ways; in heavy seas, for instance, the gunwales would twist out of true by as much as six inches.[2]

The voyage of Viking was quite an achievement, especially in light of the fact that the Gokstad ship, of which Viking was an approximate re-creation, was not really designed for sailing the open seas but for travel along the coastline of Norway. It was not until the excavation of the Skuldelev ships in 1962 that it became clear that there were ships specifically designed for oceangoing. Their sailing qualities were tested in 1984–1986, when a replica of Skuldelev 1, called Saga Siglar, circumnavigated the world captained by its owner, the Norwegian Ragnar Thorseth. Saga Siglar averaged 8 knots but could do up to 13 knots with wind behind or obliquely. In headwind, it was slow, and in such conditions it was necessary for the ship to beat to windward so as not to lose too much of the distance already covered toward the final destination. Max Vinner, who did trial runs on Saga Siglar, explains that "the technique...was to lay the leg for the tack in the direction from which the wind was expected to come after a change of wind so that it would then be possible to tack and make for the goal full and by on the new tack."[3] If the wind became so strong that the ship might capsize, the sail was lowered some way down on the mast in order to reduce the wind pressure and speed. If conditions became still worse, the options were to either turn the stern of the ship to the waves and run before the wind or, in extreme situations, take the sail in and continue with a bare mast.

Most of the navigation by Scandinavians in the Viking age was along a coast from one location to another with landfalls made at night. Only the largest trading centers had piers or wharfs, but with their shallow draft many ships did not need them and could easily be run ashore on beaches.

The cargo ships were usually anchored near landing places, and small boats were used to transport cargo and passengers to and from land.

Distances were measured in day's sailings and were based on the old Scandinavian nautical mile called *vika* (plural *vikur*), which corresponds to 6 modern nautical miles. A day's rowing was estimated at 6 *vikur* (36 nautical miles) and a day's sailing at 24 *vikur* (144 nautical miles). When in the medieval sources a ship is said to have sailed for three days, it therefore means that it covered a distance of about 18 *vikur* or 72 nautical miles, which might well have taken fewer than three days in good weather or more than three days in bad weather.

Very little is known about navigation on the open sea, but the seafarers clearly relied on sailing directions. One manuscript of *Landnamabok* (Book of settlements), an Icelandic historical work from the first half of the twelfth century, gives directions for sailing from the island of Hernar on the coast north of Bergen in Norway to Greenland:

From Hernar in Norway one is to continue sailing west to Hvarf in Greenland. This course will take one so far north of Shetland that one can just sight it in very clear weather and so far south of the Faroe Islands that the sea appears half-way up the mountain slopes and then so far south of Iceland that birds and whales will be sighted.

The quotation shows that the seafarers combined techniques of landmark navigation used in coastal sailing with those of latitude sailing. That they could fix their latitudes is fairly certain, but there is uncertainty about their methods. It is likely that they relied on simple celestial navigation based on the movements of the sun and, at night, the position of the stars, notably the Polaris, which in Old Norse is called *Leidarstjarna* (lode star). They may also have observed wave and cloud formations, flight patterns of birds, sea creatures, such as whales, and seaweed and used these observations as navigational aids. The question of whether the seafarers had any navigational instruments remains open, though it has been suggested that Norse seafarers had discovered the sun-seeking property of double refracting cordierite or Icelandic feldspar crystals. Indeed, various sources make reference to an object called a *solarsteinn* (sun-stone), but no description of its navigational use is given. Moreover, a half-disc of wood found in 1948 at an archaeological excavation of a Norse settlement site at Unartoq in Greenland has received a fair amount of attention. A number of triangles are carved around its semicircular edge, and if the disc were complete, it would be marked off into 32 sections. A number of straight and curved lines mark the surface, and in the middle there is a hole for a pin (or gnomon). Some scholars interpret this disc as a fragment of a bearing dial, others as part of a sun compass. Yet others dismiss it altogether as a navigational instrument, because such a device requires knowledge of the different angles of the sun in different seasons and at different latitudes, which the seafarers may not have had.

Land Travel and Transportation Also on-land communication increased and improved during the Viking age. Remains of roads where travelers walked or rode have been found in many places, though mostly in southern Scandinavia. The Army Road or Ox Route through the middle of Jutland, Denmark, was an especially widely used road.

The most significant improvement to communication and transportation was the construction of bridges. Several rune stones mention bridge building as acts of social charity. The inscription on the stone at Sälna in Uppland, Sweden, may serve as an example. It gives the names of three brothers, Eystein, Jorund, and Bjorn, who raised the stone and built a bridge in memory of their father and then continues with the following verse:

> Always will it stand
> while time lives on,
> this bridge firmly founded
> broad in memory of a good man.
> Lads made it
> for their father.
> No way-monument can be
> better made.[4]

Most of these rune stones, including the Sälna stone, date from the end of the Viking age, and it may well be that bridge building was a late phenomenon. The largest and earliest bridge that has so far been found is the bridge at Ravning near Jelling in Jutland, which crossed the Vejle valley. It was quite a formidable bridge: about 700 m (2,296.56 ft.) long and 5.5 m. (18 ft.) wide and made of oak timbers. It is believed that it was built at the request of King Harald Bluetooth around 980.

The bridges were helpful not only to vehicular traffic but also to those traveling on foot or on horseback, and they must have constituted the majority. Most of the horses in the Viking age were quite small, about the size of Icelandic horses or ponies. Riding equipment—bridles, spurs, saddles, and stirrups—have been found in graves, and horseshoes are mentioned in literary sources, though it is likely that calks rather than horseshoes were used. The finds show that saddles were made of wood and leather. While the bits (of which the main type was the snaffle bit) are typically undecorated, the bridles, with which the bits are sometimes combined, and the stirrups, which are sometimes formed with a set of spurs, are often highly ornamented. In addition, iron crampons for horses' hooves have been found in Sweden and Norway. They were for use on ice to prevent the horses from slipping.

Horses were used not only for riding, but along with oxen, they were also used as pack and draft animals for carts and carriages. A four-wheeled wagon was found in the Oseberg ship-grave. It is fitted with heavy wheels with a central hub and long shafts. With its elaborate carvings, which completely cover the body of the vehicle, it must, however, be regarded as a somewhat atypical specimen, and the fact that the wooden wheels show no signs of wear suggests that it was constructed for the burial and served no other practical purpose. The Oseberg wagon is the only four-wheeled wagon to survive, but depictions of similar wagons or carts in use on the tapestry found in the Oseberg grave and on the Gotland picture stones show that wheeled vehicles were commonly used. Moreover, several iron attachments for harnessing the draft animals have been found.

In the winter, sledges were used for transportation, and a number of sledges have been found, including four in the Oseberg grave. Three are beautifully carved wooden sledges evidently intended for personal transport. These large and heavy sledges were clearly drawn by horses. The fourth sledge is lighter and less ornate. It has a detachable body and appears to have been used to transport goods either by men or horses. Other means of transportation in the winter were skates. They were made from smoothed horse and cow metatarsal bones and attached to the feet with the help of leather thongs. Pointed staffs or poles enabled the skater to propel himself. Skis are known only from the Tune ship-burial on the shore of Oslo fjord in Norway, but they are frequently referred to in literary sources and must have been common. For walking in snow and on ice, people used woven or braided snowshoes and iron clampons.

King Harald Bluetooth may be credited not only with the construction of the Ravning bridge, but also with the four geometrically planned Danish fortresses: Trelleborg on Zealand, Aggersborg and Fyrkat in north Jutland, and Nonnebakken on Funen. These fortresses, all built around 980, are the oldest known fortresses in Scandinavia. The plans of the fortresses are very much alike. They consisted of circular ramparts made of timber-laced turf with an external ditch around the sections that were not naturally protected by the terrain, such as waterlogged ground or a steep slope. In the rampart were four gates, probably covered by a roof, at the four main compass points. Two roadways, paved with wood, which crossed each other at right angles at the center of the site, and which divided the area into four quadrants, linked these gates. In each of these quadrants were large, bow-sided houses with straight ends arranged in groups of four to form square courtyards. Because of the fortresses' similarity, it is believed that they were undertaken at the request of one and the same authority—a king—and are the work of the same group of engineers or builders, who evidently possessed very sophisticated surveying techniques.

Fortresses, Camps, and Earthworks

The largest of the fortresses was Aggersborg. The inner diameter of its rampart was 240 m (787.39 ft.), which made room for no fewer than 48 buildings in 12 squares within the fortress proper. It must have provided accommodation for at least 3,000 people. Trelleborg had an internal diameter of 134 m (439.6 ft.). Fyrkat and Nonnebakken were somewhat smaller with diameters of 120 m (393.69 ft.). The three fortresses—Trelleborg, Fyrkat, and Nonnebakken—all had 16 buildings in four squares, though Trelleborg had an additional 15 houses within a rampart concentric with that of the fortress itself. Cemeteries have been found outside the ramparts of Trelleborg and Fyrkat containing remains of women and children as well as men, which indicate that the fortresses did not serve primarily as barracks or training camps of Vikings, but rather that the king had the fortresses constructed for the purpose of keeping control of and maintaining peace in his country. The fact that the fortresses are situated on inland roads either far from the sea or in places where there was no convenient access to the sea further strengthens this supposition. The fortresses seem to have had a lifetime of about 30 years and were never repaired.

It appears that there was a general trend in Scandinavia in the late Viking age for the building of fortifications, and the four royal fortresses represent only one type. In Norway, King and Saint Olaf Haraldsson is said to have built a fortification at Borg (now Sarpsborg) in Østfold, and it

Trelleborg. Photo courtesy of the National Museum of Denmark.

is known that Eketorp, a fortification on the island of Öland, Sweden, which dates from around A.D. 300–400, was rebuilt around 1100. The latter was constructed of stone and had two ring walls; the inner area had a diameter of 80 m (262.46 ft.) with long buildings extending out from the middle leaving open space only in the center.

A variety of urban defenses are known to have been built, the main forms being earth ramparts, ditches, and sea barriers. The earliest date from the mid-tenth century and protected the trading centers of Hedeby and Birka. Århus and Ribe in Jutland may also have been defended at this time, and the Västergarn rampart on Gotland is believed to have been built in the tenth century as well. Sea barriers also protected some of the urban centers, such as Roskilde on Zealand and Hedeby. The Skuldelev blockage of five sunken ships provided seaward defense for Roskilde, while rows of stakes in the water protected the harbor at Hedeby.

In less densely populated areas, refugee camps offered protection for people in times of unrest. It is known that refugee camps existed, on, for example, the Danish islands Bornholm and Falster and the Swedish island Öland. The largest refugee camp in Scandinavia that is known to have been used in the Viking age is Torsburg on Gotland. It covers 112.5 hectares (277.99 acres) on a cliff plateau with a 2 km (1.24 miles) long stone wall. Its enormous size suggests that it was intended to contain the entire population of Gotland. Also found on Gotland is the fortress Bulverket situated in the middle of a shallow lake in the northern part of the island. It is a square timber construction with sides 170 m (98.42 ft.) long dating from around 1100. The structure is unique in Scandinavia, and the fortress is believed to have been built not by Gotlanders but by immigrants from the eastern side of the Baltic.

Of linear earthworks, only one is known to have functioned in the Viking age: Danevirke (Defense of the Danes), a set of ramparts protecting the southern border of Denmark against the Germans. Covering some 30 km (18.64 miles) Danevirke stretches from the head of Schlei fjord in the east to the river Treene in the west. Although it is not a continuous rampart, it nonetheless controlled the land approach to Denmark, because marshland already made areas impassable. Danevirke is first mentioned in the Frankish annals under the year 808, where it is said to have been built at the initiative of the Danish King Godfred, but by means of dendrochronology (dating on the basis of tree rings) it has been shown that the earliest phase was constructed earlier, about 737. This early construction consisted of a rampart just north of Hedeby known as the North Wall and a section of the Main Wall. It was a timber-faced rampart with a U-shaped ditch, about 7 km (4.34 miles) long, 10 m (32.8 ft.) wide, and 2 m (6.56 ft.) high. The second construction phase may be associated with King Godfred and consists of the straight wall Kovirke (Cow-work) south of Hedeby. The rampart was 6.5 km (4 miles) long, and like the North Wall it was timber faced but with buttresses and a V-shaped ditch. The third construction phase, which dates from around 968, was a rampart in zigzag line, about 10–13 km (6.2–8.07 miles) long and about 3 m (9.8 ft.) high. It comprises the Main Wall, to the west the Crooked Wall, and to the east the Connecting Wall, which incorporated the ramparts and ditches of Hedeby. This part of Danevirke was built of earth faced with turf and was likely crowned by a wooden palisade. The result was a remarkable barrier and one of the largest ancient defenses in northern Europe.

VISUAL ART

Well before the Viking age, there developed in Scandinavia an art, one aspect of which—contorted and distorted animal ornament—was to continue until the end of the Viking age, when Scandinavian artists yielded to the new Romanesque art that was to become prevalent in Europe in the later Middle Ages. Very little Viking-age art can be termed art in the primary sense—art for art's sake. Most of it is applied art and appears as decoration on functional objects used by Viking-age Scandinavians in their daily life, such as clothes, weapons, cups, sledges, ships, buildings, memorial stones, and, not least, brooches. It is typically abstract rather than naturalistic, and it is characterized by originality, vitality, and ostentation. It shows the Viking-age Scandinavians' love of splendor and their penchant for displaying wealth and rank.

Our knowledge of Viking art derives primarily from archaeological finds, but it has, of course, been recognized that organic materials, such as wood, leather, and bone, of which relatively little survives, must have been the most common materials. A large portion of the preserved objects are decorative metal items. As might be expected, the most treasured metals were gold and silver, but other materials, such as amber and walrus ivory, were also highly prized. Traces of color on rune stones, shields, furniture, and the like show that some objects were originally painted—red, blue, brown, black, and white being, it seems, the most common colors. These objects include the Gotland picture stones—large mushroom-shaped slabs of limestone erected on the island from around 500. The Gotland stones are the main examples of naturalistic art, which must originally have been an important aspect of Viking art. Individual figures (amulets) are known in metalwork and as carvings, but otherwise there is little in terms of naturalistic art for its own sake. The scenes on the Gotland picture stones appear horizontally across the stones with ribbons framing the stones and dividing the scenes. Popular motifs on the stones are a ship often filled with warriors in full sail across stylized waves and a rider, both of which are generally considered to be symbols of the journey to Odin's Valholl. These stones illustrate the existence of pictorial art during the Viking age and are paralleled, for example, in the carvings on the Oseberg cart and on the fragmentary tapestries that have been preserved. The Oseberg tapestry depicts a procession in connection with a religious ritual,

Picture stone from Hammars in Lärbro, Gotland. Printed with
permission of Antikvarisk-topografiska arkivet, Stockholm.

possibly a funeral procession, while the Swedish Överhogdal and Skog
tapestries of a later date depict a church with a bell tower, animals, people,
and gods. The oldest of all Viking-age art known to us is a little wooden
man found legless and broken in the plundered grave chamber of the
Danish King Gorm the Old and his queen when the northern mound at
Jelling was excavated in 1820. It is a small flat figure, 15 cm (5.9 in.) tall,
and carved in oak. The little man is seen in profile and has a large beltlike
circle around his waist. Originally, the figure was painted, and traces of
color—black, red, and yellow—can be seen on the largest of the fragments.

No new art style can be said to mark the beginning of the Viking age in Scandinavia; it merely grew out of the art styles of previous centuries, which are ultimately derived from the provincial art of the late Roman Empire. In 1904, the Swedish archaeologist Bernhard Salin divided the animal-style ornamentation of the entire period, that is, from around 400

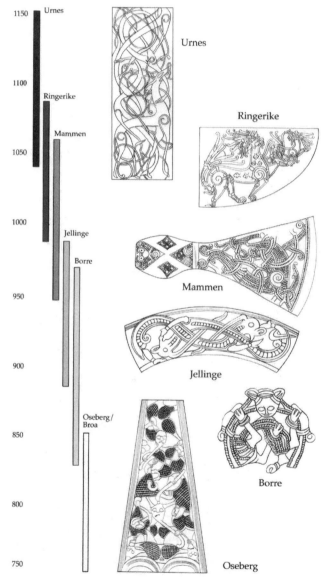

Viking art styles. From William W. Fitzhugh and Elisabeth I. Ward, eds., *Vikings: The North American Saga* (Washington, D.C.: Smithsonian Institution, 2000). Photograph courtesy of the Smithsonian National Museum of National History.

to 900, into three different styles, and his classification is still used today, though with some modifications. Migration-period ornamentation (c. 375–550), which is based on a contorted single animal seen in profile, is labeled Style I. Vendel-period ornamentation (c. 550–800), which is called Style II, is characterized by interlaced animals of ribbonlike form. It was often executed with a technique called chip carving. This technique, which appears in silver and bronze often with niello (black metallic alloys of sulfur) used to fill the incised designs, was derived from woodcarving and involves cutting a flat surface with a chisel into a series of facets, so that the objects glitter in any light. It was this style, Style II, on which the first true Viking style, referred to as Style III, was based.

The most typical examples of the earliest Viking style, which, using another classification system, is sometimes referred to as Style E (Styles A–D refer to pre-Viking-age styles), are small cast gilt-bronze bridle mounts found in a **The Broa Style** man's grave in Broa on Gotland. These mounts display three different animal motifs. The first has an elongated double-contoured body, which is frequently broken in places by an overlying framework. The head is small but with a large eye, and the feet have three claws. The second motif is quite similar to the first one, but it has no double contours. Moreover, the animal, which is often a bird, is somewhat more compact. The third motif, the so-called gripping beast, is a new one. Contrary to the other motifs, in which the animal is seen in profile, the gripping beast is seen full face. It is chunky and has large muscular shoulders and hips, and its legs end in paws which clutch or grip either itself, animals next to it, or the edge of the ornamentation border—hence the name of the design.

Other fine examples of Style E are the woodcarvings from the Oseberg ship-burial, which show the art of the Viking age in its most natural medium: wood. The carvings, which are all decorated with versions of the three animal motifs found in the Broa bridle mounts, include a ship, a cart, four sledges, and several bedposts. The most remarkable object is, of course, the ship with its carvings on the prow, the sternposts, and the crosspieces inside the prow. Here the sculptor, who is commonly referred to as "the Ship Master," has skillfully carved flat, interlaced animals deeply into the wood. Two basic motifs may be distinguished on these carvings. One is a beast with a small head seen in profile. It has a large eye, a pigtail, an open mouth, and a long neck. Its body is double contoured, and it has pierced, heart-shaped hips. This is the motif found on the prow and sternposts, and it differs from that on the crosspieces inside the prow. The animals carved here are gripping beasts clutching each other with their hands and feet. Similar ornament appears inside the top of the stem. The most sophisticated object in the Oseberg find is, however, one of several posts carved in the form of an animal head. Their practical function remains unclear, but presumably they were intended to ward off evil spirits. The post is made by a sculptor, who has been nicknamed "the Academician," and the post is considered to be his masterpiece. It has an open mouth with great, bared teeth, a square snout, and big eyes. The back of the head and neck are covered with a series of birdlike figures intertwined in an elaborate and coherent pattern.

The Borre Style

The succeeding style has been called the Borre style from the bronze bridle mounts found in the rich ship-burial at Borre in the Vestfold region of Oslo Fjord in Norway. It developed in the second half of the ninth century and was in vogue until the mid-tenth century. It is the earliest Scandinavian style to have been used in the Viking colonies in Iceland, the Isle of Man, England, and Russia. Three main motifs characterize the Borre style, which is known exclusively from metal objects. One, which is unique to the style, is a ribbon plait consisting of a symmetrical interlace pattern. It is known as a "ring-chain" and is most often found on strap ends, where it is commonly terminated by an animal mask. The second motif is a single gripping beast, now with a triangular head and distinct eyebrows, ears, and neck and with a body that has the form of a pretzel knot. The third motif consists of a backward-looking, seminaturalistic animal with spiral hips and a tail.

The Jellinge Style

The Borre style is, however, not the only successor to the Broa style, because in the third quarter of the ninth century the Jellinge style developed. For most of its history it was contemporaneous with the Borre style, though it was not as common, and occasionally the motifs of the two styles appear side by side on the same object. The Jellinge style takes its name from an engraved frieze on a small, silver, pedestal cup found in one of the royal burial mounds at Jelling in Jutland, Denmark. The frieze consists of two S-shaped animals. As in the pre-Viking styles, the head is in profile, and it has a big, round eye, a curled upper lip, and a long pigtail. The animals in Jellinge style are commonly interlaced with ribbonlike tendrils, which sprout from the limbs, and sometimes they have spirals at the shoulders and hips. The Jellinge style, which may be of Danish origin, survives in Scandinavia only in metalwork (in Britain it is found in stone sculpture), and as with the Borre style, filigree (consisting of twisted wires) and granulation (consisting of little gold or silver grains in clusters), or cast imitations of these, were much used on jewelry in the Jelling style. The style lasted until well into the second half of the tenth century, when it merged into the Mammen style.

The Mammen Style

The Mammen style developed in the last half of the tenth century and lasted until the first quarter of the eleventh century. The style is named after a wealthy man's grave from about 970 at Mammen near Jelling and identified with a beautifully produced iron ax found in the grave. It is inlaid with silver wires on both sides, one with a foliate pattern and the other with a human mask and a bird, whose head is thrown back over its body.

It has a double-contoured body, a spiral hip, and its wings and tail are drawn out into elongated, ribbonlike tendrils.

Although the ornament of the ax characterizes the Mammen style, the medium does not, for the style is usually found in bone, ivory, and stone carving. Of such carvings, the most significant work is the large three-sided memorial stone at Jelling, on which King Harald Bluetooth announced, among other things, that he had Christianized Denmark. Two of the sides have low relief carving, one of a crucified Christ (the earliest recorded in Scandinavia) entwined by plant scrolls and another of a majestic lion struggling with a snake (likewise the earliest example of this iconography in Scandinavia). The motif of an animal struggling with a snake symbolizing the struggle between good and evil is a new one in Viking art, and generally it may be said about the Mammen style that it is quite innovative. As evident from both the ax and the memorial stone, artists during this time also began to experiment with plant ornamentation, in which sculptors of previous styles had shown no interest. It is ultimately derived from the florid acanthus ornament frequently found in Carolingian and Ottonian art.

Another example of Mammen style is the Bamberg casket, which is now in a museum in Germany. Tradition has it that it was the jewel box of Queen Kunigunde, who was the daughter of the Danish King Knud the Great (995–1035) and later the wife of the German Emperor Henry II. It consists of an oak box covered with carved panels of walrus ivory, which is clasped by gilt-bronze bands nailed to the wooden base. While the Bamberg casket, which is truly an artistic masterpiece, represents a late phase of the Mammen style, the cross from Kirk Braddan in the Isle of Man is an example of an earlier phase. Of the Manx crosses, which are all made of local slate, this is one of the most genuinely Scandinavian. According to the runic inscription on one of the edges, it was raised by a man named Thorleif in memory of his son. The foliate ornament on the stone makes it a typical Mammen-style object, but influence from the Jellinge style is seen on the decorated edge, where ribbonlike animals are found.

The next phase in the development of Viking art is the Ringerike style, which may have been created in Denmark. It is named after the district of that name just north of Oslo, Norway, where a number of carved monuments made of sandstone were found. The Ringerike style, which devel- **The Ringerike Style** oped toward the end of the tenth century and lasted for about a century, grew naturally out of the Mammen style and shares many features with it, but generally it is more symmetrical, and its compositions are based on axiality. The Jelling stone is often used as a starting point in discussions of the Ringerike style, for Harald Bluetooth seems to have established a fashion for erecting decorated stone monuments, which became very common in Scandinavia in the following century.

The three main elements of the Ringerike style are the lion, the snake, and the extended tendril. Its primary innovation is the handling of the plant ornamentation, which dominates the animal ornamentation and often takes over the entire pattern. Fine examples of the Ringerike style are a gilt-bronze weather vane from Söderala in Sweden, which has at its center a large dragonlike animal with a lesser animal locked around its foot, and a stone monument possibly raised in memory of one of the Danish King Knud the Great's (r. 1016/1017–1035) men in St. Paul's churchyard in London, England, which shows the lion and snake motif. The Ringerike style also appears on the frieze on the fragments of the oldest extant church decoration in Scandinavia, the panels from Flatatunga in Iceland.

The Ringerike style has a pan-Scandinavian distribution and was very popular also in southern England, where it was used in the illumination of ecclesiastical manuscripts, and in the Viking colonies in Ireland.

The Urnes Style The final ornamental style of the Viking age is the Urnes style, which developed shortly before the mid-eleventh century. It takes its name from the woodcarvings of the little stave church in Urnes in western Norway. The church dates from the twelfth century, but the doorway, posts, planks, and gable ends on which the ornamentation was found had been reused from a mid-eleventh-century church in the same location. Because the Urnes style occurs on several eleventh-century memorial stones especially in Sweden, where it was extraordinarily popular, it is also known as the rune-stone style.

Unlike the Mammen and Ringerike styles, animals occupy the preeminent position in Urnes style; foliate ornament is now a thing of the past. These animals comprise stylized quadrupeds (some of which are lions), ribbon-shaped animals, and snakes. Winged dragons also appear; their earliest occurrence is on memorial stones in Uppland, Sweden, which also often incorporate the cross. The Urnes style is characterized by sophistication and elegance. It is asymmetric and depends for its effects on interplays of lines of different widths to form patterns of smooth and unbroken curves and loops. A small silver brooch found at Lindholm Høje on the northern shore of the Limfjord in Jutland shows the refinement and grace of the Urnes style. The openwork brooch is cast in rounded relief and inlaid with niello in the form of an animal intertwined with a snake. The animal's head bends down to touch its breast, and its body is looped and separated into two tendril-like extensions. At the bottom, a snake loops around the animal's foreleg and hindquarters.

The Urnes style remained popular in Scandinavia until the mid-twelfth century. It lasted slightly longer in England, and in Ireland it had a significant impact on the art produced there in the late eleventh and the twelfth centuries.

NOTES

1. Ibn Fadlan's statement is quoted from H. M. Smyser, "Ibn Fadlān's Account of the Rūs with Some Commentary and Some Allusions to *Beowulf*," in *Franciplegius:*

Medieval and Linguistic Studies in Honor of Francis Peabody Magoun, Jr., ed. Jess B. Bessinger, Jr. and Robert P. Creed (New York: New York University Press, 1965), p. 95.

2. Magnus Andersen's report is quoted from Magnus Magnusson, *Vikings!* (New York: E. P. Dutton, 1980), p. 39.

3. Max Vinner is quoted from his article "*Unnasigling*—the Seaworthiness of the Merchant Vessel," in *Viking Voyages to North America,* ed. Birthe L. Clausen (Roskilde, Denmark: The Viking Ship Museum, 1993), p. 102.

4. The verse from the stone at Sälna is quoted from R. I. Page, *Runes* (London: British Museum Publications, 1987), p. 50.

6

Political Life

SOCIAL STRUCTURE

Abroad, the Vikings let it be known that they were all equal. Dudo of St.-Quentin (d. before 1043) tells in his *De moribus et actis primorum normanniae ducum* (Concerning the deaths and deeds of the first Norman dukes) that when in the late tenth century a messenger from the Franks, who was standing on the bank of the river Eure in France, saluted the approaching Viking ships and asked the name of the Vikings' master, they responded that they didn't have any and that they were all equals.

Nonetheless, there were significant differences, especially between those who were free and those who were not. The general picture of Scandinavian society during the Viking age is commonly sought in the eddic poem *Rigsthula* (List of Rig), which provides a mythological explanation of the origin of three distinct social classes: slaves, free men, and nobles. The poem has been assigned by some to the tenth or eleventh century, while others have maintained that it dates from the eleventh or twelfth century. It survives incomplete in a manuscript from the mid-fourteenth century.

The poem tells that Rig—who is in reality the pagan god Heimdall—went a journey, and as he walked along the seashore he came first to a married couple named Ai (great-grandfather) and Edda (great-grandmother), who lived in a poor hut. They entertained him with coarse bread and boiled calf meat, and Rig spent three nights with them, sharing their bed, and then went on his way. Nine months later Edda gave birth to a dark-skinned boy named Thraell (thrall), who grew up with rough hands, thick fingers, an ugly face, and a crooked back. He was a physical laborer and married an unattractive woman by the name of Thir (bondwoman). The two had many children with ugly names, who did hard manual work:

> Children they had, they lived and they were happy;
> I think they were called Weatherbeaten and Stableboy,
> Stout and Sticky, Rough, Badbreath,
> Stumpy, Fatty, Sluggard and Greyish,
> Lout and Longlegs; they established farms,
> put dung on the fields, worked with swine,
> looked after goats, dug the turf.
>
> Their daughters were Stumpina and Podgy,
> Bulgy-calves and Bellows-nose,
> Noisy and Bondwoman, Great-gabbler,
> Raggedy-hips and Crane-legs.
> From them are descended all the race of slaves.[1]

Next, Rig came to the hall of Afi (grandfather) and Amma (grandmother). There was fire on the floor, and both were at work. Afi, with hair above his brows and a well-trimmed beard, was whittling wood for a cross beam; Amma, with a headdress on her head, a smock on her body, a kerchief round her neck, and brooches at her shoulders, was spinning. Rig spent three nights with them, sharing their bed, and then went on his way. Nine months later Amma gave birth to a son named Karl (farmer). When he grew up, he tamed oxen, worked the harrow, built houses, threw up barns, made carts, and drove the plough. Karl married a woman "with keys at her belt in a goatskin-kirtle," and the couple had children with attractive names:

> Children they had, they lived and they were happy,
> called Man and Soldier, Lad, Thane and Smith,
> Broad, Yeoman, Boundbeard,
> Dweller, Boddi, Smoothbeard and Fellow.
>
> And these were called by other names:
> Lady, Bride, Sensible, Wise, Speaker,
> Dame, Fanny, Wife, Shy, Sparky,
> from them descend all the race of farmers.[2]

Finally, Rig came to the hall of Fadir (father) and Modir (mother). The doors were facing south.

> In he stepped, the floors were strewn with straw;
> there sat the couple looking into one another's eyes,
> Fadir and Modir, busy with their fingers.
>
> There sat the householder and twisted bow-strings,
> bent elm, shaped arrows,

and the lady of the house was admiring her arms,
stroking the material, straightening the sleeves.

Her head-dress was set straight, there was a pendant on her breast,
a short, full cape and a blue-stitched blouse;
her brow was brighter, her breasts more shining,
her neck was whiter than freshly fallen snow.[3]

At Fadir and Modir's house, Rig was served at table and lavishly entertained with expensive food and drink. Rig spent three nights with them, sharing their bed, and then went on his way. Nine months later, Modir gave birth to a son named Jarl (earl) and wrapped him in silk. He was very handsome; his hair was blond, his cheeks were bright, and his eyes glittered like those of a serpent. He grew up skilled with the bow, the spear, and the horse. One day, Rig came to him from under a bush; he acknowledged his son, gave him his own name, and taught him the runes. His wife, a "slender-fingered girl, radiant and wise," was called Erna, and they had twelve sons with beautiful names:

Son was the eldest and Child the second,
Baby and Noble, Heir and Offspring,
Descendant and Kinsman—they played together—
Sonny and Lad—at swimming and chequers—
Lineage one was called, Kon was the youngest.[4]

Young Kon was the noblest of all of them. He knew the runes, could blunt weapons, and understood the speech of birds. The poem is incomplete, and where it breaks off, young Kon, who, as his name implies (Kon + *ung* [young] = *konung* [king]), is clearly destined to become king, is about to take off and conquer other lands at the urging of a crow.

Obviously, the poem's description of the divinely arranged social structure of Viking-age Scandinavia is somewhat simplistic. Especially the middle group—free men—comprised a wide spectrum of people. There were people who were poor and probably landless, living by occasional work and yet not slaves; as well as people, such as chieftains and warriors, who were wealthy and powerful and yet were not nobles. Nonetheless, the tripartite structure that the poem sanctions is a convenient one.

The poet of *Rigsthula* shows considerable class consciousness. He was clearly sympathetic to the free men, the farmers, who **Slaves** are mentioned with respect. The slaves, on the other hand, are portrayed as crude, almost bestial, creatures. Indeed, in Viking-age Scandinavia the slaves were at the very bottom of the social scale. Slaves had no legal rights whatsoever. They could own nothing and were property like livestock. In fact, sacrificed slaves have been found in Viking-age graves. Excavations of a tenth-century grave near Stengade on the island of Langeland in Denmark, for example, revealed a wealthy farmer, who had been accompanied by a decapitated slave; and in the royal mound of Oseberg in Norway, the noble lady was similarly accompanied by what must have been a young slave woman. Slaves could be purchased and sold and used to pay off debts. The price of a slave varied according to his or her skills, age, health, and looks. They were not protected by law against violent abuse; the laws did not punish owners for injuring or killing their slaves, and if someone injured or killed another man's slave, he had to pay market-value compensation to the slave's owner and not to the slave's relatives. By extension, the owner was accountable for injuries committed by his slave unless the slave had escaped, though for some minor crimes slaves were physically punished.

Some areas of Scandinavia recognized slave marriage, but generally it appears to have had little, if any, legal standing. Children born to slaves belonged to the mother's owners or were split between the mother's and father's owners. Because slavery was hereditary, the children of slaves also became slaves. The number of slaves must have increased by the addition of captives once Viking raids became common, though most of these slaves were sold in European or eastern markets. The many references to slaves in the literary sources suggest that they were an important segment of society. Unfortunately, archaeology can tell us nothing about their numbers and very little about their living conditions. Most likely, only the more privileged had slaves on their estates, where they were members of the household. They probably did more or less the same work as family members or hired laborers and served in a variety of capacities, including those of cook, cleaner, washerwoman, farmhand, craftsman, and messenger. The more unpleasant types of work, such as dunging fields, herding pigs, and digging peat, were probably reserved for slaves. It is also possible that slave labor was used in such large construction or building projects as Danevirke and the circular fortresses.

Occasionally, slaves were freed by their owners. A rune stone from Hørning in Jutland, Denmark, was raised by a freed slave. In the inscription, the freed slave, Toki, acknowledges his gratitude to his master, who not only set him free but evidently also helped him financially to get established as a smith:

> Toki the smith raised the stone in memory of
> Thorgisl Gudmund's son who gave him
> gold and his freedom.[5]

Slaves could also purchase themselves or their relatives' freedom. Most of the freed slaves, who had lower status than the fully free, probably lived as cottagers or as landless farm workers or servants for their former owners.

Free Men The free men were the backbone of the Scandinavian community, and they formed the bulk of society. They comprised a varied group, and there were different ranks of free men.

The difference in social status among free men, which was largely dependent upon ancestry and wealth, is evident from Viking-age graves and is also given clear expression in the laws in terms of the compensation (*wergild*) that a man was obliged to pay if he committed a crime or that would be owed to him if he suffered injury at the hands of another man.

Most of the free men were farmers: independent farmers on inherited land, independent farmers on leased land, and independent farmers on bought land. The independent farmers on inherited family land (called *odal*) made up the most important class, and some of them owned very large tracts of land. Such farmers were typically very influential and powerful and often served as chieftains. The lawyers and (pagan) priests were also drawn from this particular class of farmers. The tenant farmers, who appear to have become fairly numerous during the Viking age, were probably to quite some extent made up of freed slaves or free men with no capital. They usually paid an annual rent in cash or kind to the landowner. Other free men worked as farmhands or servants or had more specialized occupations (smiths, carpenters, weapon makers, jewelers, etc.). The number of craftsmen appears to have gradually increased during the Viking age as a result of advances in material standards and the growth of towns. Yet other free men were merchants or professional warriors.

The free men had legal protection and played a role in the administration of the law. They also had the right to bear arms, and no doubt the bands of Viking raiders and traders came from this class of people. Such bands were called *felag*. They were essentially partnerships or guilds, in which the members owed each other mutual obligations. The *felag* were not limited to raiding and trading activities but could also involve, for example, the sharing of capital in farming ventures or the joint ownership of a boat or a ship.

Among the free men, there were, of course, also poor people. They were the responsibility—at least in theory—of their relatives. This is clearly stated in the laws of the Icelandic free state, collectively known as *Gragas* (gray goose), and one must assume that these stipulations are reflective of Viking-age conditions:

It is so prescribed that every man here in the country has to maintain his own dependents. A man must first maintain his mother. And if he can manage more, then he is to maintain his father. If he can do better, then he is to maintain his children. If he can do better, then he is to maintain his brothers and sisters. If he can do better, then he is to maintain those people from whom he has the right to inherit and those he has taken on by inheritance-trade. If he can do better, then he is to maintain his freedman, one to whom he gave freedom.[6]

If a man was not in a financial position to care for his mother or father, the following rules applied:

If he does not have means enough, then he is to go into debt-bondage [bondservice] for his mother. If his father now has greater need of maintenance, he is to go into debt-bondage for him. If he has gone into debt-bondage for his father but then his mother needs maintenance later on, his father is to pass to his kinsmen for maintenance and he is to go into debt-bondage for his mother. If he does not have the means to maintain them, he is to go to the home of their closest kinsman with means enough to maintain them.[7]

It is difficult to know what kind of help or support was available to poor people if there were no relatives or if those relatives were already destitute. Organized poor relief did not come into existence until Christian times. Iceland, in particular, had a sophisticated system to help its financially disadvantaged citizens. The country was divided geographically into *hreppar* (sing. *hrepp*), each unit comprising at least 20 assembly-attending farmers. The role of these *hreppar* was, among other things, to provide for paupers whose relatives were unable to provide economic help. Each assembly-attending farmer had to take care of the pauper for a specific period of time relative to his means. In this manner, the pauper moved between the larger farms in a *hrepp*. The *hreppar* later derived some income for poor relief through the introduction of the tithe law in 1096, which was the first Icelandic tax to be levied according to means. Ten percent of a man's possessions were to be paid to the church, and of this 10 percent one-quarter should go to the poor. The same *hrepp*-system also served as a kind of insurance to circumvent the need for poor relief. If a man lost a quarter or more of his livestock through disease or if he lost three farm buildings (livingroom, kitchen, and pantry) through fire, the farmers jointly covered half the damage.

Aristocracy   The third class consisted of aristocrats, whom the poet of *Rigsthula* portrays as living in luxury. They were the ruling caste, and to this group belonged the people with wealth, land, and rank.

It is generally assumed that before the Viking age there were a considerable number of petty kingdoms and independent earldoms in Scandinavia. This we have largely on the authority of the Danish historian Saxo Grammaticus, who in his *Gesta Danorum* (Deeds of the Danes) from the early thirteenth century, claims that there were many kings, princes, and earls (*reges, reguli, praefecti,* and *duces*). Very little, if anything, is known about these petty kings and kingdoms; we do not know the extent of the kings' powers and the size of their territories. Presumably, they were warriors who had gathered bands of men around them and united areas of the country.

The title of king was probably used quite freely, though certainly some regulations applied as to how and on whom it could be bestowed. The succession pattern reveals two principles. One required that a king be related by blood to a previous king. In fact, the word "king" (in Old Norse *konung*) is believed to be derived from the word related to "kin." This principle may have its origin in the belief that the kings were descended from pagan gods. The idea of "sacral kingship" is especially noticeable in Sweden, where the Yngling clan of kings traced their descent through a long list of ancestors back to Frey. The other principle, election, gave leading chieftains the privilege of choosing a suitable candidate. Often, there were two or more contenders for the title, though joint rule was by no means uncommon. It was not until the very end of the Viking age, when Denmark, Norway, and Sweden had taken shape as kingdoms, that the notion of vertical lineage within a single dynasty was promoted. The aim was succession through primogeniture, but it was not achieved until well after the Viking age.

In the course of the Viking age, the rule of these petty kings was gradually replaced by politically powerful kings, who eventually unified the three Scandinavian countries. To a great extent, the introduction of Christianity was responsible for speeding up the progress of this centralization, for the church needed the support of a centralized power. In addition, there must have been a general desire among the population for peace and prosperity, which could only be achieved by the consolidation of authority.

Denmark

The process of the unification remains largely obscure, and we do not know exactly when it was completed. The unification of Denmark appears to have begun before 800 and was prompted by the existence of hostile neighbors. King Godfred, who was instrumental in the construction of Danevirke, was clearly strong enough to secure a basis of his royal authority in south Jutland. It was not until the mid-tenth century, however, that all of Denmark was unified and became a kingdom identifiable with that of today. The reawakening of interest in the consolidation of Danish power probably began under King Gorm the Old (d. c. 958), who most likely had authority throughout Jutland. His son, Harald Bluetooth (d. c. 987), was successful in increasing Danish royal authority, and on the famous Jelling stone he claims that he "won all Denmark for himself." What this phrase really means has been a matter of speculation, but it is possible that it implies the inclusion of the islands east of the Great Belt to the Jelling-based kingdom of Jutland. Certainly, the four Danish fortresses—Trellborg, Aggersborg, Fyrkat, and Nonnebakken (see chapter 5)—which are considered to have been constructed at his initiative, confirm that he was an efficient and powerful ruler. On the Jelling stone, Harald Bluetooth claims to have also won Norway, and while the details concerning his rule of Norway are unclear, it is a fact that the Norwegian Earl Hakon of Lade (d. c. 995) acknowledged him as his superior. Around 987, King Harald Bluetooth was driven into exile by a revolt and replaced by his son Sven Forkbeard (d. 1014). He secured Danish overlordship of Norway when in 999/1000 he and his allies won victory over the Norwegian King Olaf Tryggvason in the battle of Svold in Norway. He also led several raids on England, and one such raid, in 1013, achieved the conquest of England. Of all the Danish kings during the Viking age, Knud the Great (r. 1016/1017–1035) was, however, the most powerful, for he was the one who came closest to establishing a North Sea empire. For a number of years, he was king of Denmark and England as well as of Norway and perhaps parts of Sweden, but because of the fragile political structure of his domain, the empire fell apart shortly after his death.

Norway

Norway was more difficult to unite because of its size and long coast, which encouraged the proliferation of petty kingdoms. The king normally credited with the unification of Norway is Harald Fairhair (d. 930–940). According to his saga by Snorri Sturluson in *Heimskringla* (Disc of the world), he inherited his father's kingdom of Vestfold on the coast southwest of modern Oslo at the age of 10. His ambition was to become king of all of Norway, and he vowed not to cut or comb his hair until he had reached his goal. An important step in that direction was the battle of Havsfjord in the last years of the ninth century, in which Harald won victory over an alliance of petty kings and earls, but his kingdom included only the southern part of Norway and the coastal regions, not northern Norway. Before his death, King Harald Fairhair assigned his son Erik Bloodaxe, who had been joint ruler, the kingship, but because of his unpopularity he was forced into exile. He was succeeded by his half-brother Hakon the Good, who was also nicknamed "foster-son of Aethelstan" due to his upbringing at the court of King Aethelstan of Wessex (r. 925–939). The years of his reign were marked by struggles against the sons of Erik Bloodaxe, who replaced him when in one of their onslaughts around 960 he was killed. These sons under the leadership of Harald Grey-cloak (d. c. 970) managed to exercise considerable control over the Lade earldom and even secured for themselves the tribute paid to the earls from northern Norway. It appears, however, that their Danish uncle, King Harald Bluetooth, found their reign too independent; in any case, he drove out Harald Grey-cloak and appointed Earl Hakon of Lade to rule the country under his suzerainty. Eventually, Earl Hakon renounced the Danish allegiance, and consequently Norway enjoyed a short period of independence. He was succeeded by Olaf Tryggvason (r. 995–999/1000), a great-grandson of King Harald Fairhair, who established himself in the wealthy region of Trøndelag and gradually expanded royal territorial control to comprise the Norwegian coast from the south to Halogaland in the north. As noted above, he died in the battle of Svold, where he fought Sven Forkbeard (who had been forced to give up the Oslo fjord or Viken [the Inlet] as it used to be called), the Swedish King Olof Skotkonung (r. c. 995–1022) and Erik, the son of Earl Hakon of Lade. With the appointment of Olaf Haraldsson (r. 1015–1030), who was also a descendant of King Harald Fairhair, and who had engaged in Viking raids for many years, as king, the process of unifying Norway began again, and within a year he had defeated the Danish and Swedish kings. But because of his forceful behavior, he became very unpopular among the local chieftains, who eventually joined forces with King Knud the Great and his Norwegian vassal Earl Hakon. They managed to drive King Olaf into exile, and he fled to Prince Yaroslav of Novgorod. When two years later, in 1030, King Olaf received the news that Earl Hakon had died, he assembled an army in Sweden and continued to Norway, where he fell in battle at Stiklestad near Trondheim. It was not until the disintegration of the Danish North Sea Empire following the death of Knud the Great that Norwegian kings were able to control all of Norway on a more permanent basis. Under Olaf Haraldsson's son Magnus (r. 1035–1047), who had fled to Novgorod with his father in 1028, and who was brought back in 1035, and his coregent and successor Harald Hardruler (r. 1046–1066), the inland regions, Upplönd and Trøndelag, were brought under royal rule. Southward Norwegian territory was secured through Bohuslän to the mouth of the Göta River.

Sweden

Very little is known about Swedish kings in the Viking age, and it is difficult to ascertain how the unification of Sweden came about, for the source material documenting the process is scanty. King Olof Skotkonung is the first king known to have ruled over both the Svear, who occupied the provinces around Lake Mälaren, and the Götar, who occupied the territory around Lake Vänern and Lake Vättern (Scania and Halland belonged to Denmark). The first who is known to have acted as king over all of Sweden was Knut Eriksson (r. c. 1172–1195/1196), who was also the first to have coins struck in his name in the provinces of both the Svear and the Götar.

Duties of the King

The king was the head of state in international relations and served as a representative of his country. He functioned primarily as a military leader, though it was not until the end of the Viking age that Scandinavian kings themselves led and participated in attacks on the British Isles. Their kingdoms were too unstable to permit them to be away for long periods of time. The king's main duty was to maintain peace at home and protect his subjects not only from foreign attacks but also from unruly local chieftains. As a military leader, the king's powers were based on the *leidang* (see below), which was a social duty, and on his *hird*, an Anglo-Saxon word meaning "household" that had become adopted in Scandinavia by the eleventh century as a term for the retinue accompanying kings, earls, or other rulers. The *hird* was essentially a private warrior organization, a nucleus of armed followers, and most of its members probably lived in close proximity to the king. Although some form of contract must have existed between the king and the members of his *hird,* the fundamental tie was that of personal loyalty to the king. The king's bodyguards and standard-bearer (an especially talented man whose task it was to keep the standard from falling) were almost certainly drawn from the *hird*. This loyalty is succinctly expressed in the Danish nobleman Sven Aggesen's (b. c. 1140–1150) account of the law of the *hird*, the *Lex castrensis* or *Vederlov* (penalty-law), which may go back to King Knud the Great and his *hird*, the *Thingmannalid* or *Tinglid* (as it is called in Icelandic and Danish sources) in the 1020s:

> But while the law had to be made to cover many matters, it came into being primarily as a result of the respect in which the prince was held. Just as he laid down the pattern and rule of obedience for his men, so his own conduct should be gracious and familiar. Therefore it was enacted that the king with an army in attendance, or anyone else entitled to the same honor, should himself display the loyalty he demanded from them. He should present a cheerful countenance, and deny none of them a courteous reception. He was also to give them the reward of their labor and pay his warriors their wages without delay or any kind of argument, whenever it was customary or when they were short of money. Once they had received their pay, the men would show the same goodness and generosity in return towards their lords, and would be prepared to obey whatever commands they gave and not fail to carry out their orders.[8]

The most detailed information about the composition of the *hird* is found in the *Hirdskra*, a Norwegian code from around 1270. By that time, the hird was a three-tier organization of knights, officials, and servants. The knights (or so-called *hirdmen*) caroused with the king in his hall and received gifts of booty from the royal hand. This group was hierarchical and divided into an elite of men typically drawn from leading families; landed men; *skutilsveinar* (men who served at the royal table); and ordinary *hirdmen*. The officials, who were called *gestir* (guests), were of a lower order and received less pay. They functioned as a kind of police force. The servants were referred to as *kertisveinar* (candle-boys). They were young men or boys, apprentices, recruited from the better families in the kingdom, who worked as pages.

In essence, the *hird* served as protection for the king. The members of the *hird*—often referred to collectively as a *lid*—enforced the king's will and fought on his behalf. It is no doubt against this background that the construction of the four circular fortresses—Trelleborg, Aggersborg, Fyrkat, and Nonnebakken—in Denmark must be seen. These carefully planned fortresses were centers of royal authority built in times of unrest to keep provincial chieftains in check and maintain control of the kingdom. They may also have been useful military posts when the country was threatened by attacks from foreign forces.

The king also served as a religious leader. In pagan times, it was the king who conducted the major sacrifices to the gods in order to ensure peace and prosperity in the country. We know that Lejre on Zealand in Denmark, Uppsala in Sweden, and Trondheim in Norway were important religious centers, and these locations may also have served as permanent royal residences. Generally, the king was held responsible for peace and good harvests in his country. The king's mystical importance is demonstrated by the (apocryphal) story of Halfdan the Black, Harald Fairhair's father, a petty king of Norway, whose dead body was divided into four parts at the request of the neighboring provinces, because the inhabitants believed that the presence of the king's body in their province would bring good harvests. There are also stories about kings failing in their duty to bring about prosperity. Such kings were, according to Snorri Sturluson, the sons of the Norwegian King Erik Bloodaxe. In his saga about Harald Grey-cloak in *Heimskringla*, Snorri Sturluson reports:

During the time when the sons of Gunnhild [Erik Bloodaxe's wife] ruled in Norway there were bad seasons, and they became worse the longer they ruled, and the farmers attributed that to the kings, and also complained that they were grasping and treated the farmers harshly. It went so far that the people in all parts hardly had any grain or fish. In Halogaland there was such famine and starvation that scarcely any grain grew there. The snow lay in all parts in midsummer, and the cattle had to stay in their stalls.[9]

The king had no absolute authority as lawmaker and judge. Laws were established and decisions made by free men at the assemblies (*thing*s), though it is reasonable to assume that the king played an important role in the maintenance of law and order and in the execution of legal decisions. An example of the power of the free men and their control is found in Snorri Sturluson's saga of the Norwegian King Harald Hardruler (r. 1046–1066) in *Heimskringla*. King Harald Hardruler's reign was characterized by his repeated campaigns against the Danish King Sven Estridsen, which included the burning of Hedeby in 1049. At the initiative of and under pressure from the free men, who were tired of the hostilities, the two kings eventually reached a treaty in 1064:

That same winter, messages and emissaries fared between Norway and Denmark, with the intent that both Norwegians and Danes wished to arrange for peace and agreements between them and prayed the kings to be agreeable to that. These exchanges of messages seemed likely to bring about an agreement, and the result was that a meeting to come to terms about peace was set...between King Harald and King Sven... And when the kings met, men began to talk about peace between them; and no sooner was this matter broached than many complained about the great havoc they had suffered from pillage, harrying, and loss of life... Finally the most eminent men and the wisest intervened. Then a reconciliation of the two kings was brought about to this effect that Harald was to have Norway, and Sven, Denmark, to the boundaries which had been heretofore between Norway and Denmark. Neither was to make amends to the other. Incursions were to stop, and he who had made gains was to hold onto them. And this peace was to be in force as long as they lived. This agreement was confirmed by oaths...King Harald fared north to Norway with his force, and King Sven sailed south to Denmark.[10]

Royal structures, such as the Danish fortresses and the Jelling monuments, suggest that the king must have had considerable funds at his dis-
posal. The economic foundation of the crown was primarily revenues
from land ownership and buildings on estates throughout the country,
some of which may have served as temporary royal residences during the
king's travels around the kingdom, but income was also derived from
trading, fines, shares of property confiscated from outlaws, minting at
home, and tributes and tolls abroad. Sven Forkbeard and Olaf Tryggvason
also collected huge Danegelds (literally "Danes' pay," that is, cash paid to
the Vikings to depart in peace) in England, and in his *Islendingabok* Ari
Thorgilsson reports that the kings of Norway from Harald Fairhair to Olaf
Haraldsson levied tax on emigrants from Norway to Iceland.

LAW

About the legal systems of the Viking-age Scandinavians we know next
to nothing. Contemporary primary sources have little, if anything, to say
about their laws, and no vernacular legal codes from the Viking age survive. The written laws were not codified until the twelfth and thirteenth
centuries. The earliest legal text is the Norwegian law of the Gulathing,
which was established around 950 and held in Gulen south of the mouth
of the Sogn fjord in western Norway. The text survives in a version from
the second half of the thirteenth century. The earliest Swedish and Danish
law codes that have been preserved are of an even later date. It is, of
course, probable that these laws contain older provisions reflective of
Viking-age customs and regulations, but it is difficult to identify the old
material and extract it from the new.

That laws were important to Viking-age Scandinavians is beyond
doubt. The modern English word "law" is an Anglo-Saxon loan of the Old
Norse *log* (meaning "what was laid down or settled"). It would seem
peculiar if the Anglo-Saxons borrowed such a word from a people that did
not have a reputation for legal-mindedness. In fact, in his saga of King
Harald Fairhair's son, King Hakon the Good, in his *Heimskringla,* Snorri
Sturluson emphasizes the king's attention to legislation:

King Hakon was a most cheerful person, very eloquent, and most kindly disposed.
He was a man of keen understanding and laid great stress on legislation. He
devised the Gulathings Law with the help of Thorleif the Wise; and the
Frostathings Law, with the advice of Earl Sigurd and other men from the Trondheim District who were accounted wisest. But the Heidsævis Law had been given
by Halfdan the Black [Harald Fairhair's father].[11]

It is impossible to ascertain whether King Hakon the Good devised the
laws of the Gulathing and the Frostathing or whether he merely altered
existing laws to suit the needs of the new monarchy, but the latter seems
more likely.

Only for Iceland do we have an account of how a legal code came into existence and was accepted. It is related in *Islendingabok* (Book of Icelanders) that when Iceland had been widely settled, a Norwegian by the name of Ulfljot was sent home to Norway to lay the basis of the Icelandic legislation using the law of the Gulathing as his point of departure. *Landnamabok* (Book of settlements) tells that he returned to Iceland after three years with a collection of laws that he had adapted for the conditions in Iceland. Ulfljot's laws have not been preserved, but *Landnamabok* provides some information about them:

At the beginning of that heathen law it says that men should not have ships with animal figure-heads at sea, but if they had them, they should unship them before they came in sight of land, and not sail near the land with figure-heads with jaws gaping wide or grinning muzzles, which would terrify the "land-spirits."

A ring of at least two ounces [of silver] should lie on the altar of every main temple. Every "priest" should have such a ring on his arm at all legal moots that he had to inaugurate himself. First it must be reddened in the blood of the cattle that he himself had sacrificed there. Every man who needed to take part in pleading before the court must first swear an oath on the ring and give the names of two or more witnesses. "I name witnesses to this," he must say, "that I swear my oath on the ring, an oath at law. So help me Frey and Njord and the Allpowerful God that I shall pursue this case—or defend it—or bear witness—or give verdict—or pass judgment, as I know to be most just and most true and most in accordance with the law. And all matters that come under my jurisdiction I shall determine lawfully as long as I am at this meeting."[12]

By the time Ulfljot returned to Iceland, the Althing, the General Assembly, had been established. It was set up in 930, and it met every summer on Thingvellir, the plains to the north of the great lake of Thingvallavatn in the southwestern part of Iceland. There were 36 principalities in Iceland at the time, and one chieftain in each, who then became a member of the assembly with the right to vote. These chieftains had the title of *godi* (plural *godar*), a word that is derived from the Old Norse *god* (meaning "god"). The title therefore shows that the chieftains fulfilled both religious and secular functions. The office of a *godi* was known as a *godord*, which was regarded as the *godi*'s personal possession, and between the *godord* and the Althing there was only one authority, the spring-assembly, which was a district meeting held before the Althing where local affairs and minor disputes were settled. The president of the Althing was the lawspeaker, who was the Icelandic state's highest and only secular official. It was his duty to know the law by heart and proclaim it at the Althing over a three-year period, for the laws were not put into writing until 1117. The Althing had both legislative and judiciary power, but there was no common executive power, only private. The Icelandic free state was an oligarchy, a union of chieftains without a king. Some time after 960 the country was divided into four quarters named after the four quarters of the compass. The spring-assemblies were retained and new quarter-assemblies established. There were three assemblies in the southern, eastern, and western quarters, but the northern quarter had four. Consequently, the northern quarter gained three new *godords*, and the number of *godar* rose to 39. *Landnamabok* reports as follows:

Then the land was divided into Quarters. And there should be three legal assemblies for each Quarter, and three main temples in each *thing* [assembly] district. Men were elected for their wisdom and righteousness to keep the temples. They had the duty of naming judges at the assemblies and ordering the legal cases. So they were called *godar*. Everyone must pay a temple tax as now they pay tithes to the church.[13]

The *Thing*   From this quotation and other pieces of information in the literary sources, it is evident that in the Viking age the laws were based upon the proceedings of the assemblies of free men, the so-called *things*. Slaves and children did not participate and women only occasionally as companions. The *things* were normally held in the open air within a fenced-off area. They were held at regular intervals and could be weekly, biweekly, quarterly, or annual. In densely populated areas, the *things* were typically held more frequently than in sparsely populated regions. The *things* could also be convoked by a secular or religious authority.

The *thing* could be an assembly of all free men in a district or a representative assembly of a larger region or province, and it convened for special purposes. The local *things*, about which little is known, were presumably convoked to decide on matters such as pasture rights, use of forests, construction of bridges, and to settle disputes between neighbors or families. Moreover, each community obviously had an interest in agreeing upon a tariff of payment for manslaughter *(wergild)* as an alternative to the traditional blood feud among the families concerned. The regional *things* were comprised of local chieftains, and such *things* made decisions regarding jurisdiction and defense, and they also decided on cases that could not be agreed upon at local *things*. It is known that pretenders to the throne convoked regional *things* in order to be recognized as kings. Only Iceland had a national *thing* in the Viking age.

Legal Procedure   There does not seem to have been any kind of proper trial or specific procedure relating to trial, for in small communities the nature of the crime and the identity of the criminal were usually well known, but the proceedings were nonetheless quite ritualistic, and accusations and responses were made using traditional formulas. Proof of innocence or guilt was demonstrated by producing witnesses, usually two or three free men, who were formally called by a principal in the suit. In some cases, compurgation (the practice of clearing an accused person of a charge by having a number of people swear to a belief in his innocence) was resorted to in order to strengthen a testimony. Another, though probably less common, method was to subject the accused to an ordeal in order to determine his or her innocence. The most frequent type was the ordeal of carrying hot iron, which was probably introduced from abroad. If the suspect's hands were not burned, he was declared innocent. For women, the ordeal of taking stones from the bottom of a cauldron of boiling water seems to have been the norm. Decisions could also be reached by a duel (*holmganga*) between parties to a dispute. As the name *holmganga* (island-going) implies, the duel was typically held on an island, and it was governed by very specific rules. Weapons varied, but the sword seems to have been common. Dueling was often occasioned by the breakdown of the legal proceedings or a judgment unacceptable to one party. In essence, therefore, dueling was recognition that the dispute had to be settled by a superior force or by the intervention of the gods.

Little is known about the manner of judgment, but consent to the verdict was expressed audibly by the *thing* through "weapon-taking," which entailed the brandishing of weapons.

CRIME AND PUNISHMENT

The *thing*s had no executive power. The individuals who won a legal judgment against others were responsible for enforcing the penalty. The intended effect of the laws and regulations was therefore dependent upon pressures from the society at large. This society was based on a system of kinship, and relatives protected and avenged one another. An injury or insult inflicted by an outside party against a member of a family was considered an injury or insult against the family as a whole, and it fell to the head of the family to take legal action or revenge. The revenge could be inflicted on the perpetrator, but it could also be inflicted on one of his relatives. If a woman or a child committed a crime, the husband or guardian was responsible. The same applied to slaves, for whom the owner was liable.

The most common punishment for a crime or an offense was a fine. A large portion of the Old Norwegian law, the Danish and **Fines** Swedish provincial laws, and the laws of the Icelandic free state (*Gragas*) was devoted to cataloguing the fines that could be imposed for different infractions. The imposition of fines evidently functioned as an important method of settling disputes, especially between two families. The fines also served as a means of limiting insult and violence and circumventing informal retribution for injuries, that is, blood vengeance, which, judging from the Sagas of Icelanders, was very common in Iceland. Because most crimes were, at least originally, considered to be an encroachment on a person's property, reputation, or rights, fines were granted to the man instituting the suit both as financial compensation for the damage he had suffered and as moral satisfaction.

Outlawry
Another kind of penalty that could be imposed was outlawry. It was used primarily for crimes that could not be atoned for with fines, though sometimes fines did replace outlawry. Similarly, outlawry could be imposed if fines were not paid.

The literary sources distinguish between two types of outlawry. One is "full outlawry." The laws of the Icelandic free state call it *skoggang* (forest-going), which obviously refers to outlaws' hideouts in the wilderness as outcasts from society. In Iceland, full outlawry was the ultimate punishment, for the laws made no provisions for the imposition of capital punishment. However, outlawry could amount to a death sentence, for an outlaw could be killed with impunity, that is, with no vengeance expected, and he had a price on his head—even if he managed to escape abroad. If he succeeded in leaving Iceland, he could never return. The outlaw also lost his property, from which compensation to the prosecutor was paid as well as an allowance for the outlaw's dependents. A full outlaw was denied burial in a churchyard, and children born to an outlaw had no inheritance rights. In certain cases, full outlaws could obtain reduction of their sentences or reprieve by killing other outlaws. Such rules probably created distrust among outlaws and kept them from banding together.

The other type of outlawry was more restricted in that it banished an individual from a specific region or province. It is mentioned in the Swedish provincial laws and appears to be quite similar to the *heradssekt* (district outlawry) or *fjordungsutlegd* (quarter outlawry) referred to in the Sagas of Icelanders. Curiously, this type of outlawry is not mentioned in *Gragas*, which instead refers to "lesser outlawry." It involved payment of a so-called life-ring (originally a silver ring, but later one *mork*) to a chieftain, forfeit of the lesser outlaw's property, and a three-year exile from Iceland. While abroad, the lesser outlaw had legal immunity from attack, and when he returned to Iceland he could resume his position as a full member of society. If a lesser outlaw failed to leave the country within three years, he became a full outlaw.

Capital Punishment
According to Adam of Bremen's *Gesta Hammaburgensis ecclesiae pontificum* (Activities of the prelates of the Church of Hamburg), the infliction of capital punishment was practiced in Denmark and Sweden for rapists, robbers, slanderers, and adulterers. About the Danes he says:

In many other respects, indeed, both in their laws and in their customs, do the Danes run contrary to what is fair and good. None of these points appears to me worth discussing, unless it be that they immediately sell women who have been violated and that men who have been caught betraying his royal majesty or in some other crime would rather be beheaded than flogged. No kind of punishment exists among them other than the ax and servitude, and then it is glorious for a man who is convicted to take his punishment joyfully.[14]

About the Swedes he reports as follows:

If a man knows another man's wife, or by violence ravishes a virgin, or spoils another of his goods, or does him an injury, capital punishment is inflicted on him.[15]

The testimony of Adam of Bremen is confirmed by the Danish and Swedish provincial laws, which list beheading, hanging, breaking on the wheel, burning, stoning, and live burial as forms of capital punishment. To this may be added drowning or sinking in a bog, which—in Norwegian law—was prescribed for sorcery.

The execution was probably undertaken, at least originally, by the prosecutors. Immediate revenge by the offended party was permissible when the criminal was caught in the act of, for instance, adultery, rape, or theft.

Corporal punishment, such as flogging or mutilation, was mainly reserved for slaves, though in the Swedish provincial laws it appears to have been the most common punishment after fines. *Gragas,* for example, prescribes mutilation if a slave outlawed for killing his master or mistress is captured:

Corporal Punishment

When a slave becomes an outlaw because of killing his master or mistress, then those who capture him are to take him, given it is within the same Quarter, to the man who got that outlaw condemned, and he is to cut off the outlaw's hands and feet and let him live as long as he may.[16]

Later, corporal punishment also appears to have been used as a penalty for petty theft, outstanding debts, and specific sex crimes.

WARFARE

In all of the Scandinavian countries the art of war was based on the *leidang* (levy) system. The term designates any military expedition, but because of the topography of the three countries—mountainous barriers in Norway, impenetrable forests in Sweden, and extensive stretches of woodland in Denmark—the military attached to the sea, and the *leidang* was essentially a maritime organization, a naval levy.

The *leidang* may be characterized as a public fleet levy consisting of free men under the leadership of a monarch, who was the chief military leader. The *leidang* system was founded upon a division of the country into districts. The farmers in each district were required to provide a ship of approximately 40 oars along with men, equipment, and supplies for a ship. In origin, these districts were divided into smaller areas, and each area was responsible for providing one man per oar, who was obliged to own the necessary arms. A shipmaster was selected to be in charge of the ship, its crew, the armament, and the provisions, and he was also the commander of the ship at sea. Fines due to the king were imposed on men who did not fulfill their obligations when a levy was called.

The *leidang* does not figure in the early Viking expeditions, and the age of the levy system is unknown. Certainly, by the eleventh century, it was an established military institution, and it was with a *leidang* that Knud the Great managed to conquer England. The *leidang* system obviously owed much of its success to the quality of the ships. They were capable of moving swiftly and could be propelled by both oars and sail. Moreover, they were so light that they could be hauled over land from one river to another. By law, they were required to be uniform in construction and equipment, so that when combined the ships could serve as large fleets and constitute a formidable force.

Generally, it seems that for defensive purposes the entire levy was required to convene. When the ships had gathered, it was then a question of awaiting news of the enemy's attack and the planned place of assault. Once such information was available, the main function of the fleet was to swiftly deliver fighting units to that location. Here they would be supported by locals, for every man was obliged to turn out to fight off invaders. Even slaves were allowed to fight under such circumstances, and a slave who killed an enemy was by law granted freedom. For offensive purposes, only a part of the *leidang* was selected, because obviously some forces had to remain at home to defend the country if necessary.

Naval Battles
Battles on sea did not differ much from battles on land. In Scandinavian waters, the ships were lined up and roped together side by side to create one, two, or more lines of ships directly facing the enemy. The battle was typically begun with a volley of arrows against the enemy followed by an attempt to initiate hand-to-hand fighting on the enemy's deck with swords, spears, and axes. The victorious force was the one that succeeded in reducing the opposing force's resistance to such an extent that its ships could be cleared and taken over. The most famous naval battle in Scandinavia is no doubt the one in Svold, Norway, in which King Olaf Tryggvason was defeated and killed. On offensive campaigns in non-Scandinavian waters, the ships typically sailed in broad deployments and were put in to shore at the same time. The area was then pillaged and the opposing force—if there was one at all—attacked by a formation of men trained to fight on foot. Such was probably the procedure when in 834 the Danes struck the Netherlands for the first time. The *Annals of St-Bertin,* which give a detailed record of events in the Carolingian world during the years 830–882, describe the event as follows:

A fleet of Danes came to Frisia and laid waste a part of it. From there, they came by way of Utrecht to the *emporium* [trading place] called Dorestad and destroyed everything. They slaughtered some people, took others away captive, and burned the surrounding region.[17]

When battles were fought on land, the forces were arranged in lines with a center and wings that moved forward to hand-to-hand melee. The literary sources make reference to the deployment of forces in a wedge-shaped formation called *svin-fylking* (pig-formation); those in the forefront were called *rani* (the snout). The extent to which this kind of formation was used is unknown. It is probable that it is of continental origin and presents an imitation of the classical *porcinum caput* (swine-snout), though some sources attribute its origin to Odin, god of war, who is also said to have filled certain warriors—so-called berserkers (literally "bare-skins")—with such a rage that they fell into an ecstatic battle frenzy and threw all thoughts of safety and survival to the wind. In his *Ynglinga saga* (Saga of the Ynglings) in *Heimskringla* Snorri Sturluson describes these warriors as follows:

Land Battles

> Odin was able to cause his enemies to be blind or deaf or fearful in battle, and he could cause their swords to cut no better than wands. His own men went to battle without coats of mail and acted like mad dogs or wolves. They bit their shields and were as strong as bears or bulls. They killed people, and neither fire nor iron affected them. This is called berserker rage.[18]

These almost superhuman men were obviously greatly valued as warriors, though this positive image of berserkers is challenged by the Sagas of Icelanders, in which they are typically portrayed as rather bullying and boorish types harrying the local population by demanding their daughters or wives and presented as a challenge for the hero to sweep aside.

As with naval battles, the battles on land were initiated by a volley of arrows probably accompanied by war cries to encourage fellow warriors and terrify the enemy. According to the literary sources, it was also common for military leaders to incite their men with speeches before the battle began. Troops trained to fight on horseback appear to have been virtually nonexistent in battles during the Viking age, and cavalry does not play any significant role until the early twelfth century. The outcome of the battle was determined by the flight of the forces and/or the death of the leaders on one side. When the combat had ended, the wounded men were tended to by healers and the dead buried. The plunder was then gathered and apportioned.

WEAPONS

All free men were required to own weapons and permitted to carry them. According to the Norwegian provincial laws, a man's armaments reflected his social status. A poor freeman would have only an ax and a shield, while a wealthy man would have a shield, a helmet, and a coat of mail, in addition to the Viking-age Scandinavian's three main weapons: sword, spear, and ax.

A great number of weapons have been found in Viking-age graves from pre-Christian times, especially in Norway and Sweden. Other weapons have been found in bogs and lakes in Denmark and the southern part of Sweden; most likely they were placed there as offerings to a war god. As a result, we are well informed about weapons in the Viking age.

Swords   Of all weapons, the sword was the most prestigious. Swords were praised in skaldic poetry, and a great number of kennings were devised for them, including "snake of wounds" and "flame of Odin." Some of the more special swords were even given names, such as *Brynjubit* (Byrnie-biter) and *Fotbit* (Leg-biter). The fact that sword-hilts (the guard made of bone, antler, ivory, or metal) were often decorated with animal motifs inlaid with copper, silver, gold, or niello further demonstrates the glamour of the sword in Viking-age society. The fundamental value of the sword and its many functions are aptly described by H. R. Ellis Davidson:

The sword was closely associated with much of what was most significant in a man's life—family ties, loyalty to his lord, the duties of a king, the excitement of battle, the attainment of manhood, and the last funeral rites. It was something from which its owner was never parted throughout his life, from the moment that he received it and had the right to wear it. He carried it in the king's hall and at law meetings, although on such occasions it was forbidden to draw it, and it might be fastened down in the scabbard. At night it hung above his bed, as we know from *Beowulf* and the Icelandic sagas. A sudden attack often came at night, and to lose hold of one's sword, as King Aethelstan discovered, was a terrifying experience...It was indeed, as is said in one of the Anglo-Saxon riddles, the prince's "shoulder-companion," his close friend ever at his side, and the "warrior's comrade." Small wonder that Bersi the Dueller, famous swordsman and poet of the tenth century, declared that if he could no longer wield his sword, life held nothing more for him...For a man who could no longer rely upon his sword had become a nonentity, a helpless figure relying on others for the protection of life, property, and reputation. The time had come to hand over the guardianship of the family, with the sword, to his descendants.[19]

Double-edged swords were by far the most common. The total length of a normal sword was about 90 cm (35.43 in.), the iron blade being typically 80 cm (31.49 in.) long and the tang (a projection by which the blade is attached to the handle) 10 cm (3.93 in.) long. The blade was usually broad and tapered toward the blunted tip, for the sword was a cutting and not a thrusting weapon made for use in one hand. Many blades were made with the so-called pattern-welding technique—a laborious process that entailed welding together bars of iron, bending them, and then compressing them into a thin plate or sheet—which gave the blade an ornamented look. To this middle section edges made of specially treated iron would be welded. A groove down the center of the blade on either side served to reduce the weight of the sword and give it flexibility. The sword was carried in a scabbard suspended on the left side from a strap across the right shoulder. The scabbard was made of thin wood covered with leather and lined with wool or fabric.

Evidently, sword manufacture was a specialized task for well-trained and highly experienced smiths, and it remains a matter of debate whether swords were manufactured in Scandinavia or abroad. It is known that some sword blades, the best, were forged in the Rhine region, and many of these bear the factory mark "Ulfberth." Because a number of hilts have distinctively Scandinavian designs it is reasonable to assume that they were made and fitted in Scandinavia. Other swords clearly came to Scandinavia by trade or as booty.

Apart from the sword, the commonest weapon found in Viking-age graves is the spear, though spears are represented almost exclusively by their spearheads (the wooden shafts are seldom preserved). There were two main kinds of spear: the heavy throwing spear and the somewhat lighter thrusting spear. Both were used for fighting and hunting. The blades, which are typically leaf-shaped with shoulders toward the socket, are up to 50 cm (19.68 in.) long and have a distinct mid-rib and a hollow cone-shaped socket to fit the end of the shaft. Some of the spears had pattern-welded blades and sockets richly inlaid with silver patterns. Those of the preserved spears that have sockets with side lobes or wings are most likely Frankish and imported from the Carolingian Empire.

Spears

The third main weapon, the ax, is the one with which the Viking-age Scandinavians are typically associated in popular culture. The importance of the ax may be somewhat overrated, however, for axes are not often found with other weapons in graves, and they are not celebrated to any significant extent in skaldic poetry.

Axes

Several types of axes were used, and some of the ones that have been found in connection with settlements were probably tools rather than weapons. The earliest axes were simple woodworker's axes, but over time broad-bladed axes intended specifically for battle were manufactured. The characteristics of the battle-ax are its broad neck and thin blade, which thickens immediately behind the edge. Some of the ax-heads are beautifully ornamented. A famous example is the iron ax with silver inlay from the Mammen grave in Jutland.

Like spears, bows and arrows were used for both hunting and fighting, and it is reasonable to assume that they played an important role in battles, for they are often referred to in literary sources. Finds of Viking-age bows and arrows are rare, however. In fact, only one complete Viking-age bow has so far been discovered, in Hedeby. It is a bow, about 192 cm (75.59 in.) long and made from a bough of yew. Arrowheads are frequently found in graves sometimes alongside the dead in bundles. Arrowheads were made of iron, and most of them are tanged, though some have sockets. The arrowheads take

Bows and Arrows

various forms, but a long leaf-shaped blade seems to have been the most common shape. The shafts were made of wood with a tied-on feather. The arrows were carried in cylindrical quivers.

Defensive Equipment

The most important means of self-defense was the shield. Not many complete shields have been preserved, but they are well known from contemporary pictorial representations and from literary sources. The shield-board was usually round and flat with a hole at the center for the handgrip covered by a hemispherical iron boss. Such shields hung in rows along the gunwales of the Gokstad ship. The Gokstad shields are almost 1 m (3.28 ft.) in diameter and bound with leather at the rim. Other shields, such as those found at Birka, have metal rim-bindings. Some shields were painted. In fact, the oldest surviving skaldic poem, the *Ragnarsdrapa* (Ragnar's poem) by Bragi Boddason, is an account of the pictures and mythological subjects painted on a shield.

Other protection in the form of helmets and mail-shirts appears to have been less common and reserved for wealthy warriors. The most complete surviving Viking-age helmet comes from the tenth-century Gjermundbu grave from Ringerike in Norway. The helmet is made of iron and has the shape of a rounded cap. It consists of a series of iron plates riveted together with binding strips, and projecting below the helmet is a piece of iron that frames and protects the nose and eyes.

The best-preserved remains of a Viking-age mail-shirt also come from the Gjermundbu grave, but the shirt is so fragmentary that it is difficult to get a clear idea of what it looked like in its original form. It is possible that it was knee-length and had sleeves. The shirt is made up of small rings with overlapping ends, but that other designs existed as well is clear from a fragment of chain mail found at Lund in Scania, consisting of closed rings each linking four others, and another fragment found in the fortress at Birka, consisting of small iron plates tied together.

MILITARY ACTION AND RAIDS

It was primarily as a dreaded military force that the Scandinavians became known to the western European mainland and the British Isles in the Viking age. While it is generally agreed that the key to their military success was the ship and their navigational skills, the specific causes of the raids are less clearly understood and remain open to debate. Some have suggested as reasons an increase in population in Scandinavia, while others have pointed to the growth in international trade and, by extension, a growth in piracy along the trade routes. P. H. Sawyer has convincingly argued, however, "for the Scandinavians the Viking raids in the West were simply an extension of the activity that was normal in their own society, an extension made possible and profitable by special circumstances."[20] Adventure no doubt played a role, and the journeys were probably seen as educational for young men of good families. Certainly, the potential profits from such incursions, which might provide capital for the purchase of land or a ship, must have been a major incentive for the Scandianvians to take off in their longboats.

The ferocious raid in 793 on the church and monastery on the tiny island of Lindisfarne just off the Northumbrian coast is commonly regarded as the beginning of the Viking age in western Europe and on the British Isles. The *Anglo-Saxon Chronicle* describes the onslaught as follows:

In this year terrible portents appeared over Northumbria and miserably frightened the inhabitants; these were exceptional flashes of lightning, and fiery dragons were seen flying in the air. A great famine soon followed these signs; and a little after that in the same year on 8 January the harrying of the heathen miserably destroyed God's church in Lindisfarne by rapine and slaughter.[21]

The attack clearly came as a shock, and the famous Northumbrian priest and scholar Alcuin (d. 804) expressed his surprise and lamented the catastrophe in a letter to King Aethelred of Northumbria:

Lo, it is nearly 350 years that we and our forefathers have inhabited this most lovely land, and never before has such terror appeared in Britain as we have now suffered from a pagan race, nor was it thought that such an inroad from the sea could be made. Behold, the church of Saint Cuthbert spattered with the blood of the priests of God, despoiled of all its ornaments; a place more venerable than all in Britain is given as a prey to pagan peoples.[22]

It is easy to understand Alcuin's surprise. All over Europe, churches and monasteries had been built in exposed coastal areas in the belief that from the sea they would be safe. The Viking attack shattered this belief, showing that "such an inroad from the sea" was indeed possible.

It is no coincidence that the first aggressions had churches and monasteries as their targets. Monasteries came to be especially sought-after sites by the Vikings and were often raided in the eighth and ninth centuries. The reason is not that the Vikings were hostile to Christians and Christianity, but because the monasteries typically contained many treasures and were easy prey. Moreover, their abbots, monks, and nuns could be captured without much effort and either sold as slaves or released in return for payment.

The success of the attack on Lindisfarne by Norwegian sea rovers was such that they returned to raid Jarrow in 794 and Iona and Lambay (an island near Dublin) in 795. These raids were casual affairs, however, and stand as isolated occurrences, though it is possible that there were others that went unrecorded. It appears that at this time the Scandinavians—Norwegians in particular—were more concerned with establishing bases on the islands north and west of Scotland, that is, the Orkney and Shetland Islands and the Hebrides, as well as on the Isle of Man in the middle of the Irish Sea.

The British Isles

Viking attacks.

Orkney and Shetland Islands, the Hebrides, and the Isle of Man

On the Orkney Islands, an archipelago of some 70 islands off Scotland's north coast, the Scandinavians took over Pictish settlements, such as the Buckquoy settlement on the main island of Orkney. Buckquoy faces the Brough of Birsay, a tidal island at the northwest extremity of the Bay of Birsay, on which there stood a Pictish monastery, which was later replaced by a minster at the initiative of the greatest Orkney earl, Thorfin the Mighty (d. 1065), who also was responsible for the building of a cathedral on the island. The literary sources suggest that the Orkney earldom was established in the second half of the ninth century, and it became an important link between Norway, the Celtic regions, and the Scandinavian kingdom of York. The earl's political control over Caithness, the most northerly province of mainland Scotland, which from the late ninth century onward had a large Scandinavian settlement, resulted in considerable Celto-Nordic interaction and assimilation. Politically, the Orkney Islands belonged to Norway, as did the Shetland Islands, a group of about 100 islands northeast of the Orkneys, which were under the control of the Orkney earls. On both the Orkney and Shetland Islands, the newcomers seem to have exercised a strong cultural influence. Virtually all the place names on the islands are Scandinavian, and the language of the islands became a distinctive Scandinavian dialect known as Norn, which survived until the eighteenth century. The resident Picts have left few traces, and the question as to whether they were driven out by the Scandinavians or stayed on as subservient people remains open. Excavations at Coileagan an Udail on the island of North Uist in the Outer Hebrides, where the Scandinavians also took over what seems to have been a native settlement, revealed a small fort, which suggests that certainly there the takeover was violent. It is not clear when the Scandinavians first settled on the Isle of Man off the northwest coast of England, but it is assumed to have been slightly later. Viking graves indicate that the settlements were first made during the second half of the ninth century, and the absence of females in these graves suggests that the island was seized by Vikings who intermarried with Manx women.

Scotland and Ireland

These islands became bases for attacks upon the Scottish mainland and especially Ireland, in which the Norwegians had already shown considerable interest. At first, the raids on Ireland were sporadic, unorganized, and limited to monasteries in coastal areas or on islands, but in the 830s and 840s the attacks greatly intensified and extended far into the interior of the island via the many rivers. In 840–841, the Vikings wintered in Ireland for the first time, and in 841 they established *longports* (fortified ship camps) in Dublin and Anagassan, from where they could operate. Later, camps were established in Limerick, Waterford, Wicklow, Wexford, and Cork. In these places, the Vikings settled as traders, and some of the settlements gradually developed into towns. Dublin is the most illustrious example, and in time it became the capital of the Vikings in Ireland and one of the most important trading centers in western Europe. From these camps or bases it was easy for the Vikings to attack, and it is probably no coincidence that for 845 no fewer than six raids are recorded. The author of *Cogadh Gaedhel re Gallaibh* (The war between the Irish and the foreigners), written around 1114–1116, describes the Irish people's intense hatred of the intruders in no uncertain terms:

In a word, although there were an hundred hard-steeled iron heads on one neck, and an hundred sharp, ready, never-rusting brazen tongues in every head, and an hundred garrulous, loud, unceasing voices from every tongue, they could not recount nor narrate nor enumerate nor tell what all the people of Ireland suffered in common, both men and women, laymen and priests, old and young, noble and ignoble, of hardship and injury and oppression in every house from these ruthless, wrathful, foreign, purely pagan people.[23]

Obviously, the Irish resisted the attacks and sought to defend themselves, but the effort was not a national one, for among the Irish there were at that time many warring factions. It is interesting and no doubt telling that the most successful attack on the Vikings in Ireland came from other foreigners, Danes, who in 851 invaded Norse Dublin. In 853, however, Olaf the White, son of a Norwegian king, and Ivar the Boneless, a Dane, came to Ireland and mutually took the title of king. Under the two rulers Dublin became a powerful kingdom, but the years following Ivar's death in 873 were troublesome for the Vikings and a major defeat in 902 caused many to leave.

England

In 914, the Vikings returned to Ireland full force under the leadership of the grandsons of Ivar the Boneless, who had established themselves as kings of York in England, and from the early 920s until the early 950s Dublin was almost continually the center of a kingdom comprising both Dublin and York (which came under English sovereignty in 954). The kingdom was, however, frequently attacked, and in 980 at the battle of Tara, Dublin finally lost its political independence. The Viking settlers had to recognize the overlordship of Mael Sechnaill II, king of Meah in eastern Ireland, and were required to pay tribute to the Irish. The Vikings stayed on in Dublin as traders, and their impact on Irish economic life is evident from the fact that a number of Irish words for commerce and seafaring are borrowed from Norse. Gradually, however, the Vikings faded from the Irish scene through assimilation and conversion, though Norse was still spoken in Dublin when in 1170 it was conquered by Anglo-Normans.

While in the early decades of the ninth century the Norwegian Vikings focused on Ireland, the Danish Vikings turned their attention to England. The first serious Viking attack on England came in 835, and the target was the small island of Sheppey in the Thames. For the next 15 years, Viking raids were annual occurrences directed especially against southern and eastern England, which at this time consisted of several kingdoms: Wessex in the south, East Anglia to the east, Northumbria to the north, and Mercia in the middle. These first raids were surprise attacks of a seasonal nature, but this situation changed in 850–851 when the Vikings wintered on the island of Thanet in the Thames. From then on the Vikings became a permanent threat not only to the coastal areas but also to the inland regions. In 865, the people of Kent bought off Vikings encamped on Thanet to leave in peace, and this is the first known payment of Danegeld in England. The same year also saw the arrival of what the *Anglo-Saxon Chronicle* refers to as "a great heathen host" (numbering somewhere between 500 and 2000 Vikings) in East Anglia:

And this same year came a great heathen host to England and took up winter quarters from the East Anglians, and there were provided with horses, and they made peace with them.[24]

The event marked a turning point in the Viking incursions: the Vikings were no longer only a sea force but also a powerful and highly mobile land force. Using East Anglia as a base, the army, whose ultimate purpose was to take land and settle, spent the next decade attacking in rapid succession all the major centers in the Anglo-Saxon kingdom: York in 866, Nottingham in 867–868, Thetford in 869–870, Reading in 870, London in 871–872, Torksey in 872–873, and Repton in 873. After these victories in East Anglia, Northumbria, and Mercia, the Vikings decided to divide the army, which had stayed together since 865. One army, under the leadership of Halfdan, went to Northumbria, conquered the country the following year, and settled there. The other army, under the leadership of Guthrum, moved to Cambridge and from there to Wessex, which was by now the only independent kingdom. After attempts to invade Wessex, the Viking army was in 878 defeated by King Alfred the Great (r. 871–899), and Guthrum and his men were forced to leave Wessex and establish themselves in East Anglia and Mercia. In 886, King Alfred made a treaty with Guthrum, which established the borders between the independent Wessex and the independent part of Mercia on the one hand and the land of the Vikings (that is, Yorkshire, East Anglia, and the central and eastern Midlands) on the other. The word Danelaw is commonly used as a term for the land of the Vikings, but it never became a true political entity, and the word simply means "the law of the Danes." The treaty did not automatically bring peace to England, however. In 892, a large Viking army from the continent arrived and attempted to take land for settlement, but the newcomers were resisted, and eventually some settled in the Danelaw area while others returned to mainland Europe to continue raiding.

The process of winning back the areas occupied by Viking settlers began under King Alfred's son, Edward the Elder (r. 899–924). By the end of his reign, the Danelaw south of the Humber had come under English rule, and Edward had been accepted as the ruler of Northumbria. Gradually, Anglo-Saxon control was extended, and by the middle of the tenth century a united English kingdom had been established. The last Viking king of York was Erik Bloodaxe, who had been banished from Norway, and who was killed in 954.

A second wave of Viking activity began in England when after the death of King Edward the Martyr in 978 his brother Aethelred the Unready (r. 978–1016) succeeded to the throne. However, the incursions were now of a different nature and on a different scale. They were no longer conducted by raiders intent on plunder or settlement but by kings or princes ambitious for political and economic power. The *Anglo-Saxon Chronicle* tells of large raids in various parts of the country in the years 980–982, 988, and 991, when Olaf Tryggvason (later king of Norway) arrived and was bought off with 10,000 pounds of silver. Many more Viking attacks followed, and the sums required to buy off the invaders rapidly increased from 24,000 pounds in 1002 to 36,000 pounds in 1007 to 48,000 in 1012. By then, the kingdom's defenses were almost nonexistent. The Danish King Sven Forkbeard took advantage of the situation, and in 1013 he conquered England. His victory was short lived, however, for he died the following year and his empire subsequently fell apart. Three years later, in 1016, it was restored by his son Knud the Great. The *Encomium Emmae Reginae* (A book in praise of Queen Emma), a work from the first half of the eleventh century celebrating King Knud's wife, who was the widow of King Aethelred the Unready, contains a vivid description of Knud's fleet leaving Denmark in order to conquer England:

Then King Knud, bidding his mother and brother farewell, again sought the bounds of the encircling shore where he had already gathered a brilliant show of two hundred ships. Indeed there was so great a supply of arms there that a single one of those ships could have furnished weapons in the greatest abundance if all the rest had lacked them. For there were so many types of shields that you might have thought the hosts of all nations were at hand. Further, there was such elegant decoration on the keels that to the dazzled eyes of observers viewing from a distance they seemed made of flame rather than wood. For if at any time the sun mingled with them the radiance of its beams, here would flash the glitter of armor, there the fire of the hanging shields; burning gold on the prows, gleaming silver in the varied decorations of the vessels. In fact, so great was the magnificence of the fleet that if its commander had wished to subdue any nation, the ships alone would have terrified the enemy before their fighting-men could engage in any battle. For what adversary could gaze upon the lions, terrible in the glitter of their gold, upon the men of metal, menacing with their gilded brows, upon the dragons, flaming with refined gold, upon the bulls threatening slaughter, their horns gleaming with gold—all these on the ships—and not apprehend dread fear in face of a king of so great a fighting force? Moreover, in this great armada none among them was a slave, none a freed-man, none of low birth, none enfeebled by age; for all were noble, all strong in the power of maturity, all fully trained in any type of warfare, all of such fleetness that they despised the speed of cavalry.[25]

Knud the Great reigned over England (as well as Denmark and Norway and a part of Sweden) until 1035 and brought the English 20 years of what must have been badly needed peace. After his death, his North Sea Empire was divided among his sons, but they turned out to be incompetent rulers, and the empire quickly disintegrated. England was lost when in 1042 Edward the Confessor was elected king.

Only one more attempt was made by Scandinavians to lay claim to England. This was in 1066, when the Norwegian King Harald Hardruler (r. 1046–1066) set sail across the North Sea intent on defeating Harold Godwinsson, who in the same year had succeeded Edward the Confessor as king of England. The English king surprised the Scandinavian army at Stamford Bridge near York, however, and Harald Hardruler was killed in the battle. King Harold himself was killed only two days later by Duke William the Conqueror of Normandy (r. 1035–1087) in a battle at Hastings, which marked the beginning of Norman rule in England. The Viking age in England was then over, but the effects of the Scandinavians' presence are clear from the many Scandinavian loanwords in modern English and the numerous place-names in the Danelaw area. The loan words include *egg* (Old Norse *egg*), *skin* (Old Norse *skinn*), *call* (Old Norse *kalla*), *take* (Old Norse *taka*), and the personal pronouns *they*, *them*, and *their* (Old Norse *þeir, þeim, þeirra*), to list but a few. As far as place-names are concerned, mention may be made of the numerous names with the Scandinavian suffixes *-by* and *-þorp*.

The real Viking attacks on the western European mainland began in 834. The *Annals of St-Bertin* record for that year that a fleet of Danish Vikings came to Dorestad—the main trading center of Frisia and reputedly the biggest in northern Europe—and captured and looted the town. **The Western European Mainland** Dorestad remained a target for plunder for a number of years and was sacked several times until it was finally destroyed in 863, when the River Rhine flooded the town.

Dorestad was only a forerunner for larger, coordinated, and systematically planned attacks. In 835, the Vikings pillaged the monastery on the island of Noirmoutier at the mouth of the Loire, where, moreover, they established themselves and turned the island into fortified winter quarters that served as a base for raids in the spring and summer. In 841, they sacked Rouen on the Seine; in 842, they sacked Quentowic near modern Étables, south of Boulogne; in 843, they plundered Nantes on the Loire; and in 845, they sacked Hamburg in northern Germany, which was then a small trading post and an episcopal see. The same year, a Danish Viking called Ragnar entered the Seine with a sizable fleet and plundered Paris. He was bought off by Charles the Bald, to whom Louis the Pious had allocated the western part of the Frankish Empire, and this is the first recorded payment of Danegeld. This list of raids is far from exhaustive, and the situation on the western European mainland in the mid-ninth century can probably be summarized by the following quotation from Ermentarius, a monk from Noirmoutier, writing in the 860s:

The number of ships grows: the endless stream of Vikings never ceases to increase. Everywhere the Christians are victims of massacres, burnings, plunderings. The Vikings conquer all in their path, and no one resists them. They seize Bordeaux,

Périgueux, Limoges, Angoulême, and Toulouse. Angers, Tours, and Orléans are annihilated and an innumerable fleet sails up the Seine and the evil grows in the whole region. Rouen is laid waste, plundered, and burned, Paris, Beauvais and Meaux taken, Melun's strong fortress levelled to the ground, Chartres occupied, Evreux and Bayeux plundered, and every town besieged.[26]

Germany, the Netherlands, and France were, however, not the only countries that suffered at the hands of the Vikings. Some of the Viking expeditions went as far as the Mediterranean. The first documented raid on Spain took place in 844, when Seville and other places were conquered, but the Moors, the Muslims of Spain, turned out to be formidable enemies. The Vikings suffered a heavy defeat and were forced to use their captives to purchase escape. A second and considerably more successful raid by the Vikings on the southern world took place 15 years later. The expedition was led by two chieftains, Bjorn Ironside and Hastings, who left the Loire in 859 with a large number of ships. They pillaged along the coast of Iberia, sailed through the Straits of Gibraltar, and then headed for North Africa. Back in Spanish waters, they raided the southern coast of Spain and then sailed to the Balearic Islands (Formentera, Majorca, and Minorca). By then, winter was approaching, and the Vikings moved on to Rousillon on the southern coast of France. Suitable winter quarters were found on an island in the Camarque in the Rhône delta, and using it as a base the Vikings were able to raid Nîmes, Arles, and Valence in the spring of 861 before they sailed to Italy, where they sacked Pisa and Luna (the latter, it is said, in error for Rome). In the summer, the Vikings again made an attempt to sail through the Straits of Gibraltar, but they were defeated by a Moorish fleet. They were able to raid only one more time on their lengthy Mediterranean expedition—in Navarre they capture the prince for whose release they received a handsome sum of money—and in 862 they were back on the Loire. Further raids on Spain are mentioned in the sources, including a raid on Santiago de Compostella in 968, but generally it may be said that the Vikings showed only modest interest in the western Mediterranean.

In the years following 865, the Vikings focused primarily on England, but in 879 they returned to mainland Europe with a strong fleet, the so-called Great Army. It landed on the coast between Calais and Boulogne and raided and pillaged as it made its way. It settled in the area of Meuse and Schelde until 892 and undertook devastating raids from its bases into the neighboring regions. A great number of monasteries and towns were affected by these onslaughts, including Aix-la-Chapelle, Bonn, Cologne, and Trier. Indeed, for the year 884 an annalist of St. Vaast reported:

The northmen continue to kill and take Christian people captive; without ceasing they destroy churches and dwellings and burn towns. Along all the roads one sees bodies of the clergy and laity, of nobles and others, of women, children, and infants. There is no road on which the bodies of slain Christians are not strewn. Sorrow and despair fill the hearts of all Christians who witness this.[27]

In 881 and again in 891 the Vikings suffered heavy defeats, however, and in 892 the "Great Army" retreated. Some of the Vikings settled in England; others returned to Scandinavia. By and large this marks the end of the Viking raids in Germany and France except for the occasional local incursion; but in France the presence of the Vikings was felt until the early thirteenth century, for in 911 a treaty was agreed upon between King Charles the Simple and Rollo, the leader of a Viking army that laid siege to Chartres. The Vikings were defeated, but the king evidently saw this as a clever opportunity to enlist the Vikings as watchdogs against further attacks by Scandinavians and offered the Viking invaders the land they already occupied. In return, the Vikings swore to him oaths of allegiance as their king, and Rollo was elevated to duke. In this way, the Viking colony of Normandy (or Northmannia, meaning "the land of the northmen") came into existence, and Rollo's dynasty ruled the province in direct line till 1204 when King Philip Augustus annexed the duchy to the royal French domain and abolished the office of duke.

COLONIZATION

Not all the Scandinavians who ventured abroad came as raiders. Hunger for land rather than loot was a motive for a considerable number of Scandinavians. These Scandinavians—primarily Norwegians—came not as marauders with sword in hand, but as seafaring farmers with families, livestock, and chattels intent on building up new communities on the uninhabited islands in the North Atlantic: the Faroe Islands, Iceland, and Greenland.

Various reasons have been given for this large-scale emigration of Scandinavians in the ninth century. Some have stressed the desire for adventure and honor. Others have emphasized the limited opportunities for new land in Norway in particular and the pressures of a growing population. Medieval Icelandic sources attribute the emigration to Iceland largely to dissatisfaction with the political conditions in Norway, where Harald Fairhair's attempt to unify Norway ended the rule of many petty kings and earls, to whom the Faroe Islands and Iceland seemed attractive places of exile. While Harald Fairhair no doubt played an important role in the emigration, opposition to monarchical oppression cannot be cited as the only reason, for many of the emigrants came only indirectly from Norway via the British Isles, where at this time the Vikings were beginning to lose their foothold. They were defeated in Wessex and Mercia by Alfred the Great, and in 902 the Irish conquered Dublin. In Scotland their position was also weakened. To return to Scandinavia was undesirable, if not impossible, and so the escape route lay to the islands in the North Atlantic and to Iceland in particular.

The Faroe Islands   The Scandinavians reached the Faroe Islands, a cluster of 22 mountainous islands (of which 17 are now inhabited) between Iceland and the Shetland Islands, in the early ninth century, and their settlement there is probably contemporaneous with or occurred shortly after the Norse settlement of the Isle of Man and the Orkney and Shetland Islands. Proof of earlier settlement comes from an Irish monk by the name of Dicuil, who lived at the court of Charlemagne's successor in France. In his book on the measure of the sphere of the earth *(Liber de mensura orbis terrae)* from around 825, he describes a group of islands north of Scotland and claims that for a century Irish hermits *(papar)* had sought solitude there, but he intimates that they had abandoned their habitation on the islands when the Scandinavians started making their appearance and evidently disturbed the monks' eremitical peace. Dicuil says that he had never seen the islands mentioned by previous authors.

The first Scandinavian settlers probably came from the Norse settlements in the south, that is, the Hebrides, the Shetland Islands, the Orkney Islands, etc., but during the ninth century, more settlers came from western Norway and Celtic-speaking areas, causing the settlement to grow in size. Most likely, sheep grazing was introduced by the Irish monks—the name Faroe Islands means "sheep islands"—and wool and woolen cloth was probably exported from an early date as well as down and seabirds' feathers. Otherwise the history of the Scandinavian settlement of the Faroe Islands remains largely unknown, and our knowledge of early Faroese history comes almost exclusively from remains of buildings and burials. Evidence of Viking-age settlement has been found, for example, at the village of Kvivik, where a typical farmstead was identified, and graveyards have been excavated in the villages of Tjørnuvik and Sandur. The finds suggest that the settlers brought with them farming systems typical of Norway. Many materials, including wood and minerals, obviously had to be imported, and evidently, the settlers depended very much on communications with the surrounding world and with Norway in particular.

Iceland   In contrast, the settlement of Iceland, a volcanic island of 103,000 square km (39,768 square miles) just skirting the Arctic Circle on the north coast, is well documented. In fact, Iceland is the only society in Europe whose origins are fully known.

The colonization of Iceland began in the last quarter of the ninth century, but, like the Faroe Islands, it seems that the island had Irish visitors well before Scandinavians set foot on it. Dicuil writes that around 795 he had spoken with some Irish monks, who had sailed north from Ireland and found an island called Thule, where the summer nights were so bright that one could pick lice from one's shirt. The presence of the Irish hermits is supported by a dozen *papa* place-names and also the testimony of the historian Ari Thorgilsson, who in his *Islendingabok* reports that when the first Norse settlers arrived in Iceland they found there *papar,* who went away because they did not want to live among pagans, and who left behind Irish books, bells, and crosiers.

The traditional accounts place the "discovery" of Iceland by Scandinavians in the 860s, and one redaction of *Landnamabok* places it in the context of journeys to the Faroe Islands. It tells that a Norwegian named Naddodd set sail for the Faroe Islands but was blown off course and came to a land he did not know about. As he wanted to find out more about the country, he explored the surroundings and eventually climbed a mountain to look for signs of human habitation. Before he left, some snow fell on the mountains, and, accordingly, Naddodd called the new land Snowland. The same redaction relates that subsequently a Swede by the name of Gardar Svavarsson went in search of Snowland. He circumnavigated the new land and realized it was an island. He named it Gardarsholm (Gardar's island) and spoke highly of it. A Norwegian, Floki Vilgerdarson, was the third man to come from Scandinavia. He took family and livestock with him and settled in a fjord in the northwest of the island. He spent the summer fishing and hunting but neglected to make hay for the winter with the result that his livestock died the following winter and his attempted settlement failed. Tradition says that before leaving he climbed a mountain and saw a fjord full of ice. Angry and frustrated, he named the country Iceland and spoke badly of it in Norway; but one of his companions was of a different opinion, and it seems that Floki too changed his mind, for some years later he returned to Iceland to settle permanently.

News of the new land soon spread. Two young men in southwest Norway heard about it. They were Ingolf Arnason and Hjorleif Hrodmarsson. Because of the killing of the two sons of a powerful earl in their neighborhood, they were forced to give up their land to the earl as compensation. Because there was no longer any soil to live on in Norway, they made an expedition to Iceland to examine the island and were favorably impressed. Two years later, they moved to Iceland with their families and livestock. Tradition says that when Ingolf approached the coast of Iceland, he threw overboard the high-seat pillars he had taken with him from his home in Norway in the belief that they would direct him to his future homestead (see chapter 5). Eventually, the pillars were found near a bay on the southwest coast, where Ingolf saw white "smoke" rising from the hot springs. Accordingly, Ingolf called the bay Reykjavik (smoky bay). Hjorleif, who settled on the middle of the south coast, was killed in a revolt by his slaves, who subsequently settled on the Westman Islands south of Iceland.

Ingolf's settlement took place in 870, and the year marks the beginning of Icelandic history, the so-called Age of Settlement, 870–930, when the Althing, the Icelandic parliament, was established. During these six decades Iceland was fully settled, and in his *Islendingabok* Ari Thorgilsson reports that after that date all the land was taken. The *Landnamabok* names approximately 1,000 settlers, and it is clear that most of these were Norwegian with a small number of Celts. A few came from Sweden and Denmark. Most of the Norwegian settlers did not emigrate directly from Norway, however, but came to Iceland from the British Isles, the Hebrides, and the Orkney and Shetland Islands. The settlers in Iceland quickly established specific regulations for taking land, no doubt as a result of dissatisfaction with the large claims to land made by the first settlers. According to *Landnamabok*, no man was to lay claim to more land than he could walk around with fire in one day. For women this was different; they had to be content with the territory around which they would walk with a heifer on a spring day between sunrise and sunset.

The following decade, 930–1030, is commonly referred to as the Saga Age. This period, which is the topic of the famous Sagas of Icelanders, was one of national and cultural growth. The settlers had built up their farms and made a living from farming (with an emphasis on cattle raising) and fishing. Some of them also went abroad to take part in Viking raids or to sell their goods and purchase their necessities, for in the Saga Age the Icelanders were still a seafaring nation.

Greenland   The discovery and colonization of Greenland (the world's largest island lying mostly within the Arctic Circle) by Icelanders of Scandinavian extraction were a direct result of the Icelanders' capacity to traverse the North Atlantic. The events are documented in Ari Thorgilsson's *Islendingabok, Landnamabok,* as well as in the two so-called Vinland sagas, *Groenlendinga saga* (Saga of the Greenlanders) and *Eiriks saga rauda* (Saga of Erik the Red), which tell of the earliest settlement, though they are mainly concerned with voyages from Greenland to North America.

According to *Landnamabok*, the first sighting of Greenland took place sometime before 930 by Gunnbjorn Ulfsson, who was thrown off course on his way from Norway to Iceland. The skerries off the coast of Greenland carried his name for some time and a little later, an outlaw, Snaebjorn Holmsteinsson, visited the country and spent the winter in east Greenland.

The true pioneer and the father of the Norse settlement in Greenland was, however, Eirik Thorvaldsson or Erik the Red as he is often called. He had been outlawed from Norway to Iceland because of some killings and outlawed from Iceland for three years on account of more killings. As he had heard about Gunnbjorn's skerries, he put to sea to look for them. He sailed northwest out of Breidafjord, his home, to Greenland and from there south along the coast. On the west coast he found habitable regions, which he explored during his three years of exile, and when he returned to Iceland, he spoke favorably of the new land. According to *Landnamabok*, "he called it Greenland because he thought people would be more keen to go there if the place had an attractive name."[28] Erik the Red's propaganda produced results: in 985 or 986, prospective settlers set out in 25 ships for Greenland, though only 14 ships completed the voyage, and soon other

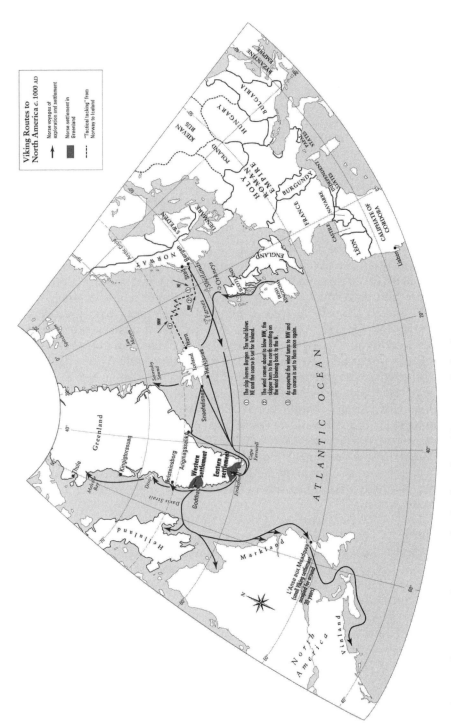

Viking Routes to
North America c. 1000 AD

Norse voyages of
exploration and settlement

Norse settlement in
Greenland

"Tactical tacking" from
Norway to Iceland

① The ship leaves Bergen. The wind blows NE and the course is set for Iceland.

② The wind comes about to blow NW, the skipper turns to the north counting on the wind blowing back to the N.

③ As expected the wind turns to NW and the course is set to Horn once again.

L'Anse aux Meadows (small Viking settlement occupied for around 20 years)

Viking explorations and an example of tacking from Norway to Iceland.

settlers followed. Presumably the settlers were people who had arrived in Iceland when most of the land had already been claimed or people who, like Erik the Red, had lost their status and saw Greenland as an opportunity to gain wealth and respect. The venture resulted in two main communities, one in the extreme southwest not far beyond Cape Farewell (now the area around Qaqortoq) and the other just below the Arctic Circle (now the area around Nuuk), called the Eastern Settlement and the Western Settlement, respectively. It has been estimated that the Norse population in Greenland numbered about 3,000. Erik the Red built his farm at Brattahlid in the Eastern Settlement, and under his leadership laws were established. He also founded an assembly, called the Althing, which met at Gardar (Igaliko), where later a church was built.

Archaeological excavations have confirmed the testimony of the literary sources about the Norse history of Greenland, and even the site of Erik the Red's farm has been identified. The finds have revealed a community that exploited all available ecological niches. The agricultural economy was based on cows, sheep, and goats, though fishing and hunting of reindeer, bears, and birds must also have played significant roles. For grain, iron, and timber, the settlers were dependent on contacts with the outside world, and for these commodities they paid with walrus and narwhal ivory, hide-ropes, pelts of polar bears, whalebones, live polar bears, and falcons—items that were highly valued in Europe in the Viking age.

The Norse settlement in Greenland lasted for only about 500 years. The last preserved record of contact between the settlers and the outside world is an entry in an Icelandic annal telling that in 1406 a Norwegian ship headed for Iceland was carried off course and landed in Greenland. The castaways did not get away until four years later. The reason for the demise of the settlement remains unknown—though disease, climatic changes, and conflicts with the Inuit have been proposed—and can only be determined through extensive archaeological excavations of the Norse settlement sites.

North America

Groenlendinga saga, which is considered the more reliable of the two Vinland sagas, tells that among the Icelandic settlers in Greenland, there was a man named Herjolf. His son, a merchant named Bjarni, came to Iceland from Norway the very summer that Herjolf immigrated to Greenland and decided to continue to his father's estate with his cargo. On his way to Greenland, he met with fog and unfavorable winds and did not know where he was for many days. When the fog lifted, he saw lands that were not Greenland, so he sailed away in a northeasterly direction and found his father's home in Greenland. Erik the Red's son Leif heard about the new land, and some time around 1000 he sailed Bjarni's route in reverse. He found the land and explored it with his men. He also gave names to the different territories they visited. First they came to Helluland (flat-stone land, probably Baffin Island), then Markland (forest-land, perhaps Labrador), and finally to Vinland (meaning either "vine land" or "meadow land" depending on the length of the *i*). Leif and his men spent the winter there, and in the spring they sailed back to Brattahlid with a load of lumber. More expeditions from Greenland to Vinland were undertaken, and of these the voyage by the wealthy trader Karlsefni is the most significant, because he sailed off with a crew of 60, including 5 women, and livestock with the intention of settling in the New World. They met and traded with the natives, but the two races eventually came to blows and the would-be colonists gave up the venture and returned to Greenland.

Archaeology has confirmed the discovery of North America by Greenlanders of Icelandic extraction. In 1960, a Norse settlement was found at L'Anse aux Meadows on the northern tip of the Great Northern Peninsula in Newfoundland. The site was excavated and revealed three building complexes characteristic of Icelandic architectural style. Artifacts found in the buildings, such as a ring-headed bronze pin, a soapstone spindle-whorl, bone needles, and, most importantly, evidence of iron manufacture, led to the conclusion that it was a Viking-age site dating from around 1000. It is generally believed that L'Anse aux Meadows was a gateway to or base for exploration and exploitation of Vinland's resources further south, and that the Norse explorers did travel further—to the St. Lawrence valley and along the Miramichi River in New Brunswick—is clear from the butternuts found on the site. Vinland itself has not been identified, but the Gulf of St. Lawrence is considered a likely candidate.

NOTES

1. *Rigsthula* is quoted from Carolyne Larrington, trans., *The Poetic Edda* (Oxford: Oxford University Press, 1996), p. 248.

2. Quoted from Larrington, trans., *The Poetic Edda,* p. 249.

3. Quoted from Larrington, trans., *The Poetic Edda,* pp. 248–50.

4. Quoted from Larrington, trans., *The Poetic Edda,* p. 251.

5. The Hørning stone inscription is quoted from R.I. Page, *Chronicles of the Vikings: Records, Memorials, and Myths* (Toronto: University of Toronto Press, 1995), p. 170.

6. *Gragas* is quoted from Andrew Dennis, Peter Foote, and Richard Perkins, trans., *Laws of Early Iceland: Gragas,* vol. 2, The University of Manitoba Press Icelandic Studies (Winnipeg: University of Manitoba Press, 2000), p. 29.

7. Quoted from Dennis, Foote, and Perkins, trans., *Laws of Early Iceland,* p. 29.

8. The quotation from Sven Aggesen is from Eric Christiansen, trans., *The Works of Sven Aggesen Twelfth-Century Danish Historian,* Viking Society for Northern Research Text Series (London: Viking Society for Northern Research, 1992), p. 36.

9. The quotations from *Heimskringla* are from Snorri Sturluson, *Heimskringla: History of the Kings of Norway,* trans. Lee M. Hollander (Austin: University of Texas Press, 1964), p. 142.

10. Sturluson, *Heimskringla,* pp. 634–36.

11. Sturluson, *Heimskringla,* p. 104.

12. *Landnamabok* is quoted from Page, *Chronicles of the Vikings,* p. 174.

13. Quoted from Page, *Chronicles of the Vikings,* p. 174.

14. Adam of Bremen is quoted from Adam of Bremen, *History of the Archbishops of Hamburg-Bremen,* trans. Francis J. Tschan, Records of Civilization: Sources and Studies, vol. 53 (New York: Columbia University Press, 1959), pp. 190–91.

15. Adam of Bremen, quoted from Adam of Bremen, *History of the Archbishops of Hamburg-Bremen,* p. 203.

16. *Gragas* is quoted from Andrew Dennis, Peter Foote, and Richard Perkins, trans., *Laws of Early Iceland: Grágás,* vol. 1, University of Manitoba Icelandic Studies (Winnipeg: University of Manitoba Press, 1980), p. 170.

17. The *Annals of St-Bertin* are quoted from Janet L. Nelson, trans., *The Annals of St-Bertin,* vol. 1, Ninth-Century Histories (Manchester: Manchester University Press, 1991), p. 30.

18. The quotation from *Ynglinga saga* is from Sturluson, *Heimskringla,* p. 10.

19. The quotation is from H. R. Ellis Davidson, *The Sword in Anglo-Saxon England: Its Archaeology and Literature* (Oxford: Clarendon Press, 1962), pp. 214–15.

20. The reference is to P. H. Sawyer, *The Age of the Vikings,* 2nd. ed. (London: Edward Arnold, 1971), p. 205.

21. *The Anglo-Saxon Chronicle* is quoted from G. N. Garmonsway, trans., *The Anglo-Saxon Chronicle,* rev. ed., Everyman's Library, no. 624 (London: J. M. Dent & Sons Ltd., 1960), pp. 55, 57.

22. Alcuin is quoted from Dorothy Whitelock, ed., *English Historical Documents, c. 500–1042,* rev. ed., English Historical Documents, vol. 1 (London: Eyre & Spottiswoode, 1979), p. 776.

23. *Cogadh Gaedhel re Gallaibh* is quoted from Magnus Magnusson, *Vikings! Expansion Westwards* (New York: E. P. Dutton, 1980), p. 152.

24. *The Anglo-Saxon Chronicle* is quoted from Garmonsway, trans., *The Anglo-Saxon Chronicle,* p. 69.

25. The *Encomium Emmae Reginae* is quoted from Page, *Chronicles of the Vikings,* p. 117.

26. Ermentarius is quoted from James Graham-Campbell, *The Viking World* (New Haven and New York: Ticknor & Fields, 1980), pp. 31–32.

27. The annalist from St Vaast is quoted from F. Donald Logan, *The Vikings in History,* 2nd. ed. (London: HarperCollins, 1991), p. 129.

28. *Landnamabok* is quoted from Hermann Pálsson and Paul Edwards, trans., *The Book of Settlements: Landnámabók,* University of Manitoba Icelandic Studies (Winnipeg: University of Manitoba Press, 1972), p. 49.

7

Recreational Life

Both climatic and occupational conditions must have allowed the Norsemen a fair amount of leisure time. Indeed, the sources, both literary and archaeological, provide evidence of a great variety of both indoor and outdoor activities that pleasantly occupied people's free time.

SPORTS

The Icelandic saga writers often mention athletic achievements when offering character portrayals of their protagonists. Although their descriptions are often exaggerated, it is clear that physical fitness and skills in sports were regarded as admirable qualities. The author of *Njals saga* (Njal's saga), for example, says as follows about the saga-hero Gunnar Hamundarson:

He was big and strong and an excellent fighter. He could swing a sword and throw a spear with either hand, if he wished, and he was so swift with a sword that there seemed to be three in the air at once. He could shoot with a bow better than anyone else, and he always hit what he aimed at. He could jump higher than his own height, in full fighting gear, and just as far backward as forward. He swam like a seal, and there was no sport in which there was any point in competing with him.[1]

Weapons training was a favorite sporting activity and probably essential for young men. Swordplay, archery, and the throwing of spears are frequently referred to in the sources. Gunnar is said to have been able to throw a spear with either hand, but the art of throwing spears with both hands at the same time and catching a spear in the air seems to have been practiced as well. Stone throwing also formed part of the training of future warriors, and it is often mentioned as being used in battles; for stone throwing a sling was sometimes used.

Tests of physical strength included wrestling, fistfighting, and the lifting of heavy stones. Among activities that involve a high degree of physical agility and balance, the sources mention mountain climbing and the ability to step from oar to oar outside the railing of a ship while it was being rowed. The Norwegian King Olaf Tryggvason was hailed as a master of both arts and was said to have excelled also in juggling with knives.

Running and jumping were activities in which children also participated. Much the same applies to swimming, which appears to have been practiced by women as well, though probably not for competitive purposes. In his saga about the sons of the Norwegian King Magnus (*Magnussona saga*) in *Heimskringla* (Disc of the world), Snorri Sturluson distinguishes between three types of swimming: diving, long-distance swimming, and a type of contest in which two swimmers try to duck each other.

Skiing and skating were the primary winter sports, although among adults skis and skates were also important means of transport on snow and ice. A passage in Snorri Sturluson's saga about the sons of King Magnus shows the use of skates in sporting contests and as tests of masculine courage. Here, in a boasting contest between King Eystein and his brother King Sigurd, the latter says to the former: "I was so good at skating that I did not know anyone who could vie with me; but you were not better at that than a cow."[2]

Horse racing and horse fighting were probably common, although only the latter is mentioned in the sources and usually because of the dissension that often occurred among the owners of the horses. The rules of horse fighting are unclear, but it seems that two stallions were pitted against one another within sight and smell of fenced-off mares. The fight frequently resulted in the death of one of the stallions.

Hunting as a sport was limited to Denmark, where it was not a particularly important source of food or wealth. A great variety of sea birds appear to have been hunted; among terrestrial birds partridges were the most important. Deer and hares were the main animals hunted for meat, while foxes were hunted for their furs and because they killed domestic animals. The weapons used were bow, spear and, later, crossbow. Stalking was the most common form of hunting, though the practice of chasing game, usually with dogs, was by no means uncommon. In addition, a variety of traps and snares was used. The right to hunt generally belonged to the owner of the land. The majority of hunters were farmers; professional hunters were found only at the courts. Gradually, hunting became a privilege of princes and nobles, who would reserve certain geographical areas for themselves; it is, however, doubtful if this had any noticeable effect on the hunting activities of the farmers.

GAMES

Icelandic sources often refer to a ball game akin to hockey called *knatt-leik*. The game is not known in the other Nordic countries, and it is believed to have come to Iceland via Norwegian emigrants from England. The rules of the game, which was popular among both children and adults, are unclear, but it is known that it was played with a bat and a little, hard ball usually on a smooth field of ice. The game could be played by two individuals or two teams, but it had to be played person against person. The game was a tough one, which often resulted in injuries, and, like horse fighting, it appears to have attracted many spectators.

Board games, called *tafl*, were a favorite indoor pastime, and archaeological finds reveal that they were played all over Scandinavia. The pieces were made of glass (clearly imported), amber, clay, stone, or, more commonly, bone. The colors vary, but it is likely that each game had pieces in two colors. It is not known how many pieces a complete set required, primarily because very few boards have been preserved and hardly any intact.

There were at least three varieties of board games: *hnefatafl*, which is probably the oldest game; *skaktafl*, which first appears in the twelfth century and may have come to Scandinavia from France and England; and *kvatrutafl*, which seems to have been less common. *Hnefatafl* was a type of "hunting game," in which one or more pieces tried to escape from a larger number of "hunters." *Skaktafl* was a kind of "war game" similar to modern chess. *Kvatrutafl* appears to have been analogous to modern backgammon. Of the three games, certainly *hnefatafl* and *kvatrutafl* were played with a die, and excavations of graves have revealed a fair number of dice (usually made of bone) from all over Scandinavia.

MUSIC AND DANCE

Very little is known about the musical life of the Scandinavians in the Viking age, but literary sources tell that music was recognized as an art and that musical proficiency was considered an accomplishment fitting for a cultured man. *Orkneyinga saga* (Saga of the Orkney Islanders), for example, tells that Earl Rognvald Kali Kolsson (d. 1158) included harp playing among his primary skills. Evidently, music was considered an accompaniment to merrymaking, for in the mythical-heroic *Bosa saga* (Saga of Bosi) it is related that Bosi (in the guise of King Godmund's harp player) played tunes at the wedding party held at King Godmund's court. According to the saga, Bosi played with such vigor that knives, dishes, and everything that wasn't held down began to move, and many people started to dance. Although the harp is the musical instrument most commonly referred to, we also hear of fiddles, lyres, and lutes. No instrumental music has survived from the Viking age and probably none was ever committed to writing.

As evident from *Bosa saga,* dancing certainly existed, and the custom of dancing at weddings is believed to be old. The practice of dancing during a wake and after a successful birth is also considered to have originated in pre-Christian times. The latter was a woman's feast, which in addition to dancing entailed drinking and the mocking of a male figure made of straw. During the twelfth century, the European ring-dance became established in Scandinavia, where it remained popular for centuries.

ENTERTAINMENT

Feasting was the most common social diversion in the Viking age. It provided respite from labor and opportunities for physical relaxation. The feasts included seasonal celebrations and commemorations of personal events. In origin both were associated with pagan sacrifices, and although Christian leaders tried to purge these ceremonial feasts of pagan elements, they retained the timing of them and associated them with commemorative days of Christianity or the feast days of saints. Typical of this endeavor is the story of the Norwegian King Olaf Tryggvason, of whom it is reported that he abolished heathen sacrifice and libations and replaced them, to please the populace, with festival toasts at Christmas and Easter, and Midsummer ale and autumn mead at Michaelmas. It is telling that the pagan name for the midwinter feast, Yule, is still used for Christmas.

Hospitality and generosity were qualities especially characteristic of the Scandinavians. In his *Gesta Hammaburgensis ecclesiae pontificum* (Activities of the prelates of the Church of Hamburg), Adam of Bremen stresses this quality, particularly among the Swedes, saying:

Although all the Hyperboreans are noted for their hospitality, our Swedes are so in particular. To deny wayfarers entertainment is to them the basest of all shameful deeds, so much so that there is strife and contention among them over who is worthy to receive a guest. They show him every courtesy for as many days as he wishes to stay, vying with one another to take him to their friends in their several houses. These good traits they have in their customs.[3]

These virtues were given expression in the hosting of parties for friends and kinsmen. Obviously, the size and grandeur of the feast depended on the occasion and the host's social and economic status. A royal feast would no doubt have been quite extravagant with an elaborate spread of food and drink and lasted several days. Indeed, Adam of Bremen says about the Danish King Sven Estridsson (r. 1047–1074) that he indulged in feasting, as was the custom among the barbarians. He also mentions that the treaty of alliance between King Sven and the archbishop of Hamburg-Bremen had been confirmed and celebrated by a sumptuous feast that lasted eight days.

The feasts probably did not differ substantially from those held elsewhere in Western Europe, but there is reason to believe that they were rowdier and involved heavier drinking. Drinking is often referred to in Icelandic sources but was probably more common in Scandinavia than in the Norse colonies in the North Atlantic, which may have had somewhat limited supplies of alcoholic beverages. The sagas, for example, relate more details of games and entertainment in Iceland but reveal more drunkenness in Norway. The appropriate way to drink was without inhibition, and competitive drinking appears to have been common. When the drinking horn was passed, a man could not refuse unless he was old or sick, and if someone tried to refuse he was penalized by being forced to drain an extra cup. The sources are silent on the matter of hangovers, but they do include descriptions of vomiting as a result of excessive drinking. A spectacular example of projectile vomiting is given in *Egils saga* (Egil's saga), where it is told that when Egil realized he could not tolerate more alcohol, he went over to his devious host, put both hands on his shoulders, and pressed him hard against a pillar. He then heaved up a vomit of massive proportions that gushed all over his host's face, into his eyes, nostrils, and mouth, and then flooded down his chest so that he was almost suffocated. The Sagas of Icelanders describe many drunken parties, but the voice of sensibility and experience speaks clearly from the eddic poem *Havamal*:

> It isn't as good as it's said to be,
> ale, for the sons of men;
> for the more he drinks, the less he knows
> about the nature of men.[4]

As is commonly known, alcohol loosens the tongue, and verbal contests appear to have been a common consequence of intoxication. As a man became drunk, he was likely to make statements he normally would have kept to himself. He might brag about himself and insult others, and such provocations would inevitably lead to new and probably more contemptuous and offensive replies. Soon a verbal duel or contest would be taking place that would increase in intensity as the men became more and more intoxicated. The goal was, of course, to improve verbal skill and performance without showing the effects of alcohol. Old Norse-Icelandic literature distinguishes between two types of flyting: *senna* and *mannjafnad*. The former is generally defined as a formal exchange of insults and threats; here one individual assails another in a verbal duel both by the insults themselves and by the wit through which they are created. The latter is defined as a formal exchange of boasts; here two individuals attempt to eclipse each other with boasting accounts of their own accomplishments.

The recital of poetry, which is closely related to verbal contests, was also a favorite form of entertainment and is also commonly associated with the consumption of alcohol. After all, Odin, the god of drink, was also the god of poetry, and Odin's mead was poetic inspiration. Storytelling, on the

Daily Life of the Vikings

other hand, probably required soberness on the part of the performer, for the stories, whether new or old ones about living kings, distant ancestors, or mythical beings, could be long and intricate. The Icelanders, in particular, were known for their ability to tell stories and were often asked to entertain at royal courts abroad.

NOTES

1. *Njals saga* is quoted from Viðar Hreinsson, ed., *The Complete Sagas of Icelanders Including 49 Tales* (Reykjavík, Iceland: Leifur Eiríksson Publishing, 1997), 3:24.

2. *Heimskringla* is quoted from Snorri Sturluson, *Heimskringla: History of the Kings of Norway*, trans. Lee M. Hollander (Austin: University of Texas Press, 1964), p. 703.

3. Adam of Bremen is quoted from Adam of Bremen, *History of the Archbishops of Hamburg-Bremen*, trans. Francis J. Tschan, Records of Civilization: Sources and Studies, vol. 53 (New York: Columbia University Press, 1959), p. 203.

4. *Havamal* is quoted from Carolyne Larrington, trans., *The Poetic Edda* (Oxford: Oxford University Press, 1996), p. 16.

8

Religious Life

Christianity was slow in gaining a foothold in Scandinavia. Denmark became officially Christian around 960. Norway and the Norse colonies in the Atlantic followed in the beginning of the eleventh century. Sweden was more resistant to the persuasion or coercion of Christian missionaries and was not fully converted until the end of the eleventh century.

During most of the Viking age, the majority of Scandinavians shared the system of beliefs and mythology that Christians derogatorily labeled heathenism or paganism. The Scandinavians themselves had no specific word for their religion. The closest word for the concept was the Old Norse *siðr* (custom), which shows how integrated religion was in everyday life.

It is reasonable to assume that there was considerable variety among the religious ideas and attitudes of the Viking-age Scandinavians, who had no universal doctrines and no central church. The multiple versions of specific myths and the conflicting representations of principal gods like Odin and Thor suggest that the pagan Scandinavian religion was subject to extensive local variation. Moreover, it would be an error to suppose that the myths and religious practices of the Scandinavians remained static or fixed at any given period of time and nonsusceptible to outside influences. Unlike Christianity, the pagan Scandinavian religion was fluid and forbearing, and it never appears to have undergone the processes of open codification that characterized Christianity from its earliest stages onward.

For Scandinavians, the Viking age in particular was a period of much cultural exchange and many cultural changes, which are likely to have affected their religious convictions and orientations. For a number of Scandinavians, these changes involved uprooting and divorce from the social organization and culture in which they had grown up. Such people were also cut off from the religion of their ancestors. While some—and this applies to many of the colonizers of the islands in the North Atlantic—carried their religious traditions with them, others rejected religious belief altogether. The sources make frequent mention of "godless men," who, according to the medieval writers, believed only in themselves, in what they could do with their own strength and wits. No doubt Christian writers of the Middle Ages made more of these unbelievers than history justified, for in their view it was better to believe in no god than to bring sacrifice to stocks and stones, idols and demons; nonetheless, the stories probably reveal the attitudes of some people toward religion and religious practices in the Viking age. Yet others—and this applies especially to those who immigrated to Christian countries such as England, Ireland, and Normandy—conformed to Christian practices, either by adding Christ to their pantheon, or by receiving the *prima signatio* (a preliminary to christening), or by professing the Christian faith through baptism.

PAGAN SCANDINAVIAN RELIGION

Sources of Knowledge   Most of our knowledge about the pre-Christian religion in Scandinavia derives from three major sources. One is the group of mythological poems of the *Poetic Edda,* recorded in Iceland shortly after the mid-thirteenth century, that is, almost three centuries after Iceland officially became Christian. The date and place of the composition of the individual poems have been sources of debate and remain largely unresolved. Some may go back to the beginning of the Viking age; others may be only a little older than the manuscript containing them. Some may have their origin in Norway or Iceland; others may be from Ireland or Greenland or other western settlements. These poems are generally considered our most direct textual witness to Scandinavian paganism, though the poems typically avoid direct articulation of key beliefs and hint instead at bits and pieces of wisdom in cryptic allusions.

Another source is skaldic poetry, the composition of which began perhaps in the ninth century. Like eddic poetry, it was not written down until the advent of Christianity. One of the characteristics of skaldic poetry is the extraordinarily frequent use of complex kennings, which sometimes present myths in miniature. The use of mythological kennings in the composition of skaldic poetry well into the thirteenth century may at least in part explain how the pagan myths survived for centuries in Iceland.

The third source is the *Prose Edda* written in the 1220s by the Icelandic politician, historian, and poet Snorri Sturluson. It remains the most valuable summary of Norse myths, although the influence of Christianity is quite apparent. However, the work was not, in the first place, designed as a treatise on mythology, but rather on prosody. As it seems, Snorri feared that the skaldic art was dying out and wished to revive and explain it (see chapter 4). His *Edda* includes rules of poetic diction, quotes from skaldic and eddic poems, and a retelling of many myths that lie behind the kennings of skaldic poetry. One section in particular, *Gylfaginning* (The deluding of Gylfi), presents a systematic account of Norse mythology.

The primary source for our understanding of the pagan Scandinavian cosmos is Snorri, who in his *Edda* specifies a cosmological model of concentric circles. The outer circle is Utgard (the outer yard), where giants and monsters live. In **The Cosmos** the inner circle is Midgard (the middle yard), surrounded by a vast ocean. Humans and gods inhabit Midgard, which is also the home of the dwarfs said to live in a northern region called Nidavellir, while somewhere below was the land of dark elves (Svartalfheim). Within Midgard are Asgard and Vanaheim, where the two tribes of gods and goddesses, called the Aesir and the Vanir, make their home. Here each god or goddess lives within his or her own sanctuary in a firmly structured community not much different from that of the wealthy farmer of the Viking age. In this horizontal model, there is, therefore, no topological distinction between Midgard and Asgard/Vanaheim and no separation between humans and gods. However, the horizontal model is supplemented by a vertical model, in which gods are placed in an upper region and humans in a lower region. A flaming rainbow bridge called Bifrost connects the two regions. Above was Valholl (castle of the slain), Odin's palace, but even here gods and men coexisted, for it was the place to where Odin's female assistants, the valkyries, brought fallen warriors, the Einherjar, to spend their afterlife. In the upper region was also Alfheim, the land of the light elves. On the lowest level lay Niflheim, the world of the dead. Its citadel was Hel presided over by a death-goddess of the same name.

At the very center of the world was a huge ash tree called Yggdrasill. Three roots supported the trunk: one passed into Asgard, a second into the realm of the frost-giants, and a third into Niflheim. Three wells lay at the base of Yggdrasill, one under each root. Under the root that reached to the world of frost-giants lay the Well of Mimir, the wisest of the Aesir. This well, in which all wisdom was stored, was where one of Odin's eyes was hidden; according to Snorri, Odin had begged for one draft from the well, but it was not granted until he placed his eye as a pledge. Under another root was the well Hvergelmir (roaring kettle), and under a third was the Well of Urd (fate), who in the eddic poem *Voluspa* (Prophecy of the seeress) is seen with two other demigoddesses or norns, Verdandi (being) and Skuld (necessity), ruling the destinies of not only humans, but also gods and giants. The three norns bring water and mud from the well to Yggdrasill every day, so that its branches will not decay, but the tree is continuously threatened by the living creatures—snakes, squirrels, stags—

that prey upon it, and in the end, at Ragnarok, it will fall just like the gods themselves.

The Pantheon

The male astral Aesir are usually identified as the principal recipients of worship among the Norsemen. Snorri gives their number as 12, excluding Odin, the All-father and head of the Aesir. Odin was the god of poetry, secret wisdom, and magic; the patron of warriors and aristocrats; and the creator of the human race, for he gave life and breath to Ask and Embla, the first man and woman, whom he made from tree trunks. Odin dwelt in Valholl with his wolves, Geri and Freki, and his ravens, Huginn and Muninn, who flew over the world every day and brought him tidings from afar. His weapon was the spear Gungnir, and he rode an eight-legged gray horse named Sleipnir. Odin's legitimate wife was the goddess Frigg, who knew the fates of men, and with her he sometimes sat on his throne looking over all the worlds. By Frigg, Odin was the father of Baldr, the most eloquent and the gentlest among the Aesir, whose death was brought about by the blind god Hod through the machinations of Loki, a cunning schemer, who both helped and hindered the gods. Part god and part demon, Loki was the son of the giant Farbauti and married to Sigyn, with whom he had a son, Narfi, but he also had issue by a giantess, Angrboda, and they turned out to be a sinister brood: the death-goddess Hel, the wolf Fenrir, and the Midgard serpent Iormungand. Snorri relates that when the gods realized that these three siblings were being raised in the realm of the giants, they pursued oracles and learned that they would bring them disaster. Accordingly, Odin threw Iormungand into the depths of the ocean, where he remained encircling the inhabited world; Hel he threw into the underworld; and Fenrir was fettered with a deceitful chain.

Another son of Odin was Thor, whose mother was Jord (earth). Thor was a warrior god and the defender of the Aesir against their natural enemies, the giants and giantesses. His weapon was the hammer Mjollnir, with which he held the forces of chaos in check. He also possessed a pair of iron gloves with which to grasp the hammer, and a belt; and when he girded himself with the belt his divine strength was doubled. Thor lived in Thrudheim (world of might). He was married to the goddess Sif, about whom little is known except that she had a son, Ull, who appears to have been a sky-god, and that her hair was of gold. Snorri tells that out of malice Loki once cut off Sif's hair, and the enraged Thor forced him to go to the black elves or dwarfs, who were considered skilled craftsmen, and prevail on them to forge a golden head of hair, which would grow like any other hair. Not only did the dwarfs forge the golden hair, but, by a ruse, Loki persuaded them to forge other treasures as well. These treasures were subsequently distributed among the gods: Odin received the spear Gungnir and the magic arm ring Draupnir, from which eight rings of equal weight dripped every ninth night; Thor received the golden hair and the hammer Mjollnir; and Frey received a golden-bristled boar and the ship Skidbladnir, which was so big that all the Aesir could board it fully armed, and which additionally always had a following wind and was built of so many pieces that it could be folded up and put in a purse.

Other sons of Odin are the courageous Ty, a god of justice and war, who lost his hand when, as a sign of good faith, he put it into Fenrir's jaws, as the wolf was chained up; Bragi, god of poetry and husband of the goddess Idun, who kept the precious apples of eternal youth which prevented the gods from growing old; and the enigmatic Heimdal, who is called the white god and said to have been born by nine maidens, all sisters. Heimdall dwelt in Himinbjorg (rocks of heaven) beside Bifrost, for he was the gods' watchman, guarding Asgard from the frost-giants. He owned Gjallarhorn (the ringing horn), whose note could be heard throughout all worlds, and at the first signs of Ragnarok, during which he and Loki kill each other, he blows his horn.

Two other gods and one other goddess lived in Asgard but were of the race of the Vanir, deities of fertility and wealth, with whom the Aesir were once at war. These are Njord and his twins, Frey and Freyja. The two were born to him by his sister, when he lived among his native tribe, which permitted incestuous unions. Njord lived in Noatun (harbor). He married the giantess Skadi, but the marriage was a failure and Skadi eventually returned to her home in the mountains. His son Frey also took his wife, Gerd, from the giant world, but in contrast to his father's marriage, Frey and Gerd's union was a happy one; indeed, the story of Frey's passion for Gerd as related in the eddic poem *Skirnismal* (Skirnir's poem) is one of the most charming Norse myths. Freyja, a goddess of love, who is known chiefly for her loose morals, married a character by the name of Od. Nothing is known about Od, but he is generally thought to be a doublet of Odin, who shared with Freyja the men who fell in battle and who learned from her the kind of magic called *seid*, which enabled its practitioners to see into the future, cause death, misfortune, and sickness, and deprive men of their wits. Freyja is sometimes referred to as the chief of the *disir*, who were tutelary goddesses attached to a person, a family, or a neighborhood, and closely connected with *fylgjur*, guardian spirits or fetches of an individual or a clan and representative of what one today would regard as inherent qualities.

These, then, were the chief gods, and beside them others about whom no myths have been preserved. They include Forseti, Baldr's son by his wife Nanna; Hoenir, a companion of Odin; Vidar and Vali, two sons of Odin; and Modi and Magni, two sons of Thor. The four last-mentioned had special parts to play, for they were to survive the Ragnarok and inherit Asgard.

In essence, Scandinavian mythology is about the continuous struggle between the gods and the giants, who may be **The Myths** regarded as personifications of the forces of order and chaos. The struggles are typically between individual gods and giants,

and most of them involve Odin and Thor, the two most famous and powerful of the Aesir. However, the two stand in sharp contrast to one another,
and in their combats with the giants they use very different means, which
serve to throw light on their characters.

Odin usually uses his immense wisdom as his weapon. His contest of
wit and lore against the giant Vafthrudnir as related in the eddic poem
Vafthrudnismal (Lay of Vafthrudnir) may serve as an example. It tells that
Odin went in disguise to the giant's court, wishing to test his wisdom. First
the giant asked Odin a few questions about the cosmos, and then god and
giant settled down to a contest of wits, on which each wagered his head. It
was Odin's turn to ask questions, and the giant competently answered 17
of them. He told of the origin of the earth, heaven, moon, and sun, of the
worlds of the dead, of life in Valholl, of Ragnarok and its sequel. But he was
defeated by the 18th question: what did Odin whisper into his son Baldr's
ear as the dead god was being placed on the funeral pyre? Only Odin knew
the answer to this, and so the giant's head was forfeit:

> No man knows what you said in bygone days
> into your son's ear;
> with doomed mouth I've spoken my ancient lore
> about the fate of the gods;
> I've been contending with Odin in wisdom;
> you'll always be the wisest of beings.[1]

The episode reveals a couple of Odin's many unattractive attributes: his
low cunning and his propensity for disguises. Such conduct may appear
peculiar for a supreme god, but it is important to bear in mind that the
gods' status did not necessarily mean that their behaviors were intended
for emulation by humans. The assumption that gods are meant to be imi-
tated is a Christian view, based on a Hellenistic notion of discipleship.

Odin's great wisdom had in large measure to do with his mastery of
poetry, which he had stolen from the giants and given to gods and
humans. Several versions of this important myth are preserved; the latest
and most lucid, that of Snorri in his *Edda*, may be summarized as follows:

When peace had been concluded between the Aesir and the Vanir, the parties signified their friendship by spitting into a vessel. From the contents they created
Kvasir, who was so wise that he could answer all questions. Kvasir travelled
widely throughout the world imparting his wisdom to others and came to the
home of two dwarfs, Fjalar and Galar. The dwarfs secretly killed him, telling the
gods that he had suffocated in intelligence because no one was sufficiently educated to ask him questions. However, the dwarfs let his blood run into three huge
vessels and mixed it with honey. Whoever drank of this mead became a poet or
learned man.

When the dwarfs later entertained the giant Gilling, they invited him to go out
to sea in a boat with them, but the dwarfs rowed onto a shoal and the boat cap-

sized. Gilling could not swim and was drowned. Enraged, Gilling's son Suttung carried the dwarfs out to a skerry below high-water level. But the dwarfs saved themselves by offering Suttung as atonement in compensation for his father the precious mead. Suttung took the mead home with him and put his daughter Gunnlod in charge of it.

The story now turns to Odin, who wanted to win the mead back from the giants. Travelling under the name of Bolverk (evil-doer), he took service with Suttung's brother Baugi. As his wages he demanded one drink of Suttung's mead, but Suttung flatly refused a single drop. Then Bolverk got out an auger called Rati, bored a hole in the rock of Suttung's castle, turned himself into the form of a snake, and crawled through the hole. He went to where Gunnlod was and slept with her for three nights. In the end, she granted him three draughts of the mead, but Bolverk emptied all three vessels. In eagle form he flew back to the Aesir, who had containers ready for him by the walls of Asgard. Odin regurgitated the mead into them, but since Sutting, also in eagle form, was close on his tail, some of it spilt on the way. Anyone could have that, and it is called the rhymester's share. "Thus," Snorri says, "we call poetry Odin's booty and find, and his drink and his gift and the Aesir's drink."[2]

While the deceitful and complex Odin used wit and cunning, that is, strategy, against the forces of chaos, the simpleminded and straightforward Thor used his hammer Mjollnir, that is, force. Among the giant enemies of Thor, Hrungnir was particularly forceful, and the myth about their encounter appears to have been especially popular. Indeed, the eddic poem *Lokasenna* (Flyting of Loki) treats it as a commonly known story, and a picture showing Thor's contest was painted on a shield given to the late ninth-century skald Thjodolf of Hvin, who described the scene in his poem *Haustlong* (Autumn long). Snorri in his *Edda* gives an extended version relating that Odin and Hrungnir had a wager together, each insisting that he had the better horse. Odin galloped off on Sleipnir and Hrungnir after him on Goldmane, and Hrungnir inadvertently found himself in Asgard, where he was offered a drink. As he got drunk, he began to boast of how he would destroy all of Asgard with all its gods and goddesses except Freyja and Sif, whom he would keep to himself. In their distress, the Aesir sent for Thor, who arrived in great rage, but Hrungnir claimed Odin's protection and agreed to fight Thor on the border of their territories. For the duel, the giants made a person of clay to support Hrungnir. Hrungnir himself had a three-spiked heart of stone and a stone head, and he was armed with a stone shield and a whetstone. As Thor drew near accompanied by his assistant Thjalfi, Thjalfi ran forward and deceitfully told Hrungnir that he had better stand on his shield in case Thor attacked him from underground. Then Thor bore down on Hrungnir with thunder and lightning and hurled his hammer at him while Hrungnir threw his whetstone. The weapons met mid-air. The whetstone split in two, and one half lodged in Thor's forehead. But the hammer completed its course and shattered Hrungnir's skull. Thor then returned home with the stone in his skull. The witch Groa was summoned and began her chant, and the stone was loosened. Thor, wanting to reward her, told her how he had once carried her husband Aurvandill in a basket out of the land of the giants. One of Aurvandill's toes had stuck out of the basket and was frozen. Thor had broken it off and hurled it into the sky, where it became a star called Aurvandill's toe. Groa was so delighted with this news that she forgot her charms and the whetstone remained in Thor's head.

The best-known myth about Thor's struggles is, however, the one detailing his fight against his most formidable enemy, Iormungand, the Midgard serpent. The story fascinated not only writers and poets, but also pictorial artists. The motif of Thor fishing for the serpent is represented on carved rune stones in Altuna in Uppland, Sweden, and in Gosforth in Cumbria, England; and in his *Ragnarsdrapa* (Ragnar's poem), which gives verbal representation to a set of pictures painted on a shield, the skald Bragi Boddason describes what was evidently a picture of Thor's fishing expedition to catch the serpent. Two main versions of the myth exist; their main point of difference is that in one Thor conquered his enemy, while in the other he failed to do so. Snorri makes mention of both conclusions in his narration of the myth, but he shows preference for the latter:

Thor...went out across Midgard having assumed the appearance of a young boy, and arrived one evening at nightfall at a certain giant's; his name was Hymir. Thor stayed there as a guest for the night. And at dawn Hymir got up and dressed and got ready to row out to sea fishing. And Thor sprang up and was soon ready and asked Hymir to let him row out to sea with him. But Hymir said there would not be much advantage in having him along since he was small and just a youth.

"And you'll get cold if I stay out as long and as far as I am used to do."

But Thor said he need not hesitate to row out from shore since it was not certain whether it would be he that would first beg to row back...He asked Hymir what they were to use as bait, but Hymir told him to get his own bait. Then Thor went off to where he could see a certain herd of oxen belonging to Hymir. He took the biggest ox, called Himinhrjot, and tore off its head and took it down to the sea. Hymir had now launched the boat. Thor went aboard and took his seat in the well of the boat, took two oars and rowed...Then Hymir said they had reached the fishing ground where he usually sat catching flat fish, but Thor said he wanted to row much further, and they did another spurt of rowing. Then Hymir said they had got so far out that it was dangerous to be further out because of the Midgard serpent. But Thor said he would row on a bit and did so, but Hymir was then very unhappy. And when Thor had shipped his oars, he got out a line that was pretty strong, and the hook was no smaller or less mighty-looking. On to this hook Thor fastened the ox-head and threw it overboard, and the hook went to the bottom...The Midgard serpent stretched its mouth round the ox-head and the hook stuck into the roof of the serpent's mouth. And when the serpent felt this, it jerked away so hard that both Thor's fists banged down on the gunwale. Then Thor got angry and summoned up his As [i.e. divine] strength, pushed down so hard that he forced both feet through the boat and braced them against the sea-bed, and then hauled the serpent up to the gunwale...And just at the moment when Thor was grasping his hammer and lifting it in the air, the giant fumbled at his bait-knife and cut Thor's line from the gunwale, and the serpent sank into the sea. But Thor threw his hammer after it, and they say that he struck off its head by the sea-bed. But I think in fact the contrary is correct to report to you that the Midgard serpent lives still and lies in the encircling sea. But Thor swung his fist and struck at Hymir's ear so that he plunged overboard and one could see the soles of his feet. But Thor waded ashore.[3]

This encounter with Iormungand was, however, not Thor's last one, for the two were destined to meet again and kill each other at Ragnarok. *Voluspa* is the primary source for the details of this struggle that led to the end of the old gods' regime, and Snorri's account is drawn primarily from this poem, although he also relied on other sources. According to Snorri, the doom is to be foreshadowed by a fierce winter (*fimbulvetr*) and by strife and bitter warfare among people. One wolf will swallow the sun and another the moon. Stars will fall from the sky, and earthquakes will cause monsters to break loose from their bonds. Iormungand will leave the sea and cause the waters to rise, and the ship Naglfar, made from the uncut nails of the dead, will break its moorings. The sons of Muspell, a fire-demon, will board the ship with Loki at the helm. Surt, the chief of demons, will come by land and ride over Bifrost to storm Asgard. Heimdal will blow his horn and the gods will arm themselves. Frey will fight with Surt and be killed. Odin will fall before Fenrir to be avenged by Vidar, who will stab the monster in the heart. The hound Garm and Tyt will kill each other as will Loki and Heimdall. Thor will fight with Iormungand and destroy him, but he will be overcome by his poisonous venom. Then Surt will fling fire in every direction: Asgard, Midgard, the land of the giants, and Niflheim will burn, and the earth will sink into the sea. However, when the Ragnarok has passed, it will rise again. Odin's sons Vidar and Vali will still be alive, as will Thor's sons Modi and Magni, who will inherit Mjollnir. Baldr and Hod will come back from the world of the dead and inhabit the divine sanctuaries. A man and a woman will survive the holocaust, and their food will be the morning dew. And from these people a new race of humans will be born.

Different people or communities probably found different gods appealing during the Viking age, depending on familial, occupational, economic, regional, and cultural factors. The Sagas of Icelanders give a number of examples of people who converted from the worship of one god to another.

The Cult of the Gods

The Norwegian and Icelandic poets as well as Snorri present Odin as the foremost god. In his *Edda*, Snorri says:

Odin is highest and most ancient of the Aesir. He rules all things, and mighty though the other gods are, yet they all submit to him like children to their father.[4]

Their reason for doing so is obvious: Odin was the patron of aristocrats and poets, who were responsible for the formal poetry that has been preserved from the pagan era. But there are also indications that the cult of Odin spread and was especially practiced during the Viking age. Unpredictable, deceitful, and cynical, Odin was the god of war, and his human clientele consisted of kings, earls, chieftains, warriors, and poets. He would thus have appealed to the Vikings and the Viking style of life. Judging from place-name evidence, Odin was especially worshipped in Denmark and southern Sweden. He was said to be the ancestor of the Danish royal Skjoldung dynasty.

The hierarchy of the gods in terms of worship is not entirely clear, but it seems that whereas the upper classes favored Odin, the farming free men showed preference for Thor, a guardian of their communities and of the stability and law of these communities. Although the place-names of western Norway and Iceland, where he was particularly popular, show that his cult was firmly established in the latter part of the ninth century, it appears that his popularity increased and that he rose in eminence especially in the late pagan period. Thor defended gods and humans against giants and monsters, and so he was considered the best suited to defend paganism against the aggression of Christ. Indeed, in his account of the pagan temple in Uppsala in Sweden, the last bastion of Nordic paganism, in his *Gesta Hammaburgensis ecclesiae pontificum* (Activities of the prelates of the Church of Hamburg), Adam of Bremen testifies to his prominence. The temple supposedly had images of three gods: Thor, the most powerful, occupied the center of the hall, flanked by Odin and Frey. According to Adam's informants, Thor ruled in the sky and governed thunder, lightning, winds, rain, fair weather, and produce of the soil, and the Swedes sacrificed to him if there was danger of pestilence or famine. Although there is little indication of Thor's role as a divine promoter of fertility in Icelandic and Norwegian myths, it may account for his popularity in communities built upon agriculture and fisheries. Frey is generally the god standing for powers of fertility, peace, and prosperity, and Adam of Bremen tells that his idol in Uppsala was fashioned with a gigantic penis. Frey was particularly associated with the Swedes and was believed to be the ancestor of the Yngling dynasty of Uppsala.

Place-names in Scandinavia also suggest that Tyt, Ull, Njord, Frigg, and Freyja were venerated, but it is impossible to know if and to what degree public worship is implied by them.

Worship   Little is known about how the gods and otherworld beings were actually worshiped. The pagan Scandinavians had no creed or dogma, and the focus of their veneration appears not to have been on belief but on securing the benevolence of their gods. This was done primarily by bringing gifts to the gods in the hope and expectation that they would give a reward. The word generally used for "worship" is the verb *blota*, which also means "sacrifice."

On the whole, cult activity seems to have been decentralized and conducted either in private or led by local chieftains or wealthy farmers either in the halls of their farms (a hall of this kind was probably called a *hof*) or out of doors at places considered sacred and where images of gods might be located. Specially consecrated places are called *ve/vi*, and the word is found as an element in many place-names in Denmark and Sweden and often compounded with names of gods, such as Odense (older Odinsve) and Ullavi. The word *horg* was also applied to places of worship, and it is found as an element in place-names over a large area, though particularly in Iceland. It is sometimes used about a pile of stones set up in the open as an altar, but later it came to be applied to small, roofed temples or shrines perhaps used mainly for private or family worship. The cult of the *disir* was generally on a small scale and may have been conducted in such shrines and in unpretentious buildings.

Three major religious festivals were held each year: one in the fall after harvest, one in mid-winter (Yule), and one in the beginning of spring. Sometimes there was a fourth festival in mid-summer. Their purpose was primarily to placate the gods, avert catastrophes, secure success in the campaigns or raids planned, and promote fertility, good harvests, and peace. No doubt systematic attention was paid to oracles in these circumstances, and the casting of lots and performing of other rites to learn about the future in connection with the sacrifices was probably common. The central part of the festivals was the sacrifice. Sacrifices could be inanimate (agricultural produce, utensils, weapons) or animate (sheep, horses, even human beings). Animal sacrifices were connected with a sacrificial meal, which established a communion between the divinities and the participants. On such occasions toasts were also drunk to individual gods and in memory of deceased kinsmen. Most likely there were also hymns to the gods and dances, though on these aspects of the festivals the sources are virtually silent.

It is known that very large, official celebrations were held at Uppsala and at Lejre in Denmark, and in both places large monuments are still visible. It is likely that they were somehow associated with royal power. The Uppsala cult was described by Adam of Bremen, who tells of contemporary conditions, while the Lejre cult was described by the German Thietmar of Merseburg around 1000, that is, about half a century after the Christianization of Denmark. According to both accounts, people gathered every nine years, and both human beings and animals were sacrificed to the gods. In Lejre, 99 humans and 99 horses along with dogs and cocks were sacrificed; in Uppsala, 9 males of every creature were slaughtered, and Adam says that a Christian informant had seen as many as 72 carcasses hanging there side by side in a grove next to the temple. Adam further relates that this feast was for all the provinces of Sweden and that no exemption from attendance was allowed; those who had embraced Christianity could, however, buy themselves off from participation.

According to Adam, priests were assigned to perform the offerings in the temple, which, Adam claims, was adorned with gold. His description of the temple is, however, believed to have been inspired by Christian worship, because temples of such splendor are not known from earlier sources. Moreover, priesthood as a sacral office appears not to have been in existence. To be sure, there were pagan Scandinavian priests in the sense of persons with priestly functions. The Sagas of Icelanders mention both men and women who performed specific tasks at cult celebrations. But priestly function appears to have been only part of a man's secular position as the head of a household or community. Women were no doubt central to domestic cult practices. Indeed, fall or midwinter sacrifices to the *disir* appear to have been particularly associated with women's religious expression.

DEATH

Death and the Afterlife
Concerning beliefs about death, there was in Viking-age Scandinavia no consistency. Different people held different beliefs, and a person might well hold views that were logically inconsistent. Some believed that life went on after death, either in the grave or burial mound or in the underworlds known as Hel or Niflheim or in Odin's Valholl. Others believed that death was simply the end. The eddic poem *Havamal* (Sayings of the High One), which is considered to express the sentiments of certainly a number of the common people in Norway and Iceland in the late Viking age, scorns mystical beliefs, such as those in a future life. According to this poem, death is the greatest calamity that can befall a man; ill health and injury are better. Even a lame man can ride a horse, a handless man drive herds, and a deaf man join in battle; it is better to be blind than burned on the funeral pyre, for a corpse is a useless object.

Although a belief in the afterlife was not universal, the many graves excavated in Scandinavia and elsewhere nonetheless testify to a widespread notion of some form of existence after death. So too does the information available about the treatment of the dead, who typically drew their final breath either on the battlefield or at home as a result of warfare, accident, illness, or, in the case of women, as a consequence of childbirth.

The profession of undertaker is a relatively modern phenomenon, and so in the Viking age it was generally the duty of the relatives to prepare the body for funeral. When someone died, the first act was usually to close the nostrils, mouth, and eyes. Often, the body was washed and the head wrapped in a cloth. If the death occurred at home, the body was sometimes carried away by a special route to the place of burial. The latter was a precaution taken if it was feared that the dead person would become an evil dead walker, who might return and harm the living. Although the dead were generally regarded as guardians watching that the family's members upheld the rights and responsibilities incumbent upon the clan, persons who had disgraced themselves in death became outcast ancestors and would typically roam as ghosts. Thorolf Clubfoot, the most famous apparition in Old Norse-Icelandic literature, is in *Eyrbyggja saga* (Saga of the people of Eyri) and is said to have been buried under huge stones, which, however, did not prevent him from visiting his old home, where he persecuted the housewife and plundered the neighborhood, killing many on his way. Consequently, the grave was opened and Thorolf Clubfoot's body moved to a headland above the sea, buried again, and fenced off. Other measures sometimes taken in such circumstances were to decapitate the body and place the head by the dead person's buttocks or feet or to break the spine of the dead person to deprive him of his mobility. The most effective cure of malevolent returns was, however, to burn the body to ashes, which were commonly thrown into the sea. Indeed, this was eventually what put a stop to Thorolf Clubfoot's hauntings.

Behind stories such as the one about Thorolf Clubfoot lies a general belief that the afterlife was inseparable from the body. This belief is shown in a number of Sagas of Icelanders; in *Laxdoela saga* (Saga of the people of Laxardal), it told of a man by the name of Hrapp that he was buried upright beneath the threshold of his home, so that he might better guard its possessions. About the bodies of the various malicious apparitions it is often reported that they were incorrupt but hideous to look at. Thorolf Clubfoot is said to have looked more like a troll than a man, and it is specified that he was black as pitch and fat as an ox.

The pre-Christian burial customs testify to the belief in the continued existence of the dead. Many people were buried with possessions for use in the afterlife, and grave goods ranged from food and drink and clothing to weapons and tools of various kinds. Sometimes the dead were accompanied by their dogs, and there is also evidence that on occasion slaves were sacrificed to attend their masters or mistresses. Other grave goods had a more symbolic function; they include horses, boats, and wagons to represent the journey to the otherworld. But when it comes to notions about the otherworlds that might receive the dead, the beliefs are varied and often hazy. Some clearly believed that the home of the dead was in the grave or burial mound. In *Eyrbyggja saga,* mention is made of a holy mountain (Helgafell), where kinsmen of a clan gathered after death. It is related that when Thorstein Cod-biter, a wealthy farmer, drowned at sea, his entrance into the mountain was witnessed by his shepherd. The shepherd saw fires burning and heard the sound of feasting and good cheer. When he listened more closely, he heard that Thorstein was being welcomed by his deceased father.

These notions probably represent the general ideas about the afterlife of settled, peaceful farmers in the Viking age. The belief in Valholl belonged to the kings and warriors of the Viking age, although it is possible that it has its origin in the idea of mountains as a dwelling place for the dead.

The fact that the name is applied to certain rocks in southern Sweden that were believed to house the dead certainly points in that direction. The medieval Icelandic poets, however, present Valholl not as a rock but as a magnificent palace, in which dead kings and warriors gathered. In this it is possible that they were inspired or influenced by accounts of magnificent buildings abroad, such as Roman amphitheaters, in the same way as notions of Hel, to which, Snorri says, wicked men go, appear to have been influenced by Christian ideas about the underworld. It is also possible, if not probable, that to some extent the poets bequeathed to the Norsemen their images of Valholl and Hel and that these images were not especially representative of popular belief.

Funerals   Native sources provide very little information about funeral rites in Viking-age Scandinavia. The most detailed description comes from the pen of the Arab traveler Ibn Fadlan, who witnessed the funeral of a Rus chieftain at the river Volga in Russia. The following is an abridged version of Ibn Fadlan's eyewitness account:

When the chieftain died, he was placed in his grave for several days while his clothes were being cut out and made ready. The chieftain's slaves and servants were then asked who would die with him. When one had volunteered, she (in this case it was a female) was held to her word and treated like a princess. Meanwhile, a ship was drawn up on posts on the shore. A bier was placed on it, and an old woman called the Angel of Death covered it with fine tapestries and cushions. This woman was also in charge of embalming the dead man and preparing him. The chieftain's body was then raised from the grave and dressed in splendid garments. It was carried into a tent on the ship and laid on the tapestry. Food and alcohol were placed next to the dead man, and two horses and two cows were cut into pieces with a sword and thrown into the ship.

While these events took place, the woman who was to die with the chieftain went to each tent in the camp and had sexual intercourse with each owner. She was then raised three times from what looked like the frame of a door. On the third occasion she claimed that she saw her master in paradise and asked to be sent to him. Accordingly, she was taken to the ship, where she took off her jewelry, drank two beakers of alcoholic beverage, and sang. The Angel of Death led her into the tent followed by six men, who all had intercourse with her. The woman was then laid by the side of the dead chieftain. Four men held her hands and legs while the Angel of Death put a rope around her neck and gave it to two men to pull. The Angel of Death repeatedly stabbed her in the chest with a dagger while the two men choked her with the rope.

The dead chieftain's closest relative, who was naked, now lit a fire under the ship. Others threw burning wood on the fire, so that everything was burnt to fine ashes. Then they built a mound on the place where the ship had stood, raised a large post in the middle of it with the names of the chieftain and the king of the Rus on it, and went away.[5]

Ibn Fadlan adds that a man of the Rus tribe, who was present, had commented that the Arabs were stupid to place their beloved in the earth where worms would eat them instead of burning them, so that the dead would go instantly to paradise.

Although some details in this account, such as the Angel of Death and the naked kinsman, have no parallels in Norse sources, archaeological finds confirm several of the funeral rites described by Ibn Fadlan.

If we are to believe Adam of Bremen, deaths and funerals were not accompanied by great displays of emotion. About the Danes he comments that "tears and plaints and other forms of compunction, by us regarded as wholesome, are by the Danes so much abominated that one may weep neither over his sins nor over his beloved dead."[6]

Both cremation and inhumation burial were practiced in Viking-age Scandinavia, though the former was more common in Denmark than elsewhere.

Burial Practices

Normally, the dead was buried in a coffin or, more elaborately, in a chamber. Those who lived in the country buried their dead on their estates, while city dwellers usually buried them in a communal cemetery inside or, more commonly, outside the city walls. The graves were usually marked by mounds (although flat graves are not infrequent), wooden posts, or stone settings of various shapes—oval (boat shaped, perhaps to symbolize death as a voyage), round, square, or triangular. Rune stones are generally not associated with graves.

The mounds could be large or small. Some of the small mounds are no more than two or three meters in diameter and no more than 0.15 m (5.9 in.) high; the largest mound in Scandinavia, the pre-Viking-age Raknehaug in Norway, is 95 m (311.67 ft.) in diameter and about 19 m (62.3 ft.) high. The large mounds were typically reserved for royalty. Notable examples of large Viking-age mounds are the two royal mounds at Jelling, the northern one with a large wooden burial chamber; and the mounds of Gokstad and Oseberg, Norway, containing unburnt ship-burials, which were common in Norway and Sweden but rare in Denmark, Iceland, and the Norse colonies.

The Oseberg ship-burial is without question the most spectacular grave in Scandinavia. The site was excavated in 1904, and the grave has generally been dated to around 800. The burial was placed in a 21.6 m (70.86 ft.) long and 5 m (16 ft.) wide ship, and originally the bodies of two women were placed in the burial chamber built onto its deck. One is of a woman 50 to 60 years old with bad arthritis, the other between 20 and 30 years old. In addition to the ship, a wagon and four sledges were found as well as wooden artifacts including troughs, ladles, chests, boxes, a plain work sledge, a hoe, a dung fork, and shovels. Oseberg also contains textiles, both imported and local, tools for textile work, metalwork, and plant remains. Because of the wealth of the burial, it is believed that it must have been for a member of the ruling dynasty, who was evidently accompanied by a female servant.

Such splendid burials as the Oseberg ship-burial are, however, the exception rather than the rule, and generally it can be said that the Scandinavian graves reveal a high degree of social stratification: graves vary according to the status and wealth of the deceased. This stratification is especially evident in market towns such as Hedeby, in which rich grave mounds filled with valuables lie beside the humble graves of poor farmers containing only insignificant grave goods or none at all.

As Christianity gradually came to replace the Scandinavian paganism, inhumation in a consecrated churchyard became the norm along with a more minimalist approach to interment. The dead were shrouded simply in a sheet and placed in a plain earth or wooden grave oriented east-west, devoid of grave goods.

CHRISTIANITY

The Scandinavians had known of Christianity for several hundred years before the conversion took place. They had become acquainted with it in the course of their raids, Anglo-Saxon and German monks had come to Scandinavia as missionaries, and some of the Scandinavians who settled abroad had even permitted themselves to be baptized.

On the whole, there appears among the pantheistic Scandinavians to have been very little genuine opposition to the new faith and to the idea of a new god. A telling example is provided by the German priest Rimbert, who in his life of Saint Ansgar described the missionary activities of the saint among the Danes and the Swedes. Rimbert relates that when Ansgar was on his second mission to Birka around the middle of the ninth century, one of the Swedes, who claimed to have been at a meeting of the gods of the land, declared that the gods objected to the introduction of a foreign god but were willing to accept the recently deceased King Erik as one of their number. According to the Swede, the gods had asked him to make this presentation to the king and the people:

You, I say, have long found us gracious towards you. With our support you have held this most fertile land—your dwelling-place—in peace and prosperity for many years. On your part you have performed sacrifices and rendered us your votive offerings. Your allegiance has been pleasing. But now you are withholding your customary sacrifices and becoming slack in your voluntary offerings. What displeases us even more, you have raised up an alien god over us. So if you want us to continue gracious to you, augment the neglected sacrifices and offer greater votive gifts. Reject the cult of another god whose teaching is contrary to ours. Do not turn to his service. In any case if you want to have more gods, if we are not adequate to your purposes, we are ready to admit to our society Erik, once your king, so that he may take his place among your gods.[7]

The matter of letting the Christian cult remain in Birka was tested by casting lots, which to the Swedes' dislike fell out in favor of the new religion. In the discussions that followed, one man advocated tolerance and drew attention to the fact that in difficult or dangerous times many of them had called on the Christian god, who had proved himself powerful and willing to help out. According to Rimbert, he was able to persuade the people gathered there to show tolerance toward Christianity:

When he had finished his speech, the whole crowd together agreed that the priests should remain with them, and that they could perform everything that was consonant with the Christian mysteries without hindrance. And so the king left the assembly, directing his officer to accompany the bishop's envoy to report the people's acceptance of what he proposed.[8]

Old Norse-Icelandic literature testifies to the existence of several individuals who were mixed in their beliefs. One of the best known is Helgi the Lean, who in *Landnamabok* is said to have believed in Christ (he was raised in Ireland) but invoked Thor to guide him at sea and when difficult decisions had to be made. It is further reported that when Helgi the Lean approached the coast of Iceland, he called on Thor to show him where to land, and the answer came that he must go to the north. But when he had established his new home, he named it Kristnes (Christ's point).

The mixture of the two religions is also discernible in archaeological finds. Representations of Thor's hammer and Christian crosses appear side by side, and a tenth-century soapstone mold for making both cross and Mjollnir amulets found at Trendgården in Himmerland, Denmark, indicates the close association of the two symbols toward the end of the pagan era. A tenth-century amulet found at Foss in southwest Iceland seems to be a hybrid of a hammer and a cross, perhaps the creation of a man of a mixed religion. A miniature silver ax is also reported to have been found at Foss; in form, it resembles the hammer and may be associated with Thor. The find at Foss throws light on an interesting passage in *Landnamabok* (Book of settlements), which tells that the Orkney migrant Einar Thorgeirsson marked his new territory in Iceland with an ax (symbolizing Thor), an eagle (symbolizing Odin), and a cross (symbolizing Christ). Most likely, Einar and his men were of a mixed belief like Helgi the Lean and placed their new land under the protection of three gods: Thor, Odin, and Christ.

As the Scandinavians became better acquainted with Christianity, they gradually came to understand that Christianity meant that only one god could and should be worshiped; but Christian concepts of guardian angels and saints probably filled the roles of several of the pagan gods and supernatural beings. Some of the latter, such as the elves and land-spirits, have, however, survived into modern times and figure prominently in folktales collected in the nineteenth century.

No doubt, there was much in Christianity that the believers in the pagan Scandinavian religion found appealing. For one thing, Christianity presented them with a just and righteous god who was not subject to Ragnarok but ruling through eternity. It gave them firm answers to questions

The larger Jelling rune stone. Face C has Scandinavia's oldest portrayal of Christ. Photo courtesy of the National Museum of Denmark.

about death, life after death, and the purpose of it all. And it provided them with an unambiguous system of moral principles or values in which goodness was rewarded and wickedness was punished. On a more practical level, Christianity required no changes in the old legal system, and, at least in its early stages, it could easily adapt itself to existing societal forms.

The Conversion   Although the conversion of the Scandinavian countries was a long process of contacts between the Scandinavians and their Christian neighbors in the south and west, it may, for practical purposes, be said to have taken place when the kings of the individual countries, who were closely linked with the traditional cults, chose to abandon pagan sacrifices in favor of Christian rites.

The Danish King Harald Klak was the first Scandinavian king to be baptized. The ceremony took place in Mainz, Germany, in 826, but since Harald Klak was exiled a year later, his conversion had little effect. Nonetheless, in the century that followed, Christianity made considerable progress: many people converted, and several churches were built, not least due to the missionary activities of Saint Ansgar. However, the German priest Poppo is the one normally credited with converting the Danes and their king, Harald Bluetooth, to Christianity. This is considered to have occurred around 960. The Saxon Widukind, a contemporary writer, relates that Poppo demonstrated the superiority of Christ by carrying a bar of red-hot iron in his bare hands without suffering any harm. By this ordeal, King Harald Bluetooth decided to convert, and on the greater Jelling rune stone he declares himself responsible for introducing Christianity into Denmark.

Although Hakon the Good, who had been fostered in England at the Christian court of King Aethelstan of Wessex, was Norway's first Christian king, the conversion of Norway is generally associated with King Olaf Tryggvason, who had led great Viking raids to the British Isles, where he had been baptized. When in 995 he became king, he set out to Christianize Norway and managed to make the entire coastal area of Norway convert.

It was not only in Norway, however, that King Olaf tried to spread Christianity. His pressure on the Icelandic chieftains was probably one of the main reasons why the Icelanders accepted the new faith at the Althing, their parliament, in 999/1000. The story of the introduction of Christianity in Iceland is very well documented and related in detail by Ari Thorgilsson in his *Islendingabok* (Book of Icelanders). Ari tells that when King Olaf's missionary Thangbrand had been exiled from Iceland because of

Tenth-century soapstone mold found in Denmark for making both the cross and Thor's-hammer amulets. Photo courtesy of the National Museum of Denmark.

his hot temper and largely failed in his attempt to convert the Icelanders, King Olaf became angry and threatened to mutilate or kill every pagan Icelander in Norway at the time. Two Icelandic chieftains, Hjalti Skeggja-son and Gissur Teitsson, happened to arrive in Norway that same summer, however. They negotiated with King Olaf and promised to see to it that the Icelanders would be Christianized in the near future. Hjalti and Gissur returned to Iceland in time for the Althing in 999/1000, where many people had gathered. The pagans remained firm, and for a while it looked as if a religious war would break out between the two factions, but eventually a number of chieftains took an initiative toward a compromise. They agreed to choose Thorgeir Thorkelsson, a moderate in the pagan group, as lawspeaker and promised to obey his verdict. According to *Islendingabok,* Thorgeir withdrew for a whole day and night to concentrate on the solution to this problem. The next day he requested that all people gather at the assembly site and stressed the need for one law and one state, for, as he said, if the law was split, the peace would be broken. He also emphasized the need for a compromise, claiming that it was unwise to leave the making of decisions up to people who wanted the most of everything. Then he delivered his verdict and declared that all people should be Christian and baptized.

In addition to Christianizing Iceland, King Olaf Tryggvason also made the Norse colonists in Greenland accept Christianity. The conversion of Norway was completed by his successor, King Olaf Haraldsson, who was declared a saint shortly after his death.

The conversion of Sweden is less clearly documented. Olof Skotkonung, king of the Götar and Svear, is generally recognized as the first Christian king, and most people in Västergötland were probably Christian by the mid-eleventh century. Indeed, under Olof Skotkonung a bishopric was established from Hamburg-Bremen, at Skara in Västergötland. However, paganism remained entrenched in Uppland, Gotland, and Småland, and pagan cults continued to be celebrated at Uppsala for many decades. Most likely, the cults were abandoned early in the twelfth century, at which time it is believed that Sweden was predominantly Christian.

The First Century of Christianity The introduction of Christianity obviously brought with it many changes. Conversion meant accepting not only Christian beliefs but also the regulations and rituals of the Christian church. Every Christian was required to know at least the *Pater noster,* the Nicene Creed, and probably also the formula for baptism (in emergency cases). Moreover, every Christian was expected to show respect for the rules of the liturgical year through periodic abstention from work and certain foods and to receive communion at least annually. The pagan practices of eating horsemeat and exposing children were forbidden, marriage within certain degrees of kinship became unlawful, and the burial of the dead was now to take place in consecrated ground.

It is hardly surprising, therefore, that the implementation of Christianity in Scandinavia took a long time, in some places almost 200 years. During that time, dioceses and parishes were established, churches built, bishops consecrated, priests trained and ordained, tithes introduced, monasteries founded, and cults of Scandinavian saints instituted. A milestone in this development was the creation in 1103/1104 of an independent Scandinavian province with Lund (in what was then Denmark) as the archbishopric. Prior to that, Scandinavia had been under the authority of the archiepiscopal church of Hamburg-Bremen, which had been formed by amalgamation after Hamburg was sacked by Scandinavian raiders in 845. Lund remained the metropolitan see of all of Scandinavia until 1153, when the papal legate Nicholaus Brekespear came to Norway to establish a Norwegian archbishop's seat in Nidaros (modern Trondheim). The Church received its own national organization with parishes and bishoprics under the leadership of the archbishop. The Norwegian church province comprised no fewer than 11 bishoprics, 5 in Norway proper—Nidaros, Bergen, Oslo, Stavanger, and Hamar—and 6 in the island communities in the west—Skalholt and Holar in Iceland, Greenland, the Faroe Islands, the Orkney and Shetland Islands, and the Hebrides and Isle of Man. In 1164, the Uppsala archbishopric was established with authority over the sees of Skara and Linköping in Götaland and of Strängnäs and Västerås on the shores of Lake Mälaren.

NOTES

1. The stanza from *Vafthrunismal* is quoted from Carolyne Larrington, trans., *The Poetic Edda* (Oxford: Oxford University Press, 1996), p. 49.

2. Snorri's *Edda* is quoted from Snorri Sturluson, *Edda,* trans. Anthony Faulkes (London: Dent & Sons, 1987), pp. 61–64.

3. Quoted from Sturluson, *Edda,* pp. 46–47.

4. Quoted from Sturluson, *Edda,* p. 21.

5. P. G. Foote and D. M. Wilson, *The Viking Achievement: The Society and Culture of Early Medieval Scandinavia* (London: Sidgwick & Jackson, 1970), pp. 408–11.

6. Adam of Bremen is quoted from Adam of Bremen, *History of the Archbishops of Hamburg-Bremen,* trans. Francis J. Tschan, Records of Civilization: Sources and Studies, vol. 53 (New York: Columbia University Press, 1959), p. 191.

7. Rimbert is quoted from R. I. Page, *Chronicles of the Vikings: Records, Memorials, and Myths* (Toronto: University of Toronto Press, 1995), pp. 228–30.

8. Rimbert, quoted from Page, *Chronicles of the Vikings,* pp. 228–30.

Glossary

Aesir   (sing. As) A family of (war) gods in pagan Scandinavian religion.

Althing   General assembly established in Iceland in 930.

amber   A hard, translucent yellow or orange fossil resin used for making jewelry and other ornamental objects.

Asgard   The home of the gods in pagan Scandinavian religion.

berserker   A warrior fighting in battle with frenzied violence and fury.

bride price   The amount that the prospective husband's family gives to the prospective wife's family at the wedding.

calk   A pointed extension on the toe or heel of a horseshoe, designed to prevent slipping.

carding   The process of brushing wool so that the fibers get untangled and run in a single direction.

compurgation   The practice of clearing an accused person of a charge by having a number of people swear to a belief in his innocence.

cottager   The smallest sort of landholding commoner, holding insufficient land to support his family without doing additional labor.

crampon   An iron spike attached to the shoe to prevent slipping when walking on ice.

Danegeld   A tax levied in England in the Viking age to finance protection against Danish invasion.

Danelaw   Commonly used as a term for the land of the Vikings in England, but it never became a true political entity, and the word simply means "the law of the Danes."

disir   (sing. *dis*) Tutelary goddesses attached to a person, a family, or a neighborhood.

distaff   A staff that holds on its cleft end the unspun wool or flax from which thread is drawn in spinning by hand.

dowry   The amount of money or land that a bride's father contributed at her wedding.

drottkvaett   Literally "court-meter"; the most common meter used in skaldic poetry.

eddic poetry   A collection of poems contained in an Icelandic manuscript from 1270–1280; the poems fall into two groups: mythological poems and heroic poems.

encrustation   The process of covering a surface with silver or copper wire pressed and hammered to form a pattern.

felag   A partnership or guild in which members owed each other mutual obligations.

filigree   Delicate ornamental work made from gold, silver, or other fine twisted wire.

fimbulvetr   A winter lasting for three years with no summer in between that precedes Ragnarok.

fornyrdislag   Literally "old-story-measure"; it is the most common narrative meter in eddic poetry, particularly in heroic poetry.

fulling   Soaking and pressing cloth in a mixture of fermented urine and hot water to shrink and thicken the cloth and reduce its oil content.

Futhark   The name of the runic alphabet.

fylgjur   (sing. *fylgja*) Guardian spirits or fetches of an individual or a clan.

galdralag   Literally "spell-measure"; one of the less commonly used meters in eddic poetry.

godi   (plur. *godar*) A chieftain.

godord   A chieftaincy.

heiti   Appellations, that is, nouns used in Old Norse-Icelandic poetry but not in everyday speech or in written prose.

Hel   The world of death in pagan Scandinavian religion presided over by a goddess of the same name.

highseat   The central section of one bench in the hall of a farmhouse and the rightful seat of the owner of the farm.

hird   The retinue accompanying kings, earls, or other rulers.

hoard   Two or more objects made of precious metal deliberately hidden in the ground.

holmganga   A duel typically held on an island and governed by very specific rules.

homespun   Wool and woolen products. It was Iceland's chief export and used as a standard exchange product.

hrepp   (plur. *hreppar*) A commune.

keelson A wooden structure resting on the keel of a ship.

kenning A term derived from the Old Norse-Icelandic verb "kenna" ("to know, recognize"), which in the phrase "kenna X vid Y" means "to call X by Y's name." It is a favorite figure in skaldic verse and is a device for introducing descriptive color or for suggesting associations.

knattleik A game played with a bat and a small hard ball on a field of ice.

Lapps A distinct people, also called Sami, inhabiting the northernmost part of Scandinavia.

leidang A naval levy.

ljodahatt Literally "song-meter"; it is a meter much used in the eddic mythological poems and especially in the didactic ones.

longhouse A hall or main room in an Icelandic farmhouse.

longport A fortified ship camp.

longship A collective, general term used for large warships with more than 32 oars.

malahatt Literally "speech-meter"; it is one of the less commonly used meters in eddic poetry.

mannjafnad A formal exchange of boasts.

mast partner A heavy block of wood resting on the crossbeam of a ship to provide additional support for the mast.

metempsychosis The transmigration of souls.

Midgard The home of gods and humans in pagan Scandinavian religion.

mork A unit of measurement, 214–217 or 257–260 grams.

Nicene Creed A formal statement of doctrine of the Christian faith.

odal A name applied to land and a technical term for inherited land bound by rules.

Pater noster The Lord's Prayer.

prima signatio A preliminary to christening.

Ragnarok The doom or twilight of the gods; the end of the world in pagan Scandinavian religion.

runes The letters of an alphabet used by ancient Germanic people, especially by the Scandinavians and Anglo-Saxons.

Rus Swedes or people of Scandinavian descent living on the upper Volga.

saga (plur. *sogur*) Medieval Icelandic and Scandinavian prose narratives usually about a famous hero or family or the exploits of heroic kings and warriors.

sauna A steam bath in which the steam is usually produced by pouring water over heated rocks.

seid A kind of magic practiced in pagan Scandinavian religion.

senna A formal exchange of insults and threats.

shieling A hut in the highland grazing pastures away from the farm, where shepherds and cowherders lived during the summer.

skald   A Scandinavian bard or court poet.

skaldic poetry   A term now used for all the early Old Norse-Icelandic alliterative poetry that is not eddic.

skein   A length of thread wound in a loose, elongated coil.

skerry   A small rocky reef or island.

stockfish   Fish, such as cod or haddock, cured by being split and air-dried.

tafl   A board game.

tang   A projection by which the blade for a sword is attached to the handle.

tapestry   Narrow strip of cloth with embroidered or woven decoration.

thing   An assembly of free men.

tithe   A tax or assessment of one tenth.

turf   Peat cuttings.

Utgard   The home of giants in pagan Scandinavian religion.

Valholl   The palace of Odin.

valkyries   Odin's female assistants.

Vanir   (sing. Van) A family of (fertility) gods in pagan Scandinavian religion.

weft   The horizontal threads interlaced through the warp in a woven fabric.

wergild   Compensation paid to the injured party for the killing of a person.

Yule   The pagan Scandinavian midwinter feast.

For Further Reading

TRANSLATIONS OF SELECTED MEDIEVAL TEXTS

Adam of Bremen. *History of the Archbishops of Hamburg-Bremen.* Trans. by Francis J. Tschan. Records of Civilization: Sources and Studies, vol. 53. New York: Columbia University Press, 1959.

Campbell, Alistair, ed. and trans. *Encomium Emmae Reginae.* Camden Society, 3d ser., vol. 72. London: Royal Historical Society, 1949.

Cross, Samuel Hazzard, and Olgerd P. Sherbowitz-Wetzor, eds. and trans. *The Russian Primary Chronicle: Laurentian Text.* Cambridge, MA: Medieval Academy of America, [n.d.].

Garmonsway, G. N., trans. *The Anglo-Saxon Chronicle.* Rev. ed. Everyman's Library, no. 624. London: J. M. Dent & Sons, 1960.

Hollander, Lee M. *The Skalds: A Selection of Their Poems with Introduction and Notes.* Ann Arbor: University of Michigan Press, 1968.

Hreinsson, Viðar, ed. *The Complete Sagas of Icelanders Including 49 Tales.* 5 vols. Reykjavík, Iceland: Leifur Eiríksson Publishing, 1997.

Larrington, Carolyne, trans. *The Poetic Edda.* Oxford: Oxford University Press, 1996.

Porphyrogenitus, Constantine. *De Administrando Imperio.* Ed. and trans. by Gy. Moravcsik and R.J.H. Jenkins. Rev. ed. Corpus fontium historiae Byzantinae 1. Washington, D.C.: Dumbarton Oaks Center for Byzantine Studies, 1967.

Smyser, H. M. "Ibn Fadlān's Account of the Rūs with Some Commentary and Some Allusions to *Beowulf.*" In *Franciplegius: Medieval and Linguistic Studies in Honor of Francis Peabody Magoun, Jr.,* ed. Jess. B. Bessinger, Jr. and Robert P. Creed, pp. 92–119. New York: New York University Press, 1965.

Sturluson, Snorri. *Edda.* Trans. Anthony Faulkes. London: Dent & Sons, 1987.

————. *Heimskringla: History of the Kings of Norway.* Trans. Lee M. Hollander. Austin: University of Texas Press, 1964.

Turville-Petre, E.O.G. *Scaldic Poetry.* Oxford: Clarendon Press, 1976.

Whitelock, Dorothy, ed. *English Historical Documents, c. 500–1042.* Rev. ed. English Historical Documents, vol. 1. London: Eyre & Spottiswoode, 1979.

REFERENCE WORKS

Graham-Campbell, James. *Viking Artefacts: A Select Catalogue.* London: British Museum Publications, 1980.

Pulsiano, Phillip, and Kirsten Wolf with Paul Acker and Donald K. Fry, eds. *Medieval Scandinavia: An Encyclopedia.* New York: Garland Publishing, 1993.

GENERAL

Almgren, Bertil, ed. *The Viking.* New York: Crescent Books, 1984.

Andersson, Thorstein, and Karl Inge Sandred, eds. *The Vikings: Proceedings of the Symposium of the Faculty of Arts of Uppsala University June 6–9, 1977.* Stockholm: Almqvist &Wiksell, 1978.

Arbman, Holger. *The Vikings.* Ed. and trans. Alan Binns. London: Thames & Hudson, 1961.

Bekker-Nielsen, Hans, Peter Foote, and Olaf Olsen, eds. *Proceedings of the Eighth Viking Congress, Århus 24–31 August 1977.* Odense, Denmark: Odense University Press, 1981.

Brøndsted, Johannes. *The Vikings.* Trans. Kalle Skov. London and Harmondsworth: Penguin Books, 1965.

Christiansen, Eric. *The Norsemen in the Viking Age.* Oxford: Blackwell, 2002.

Farrell, R. T., ed. *The Vikings.* London and Chichester: Phillimore & Co., 1982.

Fitzhugh, William W., and Elisabeth I. Ward. *Vikings: The North Atlantic Saga.* Washington and London: Smithsonian Institution Press, 2000.

Foote, Peter, and David M. Wilson. *The Viking Achievement: The Society and Culture of Early Medieval Scandinavia.* London: Sidgwick & Jackson, 1970.

Graham-Campbell, James. *The Viking World.* New Haven and New York: Ticknor & Fields, 1980.

Graham-Campbell, James, and Dafydd Kidd. *The Vikings.* London: British Museum Publications, 1980.

Jesch, Judith. *Women in the Viking Age.* Woodbridge: Boydell Press, 1991.

Jones, Gwyn. *A History of the Vikings.* Rev. ed. Oxford: Oxford University Press, 1984.

Klindt-Jensen, Ole. *The World of the Vikings.* Trans. Christopher Gibbs and George Unwin. London: Allen & Unwin, 1970.

Logan, F. Donald. *The Vikings in History.* 2nd ed. London: HarperCollins, 1991.

Magnusson, Magnus. *Vikings!* New York: E. P. Dutton, 1980.

Page, R. I. *Chronicles of the Vikings: Records, Memorials, and Myths.* Toronto: University of Toronto Press, 1995.

Roesdahl, Else. *Viking Age Denmark.* Trans. Susan Margeson and Kirsten Williams. London: British Museum, 1982.

————. *The Vikings.* Trans. Susan M. Margeson and Kirsten Williams. London: Penguin Press, 1991.

Samson, Ross, ed. *Social Approaches to Viking Studies.* Glasgow: Cruithne Press, 1991.

Sawyer, P. H. *The Age of the Vikings.* 2nd ed. London: Edward Arnold Ltd., 1971.

———. *Kings and Vikings: Scandinavia and Europe* A.D. *700–1100.* London and New York: Methuen, 1982.

———, ed. *The Oxford Illustrated History of the Vikings.* Oxford: Oxford University Press, 1997.

Sawyer, P. H., and Birgit Sawyer. *Medieval Scandinavia: From Conversion to Reformation, circa 800–1500.* Minneapolis: University of Minnesota Press, 1993.

Turville-Petre, G. *The Heroic Age of Scandinavia.* London: William Brendon and Son, 1951.

Wilson, David M. *The Vikings and Their Origins: Scandinavia in the First Millennium.* London: Thames and Hudson, 1970.

———, ed. *The Northern World: The History and Heritage of Northern Europe* A.D. *400–1100.* London: Thames and Hudson, 1980.

LANGUAGE, LITERATURE, AND RUNES

Haugen, Einar. *The Scandinavian Languages: An Introduction to their History.* London: Faber and Faber, 1976.

Jansson, Sven B. F. *Runes in Sweden.* 2nd. rev. ed. Trans. Peter G. Foote. [Stockholm]: Gidlund, 1987.

Meulengracht Sørensen, Preben. *Saga and Society: An Introduction to Old Norse Literature.* Trans. John Tucker. Odense, Denmark: Odense University Press, 1993.

Moltke, Erik. *Runes and Their Origin: Denmark and Elsewhere.* Trans. Peter G. Foote. Copenhagen: National Museum of Denmark, 1985.

Page, R. I. *Runes.* London: British Museum Publications, 1987.

Sawyer, Birgit. *The Viking-Age Rune-Stones.* Oxford: Oxford University Press, 2000.

Vikør, Lars S. *The Nordic Languages: Their Status and Interrelations.* Nordic Language Secretariat Publications, no. 14. Oslo: Novus Press, 1995.

RELIGION

Carver, Martin, ed. *The Cross Goes North: Processes of Conversion in Northern Europe,* A.D. *300–1300.* Suffolk: York Medieval Press, 2003.

Davidson, H. R. Ellis. *Gods and Myths of Northern Europe.* Harmondsworth: Penguin, 1964.

DuBois, Thomas A. *Nordic Religions in the Viking Age.* Philadelphia: University of Pennsylvania Press, 1999.

Orchard, Andy. *Dictionary of Norse Myth and Legend.* London: Cassell, 1997.

Page, R. I. *Norse Myths.* London: British Museum Publications, 1990.

Sawyer, Birgit, Peter Sawyer, and Ian Wood. *The Christianization of Scandinavia: Report of a Symposium Held at Kungälv, Sweden, 4–9 August 1985.* Alingsås, Sweden: Viktoria, 1987.

Simek, Rudolf. *Dictionary of Northern Mythology.* Trans. Angela Hall. Cambridge: D. S. Brewer, 1993.

Strömback, Dag. *The Conversion of Iceland: A Survey.* Trans. and annotated by Peter Foote. London: Viking Society of Northern Research, 1975.

Turville-Petre, E.O.G. *Myth and Religion of the North: The Religion of Ancient Scandinavia.* New York: Holt, Rinehart and Winston, 1964.

TRAVEL, TRANSPORT, AND SHIPS

Berg, Gösta. *Sledges and Wheeled Vehicles: Ethnological Studies from the View-point of Sweden.* Nordiska Museets Handlingar, no. 4. Uppsala: Almqvist & Wiksell, 1935.

Binns, Alan. *Viking Voyages: Then and Now.* London: Heinemann, 1980.

Brøgger, A. W., and Haakon Shetelig. *The Viking Ships.* Trans. Katherine John. Oslo: Dreyer, 1951.

Christensen, Arne Emil, Jr. *Boats of the North: A History of Boatbuilding in Norway.* Oslo: Det norske samlaget, 1968.

Crumlin-Pedersen, Ole. "Ships, Navigation, and Routes in the Reports of Ohtere and Wulfstan." In *Two Voyagers at the Court of King Alfred: The Ventures of Ohtere and Wulfstan Together with the Description of Northern Europe from the Old English Orosius,* ed. Niels Lund. York: Sessions, 1984.

Crumlin-Pedersen, Ole, and Max Vinner, eds. *Sailing into the Past: Proceedings of the International Seminar on Replicas of Ancient and Medieval Vessels, Roskilde, 1984.* Roskilde, Denmark: The Viking Ship Museum, 1986.

Greenhill, Basil, with John Morrison. *The Archaeology of Boats and Ships: An Introduction.* Annapolis, MD: Naval Institute Press, 1995.

Thirslund, Søren. "Navigation by the Vikings on the Open Sea." In *Viking Voyages to North America,* ed. Birthe L. Clausen, pp. 109–117. Roskilde, Denmark: The Viking Ship Museum, 1993.

Vinner, Max. "*Unnasigling*—the Seaworthiness of the Merchant Vessel." In *Viking Voyages to North America,* ed. Birthe L. Clausen, pp. 95–108. Roskilde, Denmark: The Viking Ship Museum, 1993.

ART, COINAGE, AND WEAPONS

Blackburn, M.A.S., and D.M. Metcalf, eds. *Viking-Age Coinage in the Northern Land: The Sixth Oxford Symposium on Coinage and Monetary History.* Oxford: n.p., 1981.

Malmer, Brita. *King Canute's Coinage in the Northern Countries.* The Dorothea Coke Memorial Lecture in Northern Studies delivered 30 May 1972 at University College London. London: Viking Society for Northern Research, 1972.

Peirce, Ian G. *Swords of the Viking Age.* Woodbridge: The Boydell Press, 2002.

Wilson, David M., and Ole Klindt-Jensen. *Viking Art.* Ithaca, N.Y.: Cornell University Press, 1966.

VIKINGS ABROAD

Almqvist, Bo, and David Greene, eds. *Proceedings of the Seventh Viking Congress. Dublin 15–21 August 1973.* Dundalk, Ireland: Dundalgan Press, 1976.

Bates, David. *Normandy before 1066.* London and New York: Longman, 1982.

Byock, Jesse. *Viking Age Iceland.* London: Penguin, 2001.

Corráin, D. O. *Ireland before the Normans.* Dublin: Gill and Macmillan, 1972.

Crawford, Barbara E. *Scandinavian Scotland.* Scotland in the Early Middle Ages, vol. 2. Leicester: Leicester University Press, 1987.

Fell, Christine, Peter Foote, James Graham-Campbell, and Robert Thomson, eds. *The Viking Age in the Isle of Man: Select Papers from The Ninth Viking Congress, Isle of Man, 4–14 July 1981.* London: Viking Society for Northern Research, 1983.

Fenton, Alexander, and Hermann Pálsson, eds. *The Northern and Western Isles in the Viking World: Survival, Continuity, and Change.* Edinburgh: John Donald Publishers, 1984.

Howard, Ian. *Swein Forkbeard's Invasions and the Danish Conquest of England, 991–1017.* Woodbridge: The Boydell Press, 2003.

Jochens, Jenny. *Women in Old Norse Society.* Ithaca and London: Cornell University Press, 1995.

Jones, Gwyn. *The Norse Atlantic Saga: Being the Norse Voyages of Discovery and Settlement to Iceland, Greenland, and North America.* Rev. ed. with contributions by Robert McGhee, Thomas H. McGovern and colleagues, and Birgitta Linderoth Wallace. Oxford: Oxford University Press, 1964.

Klejn, L. S. "Soviet Archaeology and the Role of the Vikings in the Early History of the Slavs." *Norwegian Archaeological Review* 6 (1973): 1–4.

Lebedeu, G. S., and V. A. Nazarenko. "The Connections Between Russians and Scandinavians in the Ninth–Eleventh Centuries." *Norwegian Archaeological Review* 6 (1973): 5–9.

Loyn, Henry. *The Vikings in Britain.* Oxford: Blackwell, 1994.

———. *The Vikings in Wales.* The Dorothea Coke Memorial Lecture in Northern Studies delivered 2 March 1976 at University College London. London: Viking Society for Northern Research, 1976.

Magnusson, Magnus. *Viking Expansion Westwards.* London: Bodley Head Ltd., 1973.

Morris, Christopher. "Viking Orkney: A Survey." In *The Pre-History of Orkney,* ed. Colin Renfrew, pp. 210–42. Edinburgh: Edinburgh University Press, 1985.

Morrison, Ian. *The North Sea Earls: The Shetland/Viking Archaeological Expedition.* London: Gentry Books, 1973.

Page, R. I. *'A Most Vile People': Early English Historians on the Vikings.* The Dorothea Coke Memorial Lecture in Northern Studies delivered 19 March 1986 at University College London. London: Viking Society for Northern Research, 1986.

Pritsak, Omeljan. *The Origin of Rus'.* Vol. 1 of *Old Scandinavian Sources Other than the Sagas.* Cambridge: Harvard University Press, 1981.

Sawyer, P. H. *From Roman Britain to Norman England.* New York: St. Martin's Press, 1978.

Smyth, Alfred P. *Scandinavian York and Dublin: The History and Archaeology of Two Related Viking Kingdoms.* 2 vols. Dublin: Templekieran Press, 1975.

Varangian Problems: Report on the First International Symposium on the Theme: The Eastern Connections of the Nordic Peoples in the Viking Period and Early Middle Ages, Moesgaard, University of Aarhus, 7th-11th October 1968. Scando-Slavica, Supplementum, no. 1. Copenhagen: Munksgaard, 1970.

Wallace, Birgitta Linderoth. "L'Anse aux Meadows, the Western Outpost." In *Viking Voyages to North America,* ed. Birthe L. Clausen, pp. 30–42. Roskilde, Denmark: The Viking Ship Museum, 1993.

Wilson, David M. *The Viking Age in the Isle of Man: The Archaeological Evidence.* Odense, Denmark: Odense University Press, 1974.

Index

About the Author

KIRSTEN WOLF is Professor and the Torger Thompson Chair of Scandinavian Studies at the University of Wisconsin, Madison.